HUMAN ALTERNATIVES: VISIONS FOR US NOW

Books by RICHARD KOSTELANETZ

AS AUTHOR
Music of Today
The Theatre of Mixed Means
Master Minds
Visual Language
Metamorphosis in the Arts

AS CO-AUTHOR AND EDITOR
The New American Arts

AS CO-FOUNDER–COMPILER
Assembling

AS EDITOR
On Contemporary Literature
Twelve from the Sixties
The Young American Writers
Beyond Left & Right
Imaged Words & Worded Images
Possibilities of Poetry
Moholy-Nagy
John Cage
Social Speculations
Human Alternatives

Human Alternatives

Visions for Us Now

Edited with an Introduction by
RICHARD KOSTELANETZ

WILLIAM MORROW AND COMPANY, INC.

NEW YORK

1971

For Morris & Suzanne Amateau,
With love, and gratitude for
aid from my very beginnings.

If it has achieved nothing else, bourgeois society at least revolutionized the means of production on a scale unprecedented in history. This technological revolution, culminating in cybernation, has created the objective, quantitative bases for a world without class rule, exploitation, toil and material want. The means now exist for the development of the rounded man, the total man, freed of guilt and the workings of authoritarian modes of training, and given over to Desire, to the sensuous apprehension of the marvelous.

—MURRAY BOOKCHIN,
"Post-Scarcity Anarchy" (1969)

It is clear that if there is to be any revival of utopian imagination in the near future, it cannot return to the old-style spatial utopias. New utopias would have to derive their form from the shifting and dissolving movement of society that is gradually replacing the fixed locations of life. They would not be rational cities evolved by a philosopher's dialectic: they would be rooted in the body as well as in the mind, in the unconscious as well as the conscious, in forests and deserts as well as in highways and buildings, in bed as well as in the symposium.

—NORTHROP FRYE,
"Varieties of Literary Utopias" (1965)

The increased capability for recovering and storing mass quantities of information, as seen in such sophistications as the computer, equips man for his decision-making task in a fashion which would invite the envy of our ancestors. For a man to be truly human he must be free to choose between alternatives. Yet freedom of choice implies knowledge of consequences of available alternatives. The conjunction of modern communications with the massing of circumstantial information in electric circuitry has provided man with this knowledge, thus freeing him and making him more truly human.

—WALTER J. ONG,
"The Spiritual Meaning of Technological Culture" (1966)

PREFACE

This, then, is one of the major tasks today of the political scientist, the philosopher, the journalist, and the prophet: To give the people an image of changes in the international system which seem small enough to be feasible yet large enough to be successful.

—KENNETH E. BOULDING,
"The Prevention of World War III" (1962)

A society without a sense of alternatives has no real future, suffering instead only regressive replications of the present; so that articulate speculations as such perform an exemplary social function. The following essays move beyond criticism to posit alternatives for man, because complaint without vision is, like windup without delivery, ultimately very frustrating, soporifically repetitious, and perhaps counter-productive. Visions of possibility inevitably serve to infuse value into the present, as well as creating a direction for humane energies; so that a sense of desired designs contributes to every dynamic society. This book of *Human Alternatives* is a sequel to *Social Speculations* (1971), itself a kind of sequel to *Beyond Left & Right* (1968); and if the first anthology, subtitled "Radical Thought for Our Times," emphasized "how we think about radical change," its successor, subtitled "Visions for Our Time," turned the corner beyond theories of change to present, as I wrote in its preface, "images of human possibility, envisioning the future that is, with increasing speed, coming into sight as the present," and that book deals primarily with the larger issues of technology and history. Taking yet another necessary step, *Human Alternatives* is more specific, more personal and perhaps more practical; for if *Social Speculations* focuses upon where mankind might go, this book is more concerned with how to get there, often devoting whole essays to what had in previous books been just passing suggestions. Both intellectually and chronologically, then, *Human Alternatives* represents an elaboration of its immediate predecessors.

This anthology is characteristically diffuse, offering not a coherent vision of incipient possibilities but a diversity of relevant alternatives, some of which contradict others; for rather than firing a single directed bullet, this book is scattershot, designed not to persuade but to bore holes through conventional social thought and perhaps open the reader's mind in several ways. (The bibliography of further readings extends this mind-expanding purpose; and those readers encountering this kind of thinking for the first time in this book might well consider its predecessors.) It is clear that the present needs social thinking that transcends old forms, whether archaic pieties or disciplinary limitations, so that intellectual gaminess and cross-fertilization as such become social necessities. "These problems require an interdisciplinary team working together over long periods of time," notes Herman Kahn; and in lieu of a research institute, this anthology becomes a similarly multi-faceted attack upon the questions of present social choices.

The presuppositions informing this collection echo those of its predecessors (as, alas, does the introduction); for although reality has changed drastically in the five years since this project was first conceived, certain generalizations about society remain pertinent. The first truth is that, to repeat, "Change is the metaphysic of our age." A second holds that, notwithstanding our increasing awareness of social failure and disparity, existence is now more amenable, to more people around the world than ever before in history; for the decline in both starvation and premature death in the past two decades, as well as the absence of engulfing wars, supplements such developments as technological dissemination and more effective distribution of material abundance, in creating a minimally satisfactory material circumstance for a greater percentage of the world's peoples. This fact remains indisputable, although some may debate, usually irrelevantly, the qualitative levels of this unprecedented prosperity. A third truth is that linear interpretations of contemporary progress are more convincing than dialectical schemes, which mistakenly assume that man's situation must get worse before it can turn better, or in spite of "seeming" better; and it is equally clear that some of the most relevant social thought today deals with how best to exploit the ongoing beneficial developments. "The crucial question confronting us now," I wrote in *Social Speculations*, "is not whether we can change the world but what kind of world do we want, as well as how to turn our choices into realities; for nearly everything even slightly credible is becoming possible, in both man and society, once we decide what and why it should be." For these and other reasons, optimism remains a more persuasive intellectual posture than pessimism, as well as the more practical outlook; and the book's introduction endeavors to define the role of this kind of alternative thinking in today's world.

Although certain characterizations of the present may remain the same, social thought must follow society in taking leaps ahead, continually offering new visions of unprecedented possibilities; for it is assumed in this book that the consideration of human alternatives should precede the formulation of policies, whether they govern social life or one's individual destiny. "Images of such alternatives," I wrote in its predecessor, "depend not only upon intellectual comprehensions of current realities, such as the pace and impact of technological development, but also upon imaginative projections that are closer in quality to 'fiction' than social analysis." Like the "social speculations" of this earlier book, the following images of human alternatives are clearly beyond "socialism" or "conservatism," as they were historically, or even currently, conceived, as well as, hopefully, beyond those familiar visions already embedded in every reader's mind. "If we are to use dichotomies," let me repeat, "it now seems more valid to divide thinkers into backward-lookers and forward-lookers—respectively, those who regard present life as similar to the past (and thus amenable to classic palliatives) and those who see today as radically different and, thus, requiring unprecedented forms of characterization and solution." The critical neglect these anthologies have suffered—less than a handful of reviews of each—persuades me to believe that this kind of thinking is unfashionable, if not unknown, in "literary" circles; yet their growing sales suggest their increasing relevance to certain readers, as well as a good reason to compile yet another sequel,

The unusual orientation of *Human Alternatives* is defined as much by its omissions as its inclusions. There is nothing here about America's international relations, because the alternatives are all fairly well articulated, if not by now oppressively familiar; and there is nothing here about minority groups, because the bias behind my thinking here is scrupulously ecumenical. In the latter respect, the assumption is, first, that the largest social problems ultimately affect everyone in the world and, secondly, that as various classes of underlings transcend their particular problem-making predicaments their sense of themselves becomes more universalized. "Racism," notes Buckminster Fuller, "is a product of tribalism, and both are falling victim to communications and world-around literacy." Little here could be classified "New Left," which tends to suffer "a disbelief in the future"—to quote an early SDS president, Todd Gitlin. The fact that most of these authors included here and their concerns are American is less a contradiction than a recognition that the United States is the world's vanguard culture, in which unprecedented realities are experienced daily and the possibilities of post-industrial society are first recognized. This new society's peculiarly similar impact upon every culture, rather than American political hegemony, explains why both American life-styles and American forward-looking thought are likely to have their influence and imitators around the world. My own position, it should become clear, may best be characterized as "techno-anarchist," since I believe, on one hand, in the saving power of technology, intelligently and considerately used, and, on the other, in both the decentralization of social power and the dissolution of constricting authorities.

The authors and/or publishers of the following selections deserve my gratitude for granting me permission to reprint their essays. Certain selections have been abridged or extracted from longer works; and footnotes have generally been deleted. Every effort has been made to trace the ownership of all copyrighted material and to make full acknowledgment of its use; so that if any error or omission has occurred, it will be duly corrected in subsequent editions, providing that notification is submitted in writing to the publisher. I should also thank William McPherson, formerly of William Morrow, for commissioning this series of books; and his successor, James Landis, for guiding both it and

its immediate predecessor through an increasingly hazardous production. My thinking in the introduction is indebted to my friends
Donald Cohen, Bernard J. Muller-Thym and Queenie Nuttree, as
well as the contributors and critics of the earlier collections; and
those to whom this book is dedicated deserve my deepest personal
gratitude.

RICHARD KOSTELANETZ

New York, N.Y.
14 May, 1971

CONTENTS

INTRODUCTION

Myths constitute the vision that the individual
has of the human situation. But within these
myths a dialectical struggle shapes up between
the tendency in man merely to accept what is
handed him from his environment and the effort
to choose and control his vision. Those who have
really changed the modern world—Rousseau,
Freud, Marx—are those who have changed its
mythology, and whatever is beneficent in their
influence has to do with giving man increased
power over his own vision.

—NORTHROP FRYE,
"Reflections in a Mirror" (1966)

It has been the assumption of these anthologies that we need to
rethink how we think about social change, because certain old
mythologies are no longer relevant to the contemporary circumstance. In the classic democratic model, people favoring a certain
reform attempt to persuade the established politicians of its desirability; and when most of the legislators are duly convinced,
the proposal becomes law—the process sometimes institutionalizing a previously radical idea. "Americans now of middle age,"
notes Richard Hofstadter in *The Progressive Historians* (1968),
"can remember how social security passed in no more than twenty
years from the status of an almost visionary social reform to a
controversial issue, and then to an established consensual position." A more militant version of this mythology assumes that if
the general public is relentlessly made aware of a certain problem
(especially one capable of inspiring feelings of guilt), they will
pressure their elected representatives to take some kind of public
action, no matter how inadequately formulated or ultimately in-

consequential. However, by the 1970s, the politicians have become besieged by innumerable proposals and the public by an abundance of appeals, most of them from narrow-minded agit-prop groups; so that both polities have become less responsive to outside (and enlightened) ideas. While the Executive Branch has been shamelessly philistine since John Kennedy's death, the Congressional bottleneck has become hopelessly clogged, the enterprise of "politics" in general becoming progressively more self-serving and conservative.

The Marxist interpretation of social change has proved no more successful; for by expropriating industries in the name of the "people," and then investing a new class of governors, socialist revolutions scarcely change the lot of the populace, or their relationship to work and authority. As in corporate America, change in ownership does not necessarily produce a radical change in functioning, for as the Cohn-Bendits observed in *Obsolete Communism* (1968), "The real meaning of revolution is not a change in management, but a change in man." Furthermore, the citizens of industrialized Communist nations have not, by and large, benefited from the increasingly pervasive post-WWII prosperity; and there is no reason, outside the realm of abstract dialectical dramatistics, why things in the non-Communist West must get worse before they can get better. "Our problem," writes the economist Robert Theobald, "is a lack of imagination to take the major leaps in understanding and policy which are essential if we are to be able to live in our totally new world." In the new mythology, therefore, social speculation should replace social criticism, a sense of opportunity overcoming the strictures of impossibility, an optimistic outlook superceding the pessimistic, and dynamic images replacing static ones.

It has been my thesis that change in our times occurs largely outside formal "politics," and often beyond the awareness of politicians, as government *at its most sensitive* becomes a sweeping operation that adjusts the laws to transformations already occurring in society. Most changes in social functioning come from the impact of a new technology, often in concert with affluence or new knowledge, or the spread of alternative ideas of human behavior. Once scientists at Bell Laboratories, for instance, invented the electronic transistor, replacing the vacuum tube, and then Japanese industry massively exploited its practical possibilities, the resulting changes included the miniaturization of radio (and its transmission), which in turn led to a more widespread dissemination of popular music (and its incendiary behavioral ideas) and even to the more effective pursuit of guerilla agitation; and thanks to the transistor, that mammoth, cumbersome new post-WWII vacuum-tube technology called "the computer" became drastically smaller and more portable, initiating its own popularization and subsequent social change. And so on and so on. The doing of more with less—actually much, much more with much, much less—also exemplifies ephemeralization, which is a key to wealth-creation and, thus, affluence. New technologies often redefine reality, overcoming certain national boundaries through its ecumenical impact, yet often, like the radio, enhancing the power of local nationalisms; for rather than forge a "global village," as Marshall McLuhan calls the planet, the new communications encompass a highly pluralistic world, closer in metamorphic form to a global *city*. For these reasons, he who wants to change the world radically would be wise to invent a desirable machine and/or manufacture it in abundance, though he will probably not be able to control or even predict the uses to which it shall be put. As certain crucial technologies have had more impact upon society than Presidents, the real "revolutionaries" today, even in underdeveloped societies, are the technological innovators. "The technologist is not a conservative like the craftsman," notes Charles Galton Darwin, "and he is always trying to cheat the human-time scale and to accelerate the rate of change." The key to much contemporary alternative thinking is the enjoyment and exploitation of new machines, yet transcending enslavement to their determining powers.

"Humanists" and other conservatives (sometimes calling themselves "radical") have mobilized prejudice against "the megamachine"; but by most humane standards the impact of technology has been more beneficial than detrimental. From the shovel to the typewriter, technologies have always extended physical functioning; but while certain new electronic machines, such as the computer and television, serve to extend the mind, other new technologies are very human-like in their structure and/or operation. The unending process of "miniaturization" usually makes technologies cheaper and more portable, further encouraging dissemination (and decentralization) of their use. The networks of technology have created a kind of second nature as powerful as primary nature; so that, as Charles DeCarlo has observed, "The rhythms of the world beat to the cycle of machines, rather than the circling of the sun." Powerful as this influence has been, the remaining truths are that machines are ultimately less responsible for "alienation" and "depersonalization" than mass organization and the circumstances of modern collaborative work, and that technology as such has less deleterious effect upon society than the ill-considered uses to which it is put. In nine contexts out of ten, the crushing antagonist is bureaucracy, along with its insensitive human agents, both of whom stand behind technology's operation. Industrial pollution, for instance, comes largely from the excessive exploitation of certain technologies, abetted by the inadequate use of others (such as those that identify and measure the causes of pollution); and to Buckminster Fuller, "pollution is nothing but resources we're not harvesting." The culprit in this case, as well as others, clearly remains those bureaucracies, whether capitalist or socialist, that are more interested in maximizing immediate output and lowering protective costs, as well as neglecting certain industrial opportunities. The more reasonable solutions for pollution today involve not less technology, but more, regardless of added expense, in addition to a general public insistance that polluting industries demonstrate more social consideration; for it is a contemporary rule that one kind of technology usually offers the most feasible palliatives for the problems that other technologies create. (Similarly, it is through technological advances, such as "the green revolution," that we eliminate the malnutrition and hunger caused by larger populations, themselves largely the result of recent advances in medicine.) Technologies also "humanize" bureaucracies, which have traditionally been centralizing and hierarchical, because the social impact of electronic communications, such as an inter-office telephone, is fundamentally decentralizing and ecumenical, giving individuals in various places and levels of society equal physical (electronic) access to the sources of information and/or the intended recipients of their messages.

Another contemporary model of social change—this one more

feasible to non-technologists—comes simply from positing a persuasive alternative for human energies, functioning independently
of "politics," which eventually makes an appropriate adjustment;
and the arsenal of suggestions includes not only the rebuilding of
old houses, so to speak, but the creation of new ones. The alternatives of the extended family, or "commune," for instance, has won
a growing number of enthusiastic adherents, as have the lobbies
for ecological concerns and comprehensive urban planning. On
another level, the increasing taste for marijuana, especially in lieu
of alcohol, has drastically changed young America's taste in music
and movies, and perhaps much else as well; and just as the laws
prohibiting alcohol were eventually repealed, so must (and will)
both the customs and legislation of America progressively adjust
to this new taste. With time and historical change, marijuana,
following behind both social security and alcohol, will become
socially legitimate. (The peril now is massive civil disobedience
that makes "criminals" out of otherwise respectable people
and leads to a socially dangerous disrespect for the law and
lawmen.) The point in this context is that the momentum
for all these changes originated and grew largely outside of
politics. What we have come to call the "counter-culture" is
actually an interlocking net of ideas for alternative living, different in crucial ways from middle-class America, and yet reflecting characteristically American aspirations; and this counter-
culture's progressively greater impact becomes a powerful motor
for social change.

As much as all establishments resist new ideas, they are nonetheless susceptible to alteration; and a sense of alternatives, at
minimum, makes decision-making on all levels better informed
and perhaps more competent. The policy scientist Herman Kahn
testifies that if any bureaucracy—even a government agency—is
given a persuasive image of how it might change, it will instinctively resist until the inevitable next crisis causes it to realize the
most persuasively articulated alternative. The sociologist Melvin
Tumin estimates that "somewhere between 10 and 20 percent of
any social-science proposal is implemented some twenty years
later in social action. This occurs primarily through the influence
it has upon college youth who push hard when, twenty years later,
they become voting adults, in positions of middle-range power to

implement some of their new visions." There is no doubt that
alternative ideas are constantly infecting the minds of people con-
trolling (or just superintending) those social levers and faucets
that can be turned one way or the other, for the ideas (and thus
their advocates) have a huge radical power in themselves, independent of any origins or contexts. Most everyone over thirty is
amazed at the widespread acceptance in the late sixties, especially
among the young, of attitudes and images that were (or would
have been) dismissed as esoterically radical only a decade before,
and these earlier alternatives have not only changed university
life drastically, but they have also infiltrated the larger community of America's educated classes—if not the Spiro Agnews,
at least their children. "Hitherto it was the mission of philosophers to interpret the world," Karl Marx observed in his *Theses
on Feuerbach* (1845), "now it is our business to change it." In
that respect, the true "elect" in our time are those who propose
or make the worlds that others will inhabit. Much as radicals gain
a rhetorical (and perhaps a dialectical) advantage in claiming
that American institutions are resistant to change, the fact is that
change, and often quite radically, indeed they do.

The key term today is "alternatives," meaning articulated options beyond the realm of current practice; and the most useful
alternatives suggest possibilities for us now. Alternative thinking
transcends social *criticism,* as well as the narrow-mindedness
peculiar to that kind of negative outlook; for once we ask such
questions as, say, whether and how the planet can support greater
populations, the answer is clearly that it can and probably should.
(Indeed, the futurologist Pat Gunkel stretches the socially concerned mind merely by estimating: "This planet can easily harbor
over a trillion people.") Alternatives at their best have breadth
and detail, one dimension complementing the other; and since
ecology takes precedence over ideology, alternatives are ideally
based upon accurate knowledge of reality, which includes assessments of both present facts and the potentialities of available
technologies. Indeed, what to do, or can be done, with (or in
response to) new technologies or situations created by them, is a
major concern of speculative thought. It is unrealistic to say, for
instance, that "the only alternative to total war is total peace,"
for a policy based upon that formulation would provide no plan

for coping with the continuing reality of limited, sub-maximal conflicts more characteristic of our time; yet it was Herman Kahn's great recognition, so often missed by his antagonistic critics, that the potential devastating power of thermonuclear weaponry means that wars cannot be fought in the old ways, for the old reasons and with the old instincts—this new reality demanding the creation of new military (though anti-militaristic) alternatives. (Similarly, nothing is more ridiculous today than conducting a U. S. "revolution" based upon a Cuban, a Chinese or an African model.)

An accurate assessment of reality is a crucial prerequisite; and not only does the modern world provide us with far more knowledge about its more complex ways than did previous cultures, but in the computer and other information technologies are superior means for handling this growing body of worldly wisdom (which sometimes assumes inundating proportions). In fact, that new kind of understanding called "systems thinking" includes "feedback loops" that generate self-knowledge, thereby enabling the process (and the processors) to benefit by experience. Furthermore, modern society is far more efficient at channeling the most relevant new knowledge to its appropriate audiences (a social development itself hastening the speed of its translation into products and action, as well as the generation of subsequent knowledge); and most of us are genuine beneficiaries of publicized advances (mostly "scientific") in our understanding of how the world works. However, empirical knowledge alone, no matter how sophisticated, is simply not sufficient in alternative social thinking, which justifiably deflates the value of precedent; for in Herman Kahn's oft-quoted phrase, "Reality has left experience far behind, and central as common sense is, it is not enough."

The necessary extra ingredient is vision, or the capacity to take the boundary-shattering, convention-transcending leap beyond the current discussions; for effective speculation has a synergetic impact upon social knowledge, endowing it with an energy greater than the sum of its parts. Definitive statements about the present may be more useful than vague hypotheses; but in discussions of the future, this bias should be reversed, approximate hypotheses becoming more valuable than definitive judgments of what is possible. "The first step of the technological or social inventor," writes the scientist Dennis Gabor, "is to visualize by an act of imagination a thing or state of things which does not yet exist and which appears to him in some way desirable." It is indicative that in no previous age were so many alternatives available, nor were they pursued before with such independence, diversity and speed; and this sense of multiple possibility represents a distinct cultural advance, by modernist standards, over unitary and/or deterministic social philosophy. (There is no doubt, for instance, that in superpower military strategy the concept of flexible response or "counterforce" is superior to "massive retaliation.") A conceptually more advanced form of alternative thinking called "scenarios" also includes consideration of the possible repercussions of several available choices, for it is likely that sweeping transformations will produce unexpected and/or unwanted results. Scenarios customarily deal with historically unprecedented realities, such as the population explosion or the existence of thermonuclear weaponry. In their concern with alternatives beyond alternatives, scenarios also cultivate an interest in surprises, or otherwise unimaginable consequences; so that, as the English biologist J. M. Fremlin puts it, "We are now, or soon will be, able to cope with *anything* that might turn up."

It should be clear by now that merely positing a viable human alternative is not only an invaluable form of "action" but also an incomparable assertion of freedom; for in the growing array of potential choices is modern man's real liberty. "For a man to be truly human he must be free to choose between alternatives," writes Father Walter J. Ong, S.J. "The conjunction of modern communications with the massing of circumstantial information in electric circuitry has provided man with this knowledge, thus freeing him and making him more human." Indeed, all this knowledge increases the power of the human mind in its age-old battle with physical matter, not only within the body but outside it; and a powerful computer, extending man's mental functioning, can be used as an alternative-generating and an alternative-consulting machine. For these and other reasons, contemporary man in post-industrial society has, by any rough criteria of measurement, more power over his destiny than his predecessors—more capacity to overcome the resistances of matter, such as nature and society, in directing the course of their lives than, say, even royalty of a century ago had available to them; and this development is not only a cultural advance, by secular standards, but also one of the great semi-acknowledged achievements of our times. Indeed, affluence and advanced knowledge are largely responsible for America's current leadership in both alternative thinking and the exploitation of alternative life-styles, often reflecting an intellectual history that includes numerous economic schemes predicated upon material abundance; and although Japan is rapidly becoming the world's second greatest power, it has little non-industrial export—not even, alas, the quality of cultural morale apparently prerequisite to its own spectacular industrialization.

Alternative social philosophy assumes that almost everything conceivable can ultimately be realized; and just as nature is susceptible to radical changes, so are we coming to accept that the human body and even "human nature" are drastically mutable. The new thinking is more concerned with human potentialities than deficiencies, and it goes beyond previous psychologies in assuming that man's mind can be verifiably improved. Since these new ideas are largely more empirical, if not more physiological, than Freudian thinking, all kinds of problems that "psycho-analysis" found knotty and complex now seem amenable to awesomely facile solutions. Yoga, dietetics, eurhythmics and the like have made us more aware of physical condition as a key to mental health, the most exaggerated formulation being Buckminster Fuller's conviction in *Nine Chains to the Moon* (1938), that most psychological difficulties can be traced "quite unromantically to mechanical maladjustments in the environment of the individual; bad plumbing of house or self-mechanism, bad sound or light control." This physiological bias also prepares the new thought to acknowledge the power of psychological drugs of all kinds to alter drastically the quality and temper of mental experience. Within the past decade new medicines have had miraculous healing effects upon, say, recurring schizophrenia, suggesting that yet newer drugs might similarly alleviate more subtle conditions, such as chronic depressions or even personality defects. Furthermore, certain hallucinogenic drugs already available also serve, deleterious reactions notwithstanding, to liberate the constrained mind for the sort of unprecedented perceptions and speculations that will become more common in the future. In these respects, psychological drugs become mental protheses, so to speak, not only repairing defects in the manner of artificial legs, driving the imagination into realms it would not otherwise go, but also giving the human mind, as the computer does in other ways, a kind of artificial supplementary intelligence. The result of optimal psychological thinking is likely to be, in Pat Gunkel's prophecy, "an increasing number of men who will be autocatalytically self-developing, -disciplining, and -controlled."

All these observations suggest that mind-change increasingly precedes change in man and society (a fact itself repudiating the Marxist prescription); and as any intelligent and self-commanding person can change his mind to his own taste, on his own time, there is no need to "wait for the revolution." Precisely because of their inexperience, the young are naturally more predisposed to alternatives than their elders (the issue of legalized marijuana typically delineating a generation gap), for the new society is largely the creation of fresh heads. For this and other reasons, education becomes increasingly important, not only to teach what is relevant information and where to find it, but also to protect against threatening ignorance by preparing the mind to deal with unfamiliar knowledge and experience. Alternative minds and alternative vision inevitably complement each other; and since our understanding of the world no longer evolves but changes instead by spectacular leaps, often moving beyond earlier categories of understanding, relevant education should emphasize the numerous processes of thinking and the various structures of knowledge, rather than specialized data (or the more recent fashion of self-discovery). "Pattern recognition is highly abstract," writes Edmund Carpenter. "It requires detachment from immediate, particular sensory experience." Since this kind of learning takes less time than the present regimen, as well as challenging more strongly the potentialities of intelligence, bright students could be accelerated into universities at a younger age. Not only should idiosyncratic waywardness be regarded more sympathetically, if not encouraged, but a continuing course in the future, at all educational levels, would unquestionably improve general morale and "stretch" sensibilities for alternative thinking and understanding. What Alvin Toffler calls "future shock" really comes from insufficient awareness of human alternatives, an intellectual unpre-

paredness itself reflecting the growing disadvantage of not antici-
pating what might happen in man and society; and it is thus
susceptible to educational palliatives. To anyone profoundly im-
mersed in futurology, which is the study of likely possibilities,
nothing can be a demoralizing surprise.

The further truth is that people in school today can expect a
lifetime in which knowledge itself will radically change—not only
in its details but its structures; so that the mark of a truly educated man will no longer be how much or even how variously he
now knows, but how quickly and how completely he can continually learn. A mind of this kind will probably be more predisposed
to consider opposites and to accept, if not generate, viable human
alternatives. It also seems probable that the new educational
technologies will become more important, electronically transmitting instruction (potentially individualized) into a home console, relieving the school, in Anthony G. Oettinger's vision, of
"the bulk of its concern today, namely the abstract and the
verbal. The school as such may concentrate instead on the concrete, the social, and the human." As Buckminster Fuller put it,
"I don't see any reason why, with television reaching not only
the children in their private homes in the slums but children in
the privacy of their homes everywhere, why we should not bring
education—school—to where the children are." Electronic media,
rather than schools, will also assume the crucial function of educating the general public in new knowledge (thereby perhaps
overcoming that short-sighted newspaper literacy which plagues
serious discussion in America); and were its pedagogic concerns
to transcend the constricting discourse of book and magazine culture, whether "highbrow" or "lowbrow," the new media may well
replace print as the primary disseminators of the new alternative
thought.

All the vehicles of human vision therefore assume an implicit
social function, encouraging us, in Herman Kahn's great epithet,
"to think about the unthinkable." In literature, for instance, the
works that are most political in this sense are those science fic-
tions (indicatively neglected by litterateurs, even those who call
themselves "radical") in which readers may inspect a diversity of
fully fleshed visions of alternative life; but any imaginative construction that either offers images of human possibility or merely

stretches the mind, whether that art be literary or non-literary, ultimately hones our sensibilities for a more congenial future. Indeed, just as vanguard artists take a leap ahead in creating new structural relationships, so does truly avant-garde work demand that its audience take a comparable leap in understanding, inevitably expanding its perceptual awareness and perhaps its imaginative capacities as well. Since artistic change generally precedes mind-change, avant-garde art in itself, regardless of its content, becomes, in Allen Ginsberg's phrase, "a typical and spiritual revolutionary catalyst." (It was surely out of a concern with psychic priorities that the poet suggests "America's political need is orgies in the park.") Just as the forging of alternatives is a primary ideology of contemporary art, so should social philosophy continually endeavor, particularly with the progress of history, to think what has not already been thought—beyond the established frame of discussion; for in both art and thought, energy is gained from new perception. It also seems likely that the mentalities capable of great innovative art will increasingly coincide with those creating the best alternative social philosophy (e.g., John Cage and L. Moholy-Nagy). It follows that just as some fresh art can be classified as technically competent but stylistically too archaic (or clichéd) for relevance, so can social thought be so divided, the kinds of qualitative distinctions relevant to one realm holding for the other; and it follows too that nothing less than the best new art and the best new social thought are necessary, for the sake of the future. It is indicative that the communities of art have always been more predisposed to alternative social thinking than, say, academics, professionals or even "intellectuals"; and it is a salutary fact that no culture has as many "serious" artists as America today. Art and social philosophy can connect at yet a further point; for as Herbert Marcuse suggests, the comprehensive alternative of regarding "society as a work of art . . . is the most Utopian, the most radical possibility of liberation today."

Though the biases of both politics and law, in contrast to art and science, cut against the grain of alternative thinking, their institutions are ultimately malleable, and destined, as noted before, to change under pressure from new technologies and ideas.

Politics in particular demands far better, more relevant thought and knowledge, suffering at nearly every level from general illiteracy, intellectual inadequacy and speculative impotence; for behind even the current militant-liberal panacea, an increase in the quantity of public funding, should stand practical thinking of considerably higher quality. (Indeed, it is increasingly clear that more money as such is an insufficient solution; for as W. David Lewis negatively speculates, "It is conceivable that we may spend billions of dollars during the coming decades on 'urban renewal' only to find in the end that this massive allocation of resources has failed to meet many of the real needs and forces operating within our society.") One political response to technology is Vladimir Zworykin's vision of exploiting the telephone system, along with a computer, to conduct a daily referendum on the issues of the day (thereby also realizing the radical idea of "participatory democracy").

Politics—meaning the kind of social power vested in governments and large institutions—will doubtlessly become more future-consciousness, responding not only to new technologies and social behavior, but also to the peaceful transfer of power to a younger generation (by and large more attuned to that new world and what Charles A. Reich calls "Consciousness III"); for not only do the currently entrenched leaders seem decades older than the incipient chiefs of the next generation, but it also seems increasingly clear that the young, especially students, are the primary radicalizing "class" in modern society, typically rebelling on behalf of human potentialities (rather than class or economic power-interests). Their impact succeeds less at transforming social structure than changing people's minds; for, as Reich perceives, "What the students discovered is that only tactics which reach people *at the level of consciousness* are effective. And so they began to develop forms of speech and action, new to America, which were designed to influence consciousness in others and in themselves." It should not be forgotten in this context that certain corporate enterprises also generate sweeping change, especially by disseminating a new technology and/or in their youthful stages, when they can be spectacularly skilled at marshalling material and human resources behind innovative intelligences and/or products; and like other forward-looking, yet instinctively conservative institutions, progressive enterprises function less as a lever of change than a shifting fulcrum continually realigning the balances of society. Economics will change too, surely capitalizing upon the facts that, as Fuller notes, "We soon will begin to generate wealth so rapidly that we can do very great things," and that a computer-assisted universal barter-àccounting could eliminate the convention called "money." "Possession," he continues, "is becoming progressively more burdensome and wasteful and therefore obsolete." And as the composer-philosopher John Cage suggests, "You could simply have other conventions which would allow people to have the things they need." There is no question, on the one hand, that in our time non-violent changes of this kind are ultimately more beneficial than violent and, on the other, that society's conservatives would be wise to insure that inevitable changes be peaceful.

The quality of politics epitomized by the Johnson and, especially, the Nixon administrations can only produce a loss of public confidence, failing not only the radical necessity of initiative but also the conservative job of preserving a culture's tenuous morale; and recent Executive leadership has taken an even more reactionary course by sabotaging so much technological research and development. Furthermore, unless there are goals informed by vision, political activity is likely to become aimless and/or egotistical and/or corrupt, this and other facts explaining why politics itself has become both less powerful and less relevant in our time. "Once we give our attention to the practice of not-being governed," notes Cage, "we notice that it is increasing."

Just as most social alternatives are above (or beneath) politics, whether Republican-Democrat or left-right, so visionary intellectuals have become socially more important than political critics or even politicians. It is inevitable that certain initiating functions previously the domain of "politics" have by now passed to social planning, defined roughly as the processes by which visions are realized, whether in society or in oneself. Planning at its most successful includes more than formulations and policies, being also concerned with the restructuring of all clogged and declining organisms; for the ultimate goal is the creation of open channels for evolutionary development. "Now the main emphases," writes Herbert A. Simon, "will not be on designing, but on devising effective design systems." New awareness, along with computer-assistance, provide good reasons for optimism about our capacities both to organize the preconditions for successful planning and to extend its durational range; for as Pat Gunkel proposes, "It is now possible, desirable and necessary to plan on time-scales exceeding our present lifetimes by decades, centuries and even millennia." Intelligent design disregards superficial or falsely formulated problems, often so conspicuously clamoring for public attention, to attack the underlying predicaments—as the author Jorge Luis Borges quipped, "Another disadvantage of fallacious problems is that they bring equally fallacious solutions." The implementations of planning can occur at any and all levels of society, bringing about widespread changes before the formal political institutions become aware of the new terrain. Nothing in man and society need be considered exempt from the pressure for change, for planning at its sagest feels no need to wait for the contingencies of politics.

By most criteria known to us, the world is getting better, materially as well as spiritually, and the surest prediction is that the immediate future will witness more of the same. The causes of changes mentioned at the beginning—technological development, new knowledge, great affluence, and alternative ideas—complement each other at increasing speed; so that, barring a cataclysm, the pace of metamorphosis can only accelerate. It is reasonable to agree with Zbigniew Brzezinski's predictions that by 1985, "Mass starvation, mass homelessness, and the rampant spread of diseases that have historically decimated entire populations will be generally eliminated." Beyond that lies an even more extraordinary possibility, becoming apparent to more of the world's peoples—as John Cage defines it, ". . . unemotional (cf. zazen, yoga) problem-solving (comprehensive design science), relating world resources to human needs so that by A.D. 2000, 100 percent of humanity will be 'haves,' " which is to say, assured of their basic material needs. The fact that people in affluent cultures are now so much more concerned about those less fortunate (rather than neglecting them, as in previous times) is itself a sign of improvement, and this genuine altruism, based upon both affluence and education, makes this moment not a nihilistic age but an ideological one (often, however, with deleterious side effects).

The philosophy of human alternatives differs from ideologies in being more concerned with preconditions—the constant positing of alternatives—than any ends more particular than a just and humane society; and its outlook is non-utopian and unsystematic. An implicit aim for alternative philosophy is an abundance of speculations equal to the unprecedented variety and pluralism of contemporary society. Though fundamentally liberal and pragmatistic in these respects, the new social philosophy links with the radical tradition in its commitments to transcendance of convention and the exploitation of persuasive visions, its championing of new forms of social order (over the current disorder) and primarily in its advocacy of rapid change. It is more ecumenical than most previous radicalisms, which envision revolution by (and in the name of) a particular class; for the unprecedented possibility in our time is a total, massive revolution, if only in the name of everyone, but by everyone who elects to participate. The new thought is also more mundane, believing, along with the anarchist philosopher Murray Bookchin, that "the goal of revolution, today, must be the liberation of daily life. Any revolution that fails to achieve this goal is counter-revolution." In contrast to the conservative emphasis upon what cannot be done to man and society, the new radicalism emphasizes comprehensive possibility, in addition to the overthrow of all in the present-becoming-past that hinders the opportunities of the future; and it capitalizes as well upon the fact that the pursuit of alternatives is a central theme of the age. The present is so different from the past that true radicals are obliged to envision a future even more different from now, and it is precisely this forward-looking quality that explains why the new social philosophy does not think much about the past-oriented problems that preoccupy, if not debilitate, the old thought. It should be clear by now that thinking about, say, what to do with affluence is more profitable, socially, than bemoaning poverty, for affluence can deal with poverty, though not vice versa. Though counter "humanist" in extolling technology, this social thought nonetheless places especially great faith in the power of mind, not only to use knowledge and imagination to generate social speculations, but also to realize and control mankind's destiny. As speculative images begin to seem more "real" than firsthand experience, the library of available alternatives becomes a kind of "third nature," having almost as much impact upon man's environment as first nature and technology; and precisely by realizing man's progressive transcendance of physical necessity, people are now more predisposed to consider extremely spiritualist (or just mentalist) possibilities.

To the suggesting of human alternatives, like the exploration of outer space, there can be no end, only new predicaments, newly visible goals, and new proposals; so that it is indicative that an alternative philosopher would say, with John Diebold, "These suggestions are by no means exhaustive; new ideas and new forms of cooperation inevitably will arise." The mythology of social thought must itself change with the times, because neither as doer nor especially as thinker can man afford to accept the status quo; and leap ahead though we have, the surest expectation is yet more radical transformations in all dimensions of existence. "New utopians," writes Northrop Frye, "would have to derive their form [of thinking] from the shifting and dissolving movement of society that is gradually replacing the fixed locations of life." And since both higher expectation and unending change are our collective fate, it is primarily by considering human alternatives and replenishing their supply that a culture can gain greater command of its destiny, its citizens shaping a present for themselves before the future shapes them.

I

Knowledge

The most serious portent of the future is that the geometrical accumulation of scientific knowledge that the world is now experiencing in effect dooms the great majority of us to live in ignorance of the forces which control our lives.

—W. WILLARD WIRTZ,
"The Challenge of Automation" (1963)

RECLASSIFICATION

by EDMUND CARPENTER

The New Communicators

I recently came across the following rules of communication, posted in a School of Journalism:

1 Know your audience and address yourself directly to it.
2 Know what you want to say and say it clearly and fully.
3 Reach the maximum audience by utilizing existing channels.

Whatever sense this may have made in a world of print, it makes no sense today. In fact, the reverse of each rule applies.

If you address yourself to an audience, you accept at the outset the basic premises which unite the audience. You put on the audience, repeating clichés familiar to it. But artists don't address themselves to audiences; they create audiences. The artist talks to himself out loud. If what he has to say is significant, others hear and are affected.

The trouble with knowing what to say, and saying it clearly and fully, is that clear speaking is generally obsolete thinking. Clear statement is like an art object: it is the afterlife of the process which called it into being. The process itself is the significant step and, especially at the beginning, is often incomplete and uncertain. Columbus's maps were vague and sketchy, but showed the right continent.

The problem with full statement is that it doesn't involve: it leaves no room for participation; it's addressed to consumer, not co-producer. Allan Kaprow posted a few small posters about Berkeley: "SUPPOSE you were interested in designing a primer, in mixed media, etc. . . . Allan Kaprow will be in Berkeley in July and August." No phone, address, dates, terms. He found, however, that those who wanted to work with him, and those he wanted to work with, located him without difficulty.

Reaching the maximum audience may be the last thing one wants to achieve. George Segal says, "I don't give myself freely to everybody. I give myself very intensely to my work, my wife, my kids, my few friends. I can't begin to give myself indiscriminately to all. It's the only thing that makes me pause about, say, Ginsberg's preachings of universal love or even California ideas about Esalen and touching."

Utilizing existing channels can wipe one out. There is a widely accepted misconception that media merely serve as neutral packages for the dissemination of raw facts. Photographers once thought that by getting their photographs published in *Life,* they would thereby reach large audiences. Gradually they discovered that the only message that came through was *Life* magazine itself and that their pictures had become but bits and pieces of that message. Unwittingly they contributed to a message far removed from the one they intended.

The same thing occurs on TV guest shows. Guests accept invitations to appear on programs in the hopes their messages will reach new and wider audiences, but, even when they are treated in a friendly manner, they generally come away with a sense of failure. Somehow the message transmitted is far removed from the message intended. The original message has been declassified by an alien medium. "Oh, what a blow that phantom gave me!" cries Don Quixote.

The young today shun the hardware of the past. Marx thought the big question was: who owns the presses? Software makes hardware obsolete, an encumbrance, creating a false sense of power and security. The young package their messages in media that fit their messages, that is, they create new media to fit their messages. In so doing, they create their own audiences. Some of these audiences may be very small at the beginning. In Houston I met film-makers producing films for audiences of no more than six. The point was that they would reach the right people in the right way with the right message.

It is one of the curiosities of a new medium, a new format, that at the moment it first appears, it's never valued, but it is believed. What it offers, I believe, is a sudden insight, an unexpected glimpse into a reality that, at most, was merely suspected but never before seen with such clarity.

Like guerrillas, the young are in a favored position; they don't need or want the hardware and audiences of yesterday.

Restraining Sight

"Shut your eyes and See." —*Joyce*

"I don't want to live life the way I see it. I'll play my life by ear." —*16-year-old New Yorker*

"If you paint, close your eyes and sing." —*Picasso*

"There's more than the eye can see. . . ." —*Popular song*

Restraining sight increases awareness through other senses: in darkness, sounds seem louder, odors stronger, flavors sharper, and surfaces more vivid. The blues singer closes her eyes; the ballad singer assumes that blank-faced, blind-eyed expression Lomax calls the Eurasian style of singing: ". . . his eyes are closed, or he gazes unseeing. . . ."

Lovers close their eyes. "Love is blind."

"Night has come. Now all the problems speak more loudly." —*Nietzsche*

Paleolithic man worked in the darkness of caverns, his paintings illuminated by flickering torch: elusive images appeared/disappeared. His art emerged as a direct response to inner light. He employed the inward eye. He had no concept of three-dimensional perspective with a vanishing point in the distance before him. For him, the vanishing point was within himself and he went through it by stepping into his art.

Hans Arp drew his curved, interpenetrating lines, which so closely resemble certain Paleolithic drawings, with half-closed eyes: ". . . under lowered lids, the inner movement streams untainted to the hand. In a darkened room it is even easier to follow the guidance of the inner movement than in the open air. A conductor of inner music, the great designer of prehistoric images worked with eyes turned upwards. So his drawings gain in transparency; open to penetration, to sudden inspiration, to recovery of the inner melody, to the circling approach; and the whole is transmuted into one great exhalation."

This is the inward quest, the search for meaning beyond the world of appearances; it's "the prophet blinded so that sight is yielded for insight."

" 'I can't believe that!' said Alice.

" 'Can't you?' the Queen said in a pitying tone. 'Try again: draw a deep breath, and close your eyes.' "

"What do you see," ask the Beatles, "when you turn out the light? I can't tell you but I know it's mine."

Step Right In

" '. . . the patriotic Archbishop of Canterbury, found it advisable—'

" 'Found what?' said the Duck.

" 'Found it,' the Mouse replied rather crossly; 'of course you know what "it" means.'

" 'I know very well what "it" means when *I* find a thing,' said the Duck; 'It's generally a frog or a worm. The question is, what did the archbishop find?' "

Literate man always felt better when it was visible. Language— at least literate languages—favored the observable and measurable. Even early mathematics dealt with the material. Newton was first branded a medieval mystic when his theory of gravity presented a non-visual bond and reversed downward gravity (i.e., collision) by outward gravity. However, his very visual example of a falling apple made his theory quickly acceptable to the many.

Before scientists turned to higher mathematics, they worked largely within the confines of verbal categories, which were, in turn, rooted in the empirical. The *Origin of Species* was essentially a literary work whose acceptance derived largely from the force of its literary persuasion. Darwin and company limited themselves to how birds and turtles looked. A fine gentleman, but daffy, you know, his gardener said of him, he stands looking at a flower for an hour, never moving.

No wonder it took thirty-five years before the significance of Mendel's discovery was recognized.

Beginning around 1900, science shifted away from the empirical to the invisible. As early as 1874, in an address to the British Association for the Advancement of Science, John Tyndall said, ". . . I cannot stop abruptly where our microscopes cease to be of use. Here the vision of the mind authoritatively supplants the vision of the eye."

Scientists ceased to be interested in the appearance of things and concentrated on the rules which govern them.

Buckminster Fuller writes: "In World War I industry suddenly went from the visible to the invisible base, from the track to the trackless, from the wire to the wireless, from visible structuring to invisible structuring in alloys. The big thing about World War I is that man went off the sensorial spectrum forever as the prime criterion of accrediting innovations. . . . All major advances since World War I have been in the infra- and ultra-sensorial frequencies of the electromagnetic spectrum. All the important technical affairs of men are invisible. . . ."

Even government has become invisible. We speak of the CIA as the invisible government. What could be more natural in a society where truth is regarded as invisible, inner structure?

X-Ray

It's not enough to say of x-ray design that it shows both inside and outside of a figure simultaneously. The question is, what does it mean to go right *inside* a form—to be in the belly of the beast? I suspect it's something like Alice going through the looking glass, or a Zuñi patient stepping into a sand painting, rolling in it, as it were. You enter, become one with what is portrayed. You are *in* the know. Notions of detached observation are meaningless here. Jonah and Ahab saw that whale in different ways.

The knower as actor and the knower as observer behold different worlds and shape them to different ends.

In order to know the illness *inside* a patient, a physician must see through the patient, that is, *dia-noses*. In psychotherapy, the therapist, through semi-hypnotic recall, re-enters the traumatic experience of the patient; he *lives* it with the patient. Similarly, in tribal shamanism, an alien spirit enters the body of a living thing, generally a person. It goes right in and takes over temporarily.

"When I'm in my painting," wrote Jackson Pollock, "I'm not aware of what I'm doing . . . there is pure harmony, an easy give and take, and the painting comes out well . . . I have no fears about making changes, destroying the image, etc., because the painting has a life of its own. I try to let it come through. It is only when I lose contact with the painting that the result is a mess."

You come to know a thing by being inside it. You get an inside view. You step into the skin of the beast and that, precisely, is what the masked and costumed dancer does. He puts on the beast.

Characters in native arts and myths are bewilderingly men and animals. Members of certain totemistic clans assert they are one with the animals from which they claim descent; some expressly declare themselves to *be* the animals in question. Tribal myths contain many references to sexual relations between men and mythical beasts.

A Tlingit myth relates how two brown bears climbed a mountain to escape drowning in a flood. Hunters killed one and took its head and skin to wear as a family crest during festivals. Another Tlingit legend describes how an ancient ancestor was captured by a bear and forced to marry her. When he finally escaped, he took a bear design as his family emblem.

This bear design served as a Tlingit house on the Northwest Coast, from circa 1840, and probably before. A gaping hole at the bottom was used as an entrance to the living quarters: one entered the bear through the vagina.

The sensation of entering a woman, being in her, is seldom expressed openly but is everywhere a subject of preoccupation. Parallels between this Tlingit house and a recent Swedish Happening—a huge, reclining female figure one entered—may be more than superficial. In many ways it's like entering a Bridget Riley walk-in, or a Light Happening ("Step right in," begins Allan Kaprow), or a performance where everyone participates *in* art.

"I wanted," recalls Miro, "to penetrate into the spirit of objects. I realized the cubists had made a great revolution, but it was strictly a plastic revolution. I wanted to go beyond the plastic aspect, to get into the spirit of the thing."

Interval

An alternate to the art of connecting events is the art of the interval. Oriental art doesn't use connections, but intervals, whether in flower arrangement or Zen poetry or dress. Free time and space are perceived as the meaningful pause. "Our grandmother did to silence," writes Pada Pereva, "what inflections do to a voice."

Practically every aspect of Japanese life asserts the integrity of the interval. The *ma* (spaces between objects in the scene or simply spacing of objects) and *kukan* (empty space) are integers, realities.

Emilio Lanier writes: "The key to Japanese culture lies in the asymmetrical intervals: spacings, rhythms of writing, designing, music, dancing, all arts. Above all it lies in the ability to see and *feel* space. . . . The *ma*, perceived as an area of change—of hue, brightness, shape—becomes symbolized in all sorts of gestures, idioms, etc., throughout all of the cultural and practical arts, and comes finally to be symbolized even more abstractly in some contexts of activity as the area of freedom. This concept of freedom possesses a non-Aristotelian dimensionality quite outside the comprehension of the West, which considers itself the chief authority on, and author of, liberty and freedom of every form.

"In contrast, practically every aspect of Western life asserts the exclusive integrity of things, objects, masses. Spaces between objects aren't perceived as integers at all; the ideal in technological machines which yield power, and in Art and Life as well, is to negate and nullify intervals into rhythmical, balanced, symmetrical patterns—all exactly alike. According to the Western Principle of Plentitude, the universe is *full:* there are no gaps, no intervals: 'Nature abhors a vacuum'—at least, Western *human* nature does."

In Japanese flower arrangement, *shuji,* in the rhythm of the tea server in *ocha,* in all the arts of design, in *Noh* and *Kabuki* drama, the interval is stressed. It calls for more participation, being incomplete.

Misako Miyamoto writes of the Noh-plays: "The audience watches the play and catches the feeling through not only the

action and words but also the intervals of the period of the
pauses. . . . There is free creation in each person's mind . . .
and the audience relates to this situation with free thinking." Of
silent intervals in speech, she says, "Especially [in] the pauses
in a tone of voice, I can feel the person's unique personality and
his joy, sorrow and other complicated feelings." On listening to a
robin in early spring: "It sang with pauses . . . I could have
time to think about the bird [in] the silent moment between one
voice and others. . . . The pauses produced the effect of the
relation between the bird and me."

The interval invites participation: it creates riddles which
involve one.

In the allsense-allatonce electric world, the interval—not the
connection—becomes the crucial technique in organization.

Symballein (to throw together) means to juxtapose, to put
together without connections: it implies interval and resonance.

It was in symbolist poetry and in the primary musical structures that the Western world first intuited the onset of the electronic age and the change-over to the art of the interval. Soon
there was a tendency for all arts to approach the condition of
music: i.e., the art of timing and interval.

Joyce in *Finnegans Wake* took over the art of the interval as a
means of retrieving that fantastic wealth of perception and experience stored in ordinary language. As used by Joyce, dispensing
with the story-line became the means of instant grasp of complex
wholes.

Waiting, Not with Patience Nor Impatience, but with Expectation

Jesse Moses, a Delaware Indian, described his fellow tribes-
man, Nekatcit: "He was not a smoker. But when he had come
into the house, made the greetings and taken a seat, he would
either suggest that we have a smoke, or just ask for one. . . .
We usually spent about ten minutes just sitting and smoking. . . .

"He explained this period of silence and smoking together as
essential, for, said he, 'See, our smoke has now filled the room;
first it was in streaks and your smoke and my smoke moved about
that way, but now it is all mixed up into one. That is like our

minds and spirit too, when we must talk. We are now ready, for we will understand one another better.' "

In such societies, children are raised to listen to silence as well as sound. Luther Standing Bear, describing his childhood as an Oglalla Dakota in the 1870's, wrote: "[Children] . . . were taught to sit still and enjoy it. They were taught to use their organs of smell, to look when apparently there was nothing to see, and to listen intently when all seemingly was quiet."

Prince Mondupe, writing of his childhood in French Guinea, says, "We learned that silences as well as sounds are significant in the forest and how to listen to the silences. . . . Deeply felt silences might be said to be the core of our Kofon religion. During these times the nature within ourselves found unity with the nature of the earth."

Emptiness

Convinced that Americans fear emptiness more than fines, a justice of the peace in Battle Creek, Michigan, devised a remarkable sentence: he forced traffic violators to sit alone in empty rooms for three to five hours. Outraged citizens made him abandon this punishment, which was regarded as unnecessarily cruel.

When we have a free day, we look forward to how we will fill it. A person who is unemployed must explain: he is ill, retired, seeking work. To do nothing is indefensible. Millionaires expect their children to work during school vacations. Welfare workers are made uneasy by Indians sitting in front of gas stations, and when we come upon an unoccupied child, we say, "What, doing nothing? Do something!"

Literate man regards silence as empty of value. He calls radio silence dead air and condemns any cocktail party marked by long silences. Silence in music is usually interrupted by applause from some oaf hoping the concert is over. A Gilbert Stuart portrait of George Washington, its background unfinished, sells for far less than an identical portrait with background complete.

Dorothy Lee writes: "In Western thought—and I speak here of the view of the unsophisticated—space is empty and has to be occupied with matter; time is empty and to be filled with activity. In both primitive and civilized non-Western cultures, on the other hand, free space and time have being and integrity. It was this conception of *nothingness* as *somethingness* that enabled the philosophers of India to perceive the integrity of non-being, to name the free space and give us the zero."

Writing of the Bedouin tribesmen, T. E. Lawrence tells how one of them took him through a deserted palace where each room had a different scent, and then called, "Come and smell the very sweetest scent of all" and led him to a gaping window where the empty wind of the desert went throbbing past. "This," he told him, "is the best: it has no taste."

Window on Chaos

Firelight doesn't dispel darkness: it illuminates things within it. Darkness remains. In masked rituals by firelight, forms appear, then disappear, merging once more with nothingness. Form is temporary. Darkness and silence are constant.

The interval may serve as a reminder of the universal vacancy that everywhere underlies human order.

For centuries the Dogon of West Africa entrenched themselves in the center of the great bend of the Niger, on the fringe of an immense rock plateau. They build their villages, a strange huddle of terraced houses and granaries, all with thatched and pointed roofs, from the debris of the cliff's rock-falls and landslides. "Looking down from above, from the brink of the plateau, is to see a fantastic lunar landscape. All color has vanished, and even contours are obliterated in waves of heat. Beyond, stretching away as far as the horizon itself, there is nothing visible but a plain of sand, dotted sparsely with bushes. The first impression is unforgettable."

One is reminded of the Hopi of Arizona. Both groups found refuge in unwanted lands—harsh deserts where subtle colors change with the light and homes blend into the landscape. Nothing stands out save man-made art: angular, geometric, hard-edged. There's nothing gentle about such art: it's an absolute denial of formlessness. Hopi and Dogon masked rituals break the emptiness of the landscape as abruptly as the blinking neon lights of Las Vegas in the Nevada desert.

Hard-Edge

"To the blind, all things are sudden." Test this yourself: move about the room with your eyes closed. All encounters become abrupt. Emptiness combines with sudden interface. Connections are lacking. The gradations, shadings and continuities of the visual world are gone.

When Gertrude Stein became acquainted with Picasso in Paris around 1905, he asked her to obtain American comic strips for him. He was studying Japanese prints at the time, but found in comic strips clearer examples of interface and interval which interested him so much. It was at this same period that he began the study of African tribal art.

Most tribal art is hard-edge art. It's art of sharp contrasts, sudden juxtapositions and superimpositions. So is children's art. It favors the strongly marked boundary lines of the icon. Gradation and continuity are shunned.

A film-maker in Canada provided young children with the means to make animated films. The result was nearly 200 films of WHAM! BANG! with figures appearing, disappearing. There were no characters in the ordinary sense; no gradations; no chiaroscuro; just abrupt encounters à la Batman of hard-edge, cartoon art.

Hard-edge art is a visual presentation, but the experience it evokes isn't visual: it's tactile. It's full of abrupt encounters, sudden interfaces. When you have interface, you have happenings. In the World of Happenings, surface and events collide and grind against each other, creating new forms, much as the action of dialogue creates new insights. It's a world of all-at-onceness where things hit each other but where there are no connections.

Soft-Edge

At first sight the world looks like a flat extension of meaningless patches of light, dark, and color jumbled into a quilt-work. Infants born without arms and legs can never see in depth. Depth is discovered by touch, then married to sight. The eye caresses *over* objects.

Tactility converts the flat world of sight into the three-dimensional world of bodies. One by one objects grow out of this chaotic world, and remain unmistakably separate once identified. Patients blind from childhood, on whom vision has been bestowed by an operation, at first shrink from the welter of additional stimulation and from the flat continuity of the world they see. In 1964, in Sicily, five brothers—all blind from birth—each acquired sight following operations: months later a picture was published which showed them holding on to one another, with downcast eyes, as the lead brother felt his way through the doorway of their home. It took time and effort before they once more recognized the objects around them as separate items.

Only sight offers the sense of flat continuity and connectedness, and only the phonetic alphabet stresses the sense of sight over all senses. Soft-edge art, that is, three-dimensional perspective and shading, has its musical counterpart: the acoustic continuity of symphonic music. By contrast, hard-edge art belongs primarily to touch. It stresses interface and interval. The eye is offended by the interval.

Over the entrance to his academy, Plato carved, "Let no man enter who has not studied geometry." By this he meant the lineal, continuous world which his friend Euclid had defined. He meant the literate, visual world of gradations and continuity.

Bishop Burnet, who died in 1715, was disturbed by the unsymmetrical arrangement of the stars: "What a beautiful hemisphere they would have made," he exclaimed, "if they had been placed in rank and order; if they had all been disposed in regular figures . . . all finished and made up into one fair piece, or great composition, according to the rules of art and symmetry."

Sight is the only sense that offers detachment. This detachment gave literate man enormous power over his environment, but led to a corresponding unwillingness to get involved. Man became a detached observer, a passive Peeping Tom. He stared out from a fixed observation post (from where I stand) and hoped the view would be unbroken and symmetrical.

Superimposition and Interpenetration

X-ray depicts (simultaneously and without favoritism) many dimensions of a *single* being. But superimposition depicts (simultaneously and without favoritism) *many* beings. All are locked together: they embrace. No form overshadows any other. Nothing dominates the foreground: in fact there's neither foreground nor background.

When the Paleolithic sketches at Pech-Merle Cavern first became known to art historians, these were judged to be interesting but deficient efforts by artists not fully human. Thanks to Hans Arp and others, today it's possible to see these interpenetrating designs for what they are: superb depictions of the essence of tribalism. In fact, how else would one depict a tribe?

I put this problem to students: sketch the seamless web of tribal life, showing the interpenetration of equal figures, including ancestors. Most were baffled: those who succeeded did so by producing drawings identical to native ones.

Literate man generally defined an object in terms of the unique space it filled, as well as its relations with objects occupying other spaces. For him, each object occupied its own space and no other. He perceived the world as made up of private spaces. In it, every man and every thing was an island.

Juxtaposition

"A line," says Miro, "has to breathe. If it doesn't, it's dead, and if you can see a corpse, you can smell it."

A basic belief common to both pre- and post-literate men is that powers reside in all things: words, objects, songs, and, particularly, people. Under certain circumstances, these unfold themselves or are released, creating change, especially when they transact with energies emanating from other properties.

Hopi farmers don't grow beans: they relate to beans so as to release the bean-ness within each seed—and thus food comes into being.

Physicists tell us that electricity isn't something conveyed by, or contained in, anything, but the conditions we observe where there are certain spatial relations between things.

Symbolist poets juxtaposed words so that energies within each reflected on the other, creating new forms. Rimbaud called these *Illuminations*. Illumination came from within.

Rouault wasn't concerned with the Renaissance technique of light on, but with light through—light emanating from the object and directed *toward* the viewer, as with stained glass windows or television. This calls for total illumination from within and converts viewer into screen.

Translation unlocks powers in language and art imprisoned by classification and convention. Yeats, Joyce, Shaw (Irish) unlocked English, as did Conrad (Pole), Nabokov (Russian), and Pound and Eliot (Americans). Poets unlock powers within words by repositioning them so they transact with one another in new ways.

"Poetry," wrote Laura Riding, "is an attempt to make language do more than express; to make it work; to redistribute intelligence by means of the word. If it succeeds in this, the problem of communication disappears. It does not treat this problem as a matter of mathematical distribution of intelligence between an abstract known and unknown represented by a concrete knower and not-knower. The distribution must take place, if at all, within the intelligence itself. Prose evades this problem by making slovenly equations which always seem successful because, being inexact, they conceal inexactness. Poetry always faces, and generally meets with, failure. But even if it fails, it is at least at the heart of the difficulty, which it treats not as a difficulty of minds but of mind."

Tribalism on Campus

Solemn faculty, assembling to discuss replacing Art 37 with Art 156, have about as much relevance to what's really happening as exiled White Russians holding court in Topeka.

Traditionally the university was an ivory tower where impractical scholars dealt with obsolete data. As the university was drawn into the war economy, this role was abandoned and ridiculed. What was overlooked was that the ivory tower offered detachment and perspective. Impracticality meant wider focus. Obsolete data meant declassified knowledge. All three aided in the discovery of fundamental patterns and processes.

The traditional university was thus an anti-environment, a counter situation designed to promote perception and awareness. Plato's Academy used writing for this purpose. Writing had a double advantage: it was then fresh and alien, and it stressed sight, the only sense that promotes detachment, all other senses serving to involve one.

Western Man long enjoyed this two-party system, using universities and art (both drawing heavily on the past) as counterpoint to the present. Humanism served as anti-environment to Renaissance mechanization. Romanticism served as counterpoint to the Industrial Revolution. Tribalism now serves this function in the Electronic Age.

But whereas Humanism and Romanticism were welcome in universities, even rooted there, Tribalism remains largely extracurricular. Thus our real university—in the sense of our culture's only strong anti-environment—exists largely apart from campuses.

Admitting Tribalism on campus involves more than merely welcoming a new subject or style. Where Tribalism is most relevant, *e.g.*, Arts, it means the total restructuring of whole areas of the university. The traditional roles of knowing teacher and unknowing pupil will have to be abandoned, along with grades. Equipment and facilities will have to become part of a service environment, available for private experimentation and play, as libraries now are. Visiting artists in residence will have to be increased in number. Administrators will play custodial roles. Above all, any art program will have to be decentralized, scattered about in many self-controlled mini-environments.

Every artist—without exception—who visited the Carnegie project at the Santa Cruz campus of the University of California made these points.

Santa Cruz, perhaps more than any other university, has moved in this direction. It consists of federated colleges with separate faculties and campuses. Grades are Pass/Fail. A fair number of students who gave me papers or worked on films or participated in various projects weren't enrolled in the University. Throughout the Santa Cruz area a large number of professional photographers, film-makers, script-writers, etc., who commute by air to distant assignments, used the University as a service environment: library, film showings, lectures, faculty and student friendships, bookstore, coffee shops, and the general dialogue of the community. There is an absence of competition among students. As one student, Fred Wiebe, noted, the challenge is personal.

But Santa Cruz stands out as an exception, and even here, change is far from complete. To be complete and successful, that change must finally come from a voluntary abdication of power. As Mead notes, "It was, in final analysis, men who gave votes to women. It will be the House of Lords that votes to abolish the House of Lords. It will be those over eighteen who must agree, if those under eighteen are to vote." Marcuse goes further. "No connection existed between the terrorist organization and the achievement of Algerian independence. The Algerian War was won for the Algerians not in Algeria but in Paris."

UCLA's film program was originally based on a formal teacher-pupil relationship with lectures, grades, and long training before a film was attempted. Almost nothing beneficial resulted. The faculty then voluntarily abdicated and assumed the role of adviser. For example, a committee of three students and two faculty sets equipment policy. Students and faculty jointly judge films for public showings. Students must first make a film before being admitted to the program. The result is that student films have improved immeasurably. Faculty films have also improved. The department is known off-campus by the films produced by students.

Traditionally, universities were judged by the fame of their faculties. They may soon be judged by the fame of their students.

COMPREHENSIVE THINKING

---

by R. BUCKMINSTER FULLER

SPECIALIZATION is in fact only a fancy form of slavery wherein the "expert" is fooled into accepting his slavery by being made to feel that he is in a socially and culturally preferred, ergo, highly secure, life-long position.

However, the big thinking in general—of a spherical Earth and

Reprinted in excerpt from William Ewald, ed., *Environment and Change*. Copyright © 1968 by Indiana University Press. By permission of the publisher.

celestial navigation, in contradistinction to a four-cornered flat world with only localized preoccupations—was retained exclusively by the great pirates. Theirs was the knowledge of the world and its resources; and of the arts of navigation and ship building and handling; and of grand logistical strategies and of nationally undetectable, therefore effectively deceptive, international exchange media and trade-balancing tricks by which the top pirate, as "the house" (in the gambler's words), always won.

Then there came a time, World War I, when the most powerful out-pirates challenged the in-pirates with the scientific and technological innovation of going under and above the sea surface and into the invisible realm of electronics and chemical warfaring. The in-pirates, in order to save themselves, had to allow their scientists to go to work on their own inscrutable terms. And in saving themselves the great pirates allowed the scientists to plunge their grand industrial strategy into the vast ranges of the electromagnetic spectrum that were utterly invisible to the pirates.

The pirates until then had ruled the world through their extraordinarily keen *senses*. They judged things for themselves and they didn't trust any one else's eyes. They trusted only that which they could personally smell, hear, touch or see. But the great pirates could not see what was going on in the vast ranges of the electro-magnetic reality. Technology was going from wire to wireless, from track to trackless, from pipe to pipeless and from visible structural muscle to the invisible chemical element strengths of metallic alloys and electro-magnetics.

The great pirates came out of that first world war unable to cope knowledgeably with what was going on in the advanced scientific frontiers of industry. The pirates delegated inspection to their "troubleshooter" experts but had to content themselves with relayed secondhand information. This forced them to appraise blindly, ergo, only opinionatedly whether this or that man really knew what he was talking about, for the great pirates could not judge for themselves. Thus they were no longer the masters. That was the end. The great pirates are extinct.

Because they had always operated secretly, and because they hoped they were not through, they of course did not announce or allow it to be announced that they were extinct. And because the public had never known of them and had been fooled into thinking of their kingly stooges and local politicians as being in *reality* the head men, *society was and is as yet unaware either that the great pirates once ran the world or that they are now utterly extinct.*

Though the pirates are extinct, all of our international trade balancing and money ratings, as well as all economic accounting in both the capitalistic and communistic countries, hold strictly to the rules, value systems, terminology, and concepts established by those great pirates.

Powerful though many successors to the great pirates' fragmented dominions may be, no one government, religion, or enterprise now holds the world's physical or metaphysical initiatives. The metaphysical initiative, too, has gone into competitive confusion between old religions and more recent political or scientific ideologies. These competitors are already so heavily weighted with physical investments and proprietary expediencies as to vitiate any metaphysical initiative. A new, physically uncompromised metaphysical initiative of unbiased integrity could unify the world. It could and probably will be provided by the utterly impersonal problem solutions of the computers, to whose superhumanly calculative capabilities all political, scientific, and religious leaders can face-savingly acquiesce. Abraham Lincoln's concept of "Right triumphing over Might" was realized when Einstein as metaphysical intellect wrote the equation of physical universe $E = mc^2$ and thus comprehended it. Thus the metaphysical took the measure of and mastered the physical. That relationship seems by experience to be irreversible. Nothing in our experience suggests that energy could comprehend and write the equation of intellect.

The great pirates did run the world. They were the first and last to do so. They were *world men* and they ran the world with ruthless and brilliant pragmatism based on the information of their specialist servants.

First came their Royal Society scientific servants with their "Great Second Law of Thermodynamics" whose "entropy" showed that every energy machine kept losing energy and eventually "ran down"; ergo, in their pre-speed-of-light-measurement misconception of an omni-simultaneous, instant, universe, that universe as an energy machine must also be "running down." Thus the energy wealth and life support were erroneously thought to be continually depleted.

Next came Thomas Malthus, professor of political economics of the great pirates' East India Company, who said that man was multiplying himself at a geometrical rate and that food was multiplying only at an arithmetical rate.

And last, thirty-five years later, came the great pirates' biological specialist servant, Charles Darwin, who, explaining his theory of animate evolution, said that survival was only for the fittest.

Quite clearly to the great pirates it was a scientific fact that there was not only not enough to go around but apparently not enough to go around for even one percent of humanity to live at a satisfactorily sustaining standard of living. And due to entropy the inadequacy would always increase. So survival, they said, was obviously a cruel and almost hopeless battle. They ran the world on the basis that these Malthusian-Darwinian entropy concepts were absolute scientific laws, for that was what their scientifically respected, intellectual, slave specialists had told them.

Then we have the great pragmatic ideologist Marx running into that entropic-Malthusian-Darwinian information and saying, "Well, the workers who produce things are the fittest because they are the only ones who know how to physically produce and therefore they ought to be the ones to survive." That was the beginning of the great "class warfare."

All of the ideologies range somewhere between the great pirates and the Marxists. But all of them assume that there is not enough to go around. And that has been the rationalized working hypothesis of all the great sovereign claims to great areas of the Earth. Because of their respective exclusivities all the class warfare ideologies have become extinct. Capitalism and socialism are mutually extinct. Science now finds there can be ample for all, but only if the sovereign fences are completely removed. The basic you-or-me-not-enough-for-both-ergo-someone-must-die tenets of the class warfaring are extinct.

Now let us examine more closely what we know scientifically about extinction.

At the meeting of the annual Congress of the American Association for the Advancement of Science held approximately eight years ago in Philadelphia, two papers were presented in widely separated parts of the Congress. One was presented in anthropology and the other in biology. Though the two author-scientists knew nothing of each other's efforts, they were closely related. The one in anthropology examined the case histories of all the known *human tribes* that had become extinct. The biological paper investigated the case histories of all the known *biological species* that had become extinct. Both scientists sought for a common cause of extinction. Both found a cause, and when the two papers were accidentally brought together it was discovered that the researchers had found the same causes. *Extinction* in both cases *was the consequence of over-specialization.*

How does that come about? We can develop faster and faster running horses as specialists. To do so we inbreed by mating two fast-running horses. By concentrating certain genes, the probability of their dominance is increased. But in doing so we *breed out or sacrifice general adaptability.* Inbreeding and specialization always do away with general adaptability.

There is a major pattern of energy in the universe wherein the very large events—earthquakes, and so forth—occur in any one area of universe very much less frequently than do the small-energy events. At any tropical land there are many more insects than there are earthquakes. In the patterning of total evolutionary events, there comes a time, once in a while, amongst the myriad of low-energy events, when a large-energy event occurs and is so disturbing that with their general adaptability lost, the ultra-specialized creatures perish.

I will give you a typical history, that of a type of bird that lived on a special variety of micro-marine life. These birds flying around gradually discovered that there are certain places in which that particular marine life tends to pocket, in the marshes along certain ocean shores of certain lands. So, instead of flying aimlessly for chance finding of that marine life, they go to where it is concentrated in those marshes. After a while, the water begins to recede in the marshes, because the Earth's polar ice cap is beginning to increase.

So only the birds with very long beaks can reach down deep enough in the marsh holes to get at the marine life. Hence the unfed, short-billed birds die off. This leaves only the long-beakers. When the birds' inborn drive to reproduce occurs there are only other long-beakers surviving with whom to breed. This concentrates their long-beak genes. So with continually receding waters and generation to generation inbreeding, longer and longer beaked birds are produced. The waters keep receding and the beaks of successive generations of the birds get bigger and bigger. The long-beakers seemed to be prospering when all at once there was a great fire in the marshes and it was discovered that because their beaks had become so heavy they could no longer fly. They could not escape the flames by flying out of the marsh. Waddling on their legs they were too slow to escape and so they perished. This is typical of the way in which extinction occurs through over-specialization.

When, as we have seen, the great pirates let their scientists have free rein in World War I, the pirates themselves became so preoccupied with harvesting enormous wealth that they not only lost track of what the scientists were doing within the vast invisible world but they inadvertently abandoned their own comprehensivity and also became severe specialists as industrial production money makers, thus they compounded their own acceleration to extinction in the world paralyzing economic crash of 1929.

But society never knew that the great pirates had been running the world. Nor did society realize in 1929 that the great pirates had become extinct. However, world society was fully and painfully aware of the economic paralysis. Society consisted then, as now, almost entirely of specialized slaves in education, management, science, office routines, craft, farming, pick-and-shovel labor, and their families. Our world society now has none of the comprehensive and realistic world knowledge that the great pirates had.

Because world societies thought mistakenly of their local politicians (who were only the stooges of the great pirates) as being realistically the head men, society went to them to get the industrial and economic machinery going again. Because industry is inherently world-coordinate these world economic depression events of the 1920–30's meant that each of the local head politicians of a number of countries was asked separately to make the world work. On this basis the world-around inventory of resources was no longer integratable. Each of the political leaders' mandates was given from different ideological groups and their differing viewpoints and resource difficulties led inevitably to World War II.

The politicians, having an automatic bias, were committed to defend and aid only their own side. Each assumed the validity of the Malthusian-Darwinian-You-or-Me-to-the-death struggle. Because of the working concept that there was not enough to go around, the most aggressive political leaders exercised their political leadership by heading their countries into war to overcome the rest of the world, thus to dispose of the unsupportable excess population through decimation and starvation—the age-old lethal formula of ignorant men.

Thus we had all our world society *specializing,* whether under Fascism, Communism, or Capitalism. All the great ideological groups assumed Armageddon.

Getting ready for the assumed inexorable Armageddon, each applied science and all of the great scientific specialization capabilities only toward weaponry, thus developing the ability to totally destroy themselves with no comprehensively organized oppositional thinking capability and initiative powerful enough to coordinate and prevent it. Thus by 1946, we were on the swift way to extinction despite the inauguration of the United Nations, to which none of the exclusive sovereign prerogatives were surrendered.

Suddenly, unrecognized as such by society, the evolutionary antibody to the *extinction of humanity through specialization* appeared in the form of the *computer* and its comprehensively commanded *automation,* which made man obsolete as a physical production and control specialist—and just in time. The computer as super-specialist can persevere, day and night, day after day, in picking out the pink from the blue at superhumanly sustainable speeds. The computer can also operate in degrees of cold or heat at which man would perish.

Man is going to be displaced altogether as a specialist by the computer. Man himself is being forced to reestablish, employ, and enjoy his innate "comprehensivity." Coping with the totality of spaceship Earth and Universe is ahead for all of us. Evolution is apparently intent that man fulfill a much greater destiny than that of being a simple muscle and reflex machine, i.e., a slave automaton.

Evolution consists of many great revolutionary events taking place quite independently of man's consciously attempting to bring them about. Man is very vain and he likes to feel that he is responsible for all the favorable things that happen and innocent of all the unfavorable happenings. But all the larger evolutionary patternings seeming favorable or unfavorable to man's conditioned reflexing are transpiring transcendentally to any of man's conscious planning or contriving.

To disclose to you your own vanity of reflexing, I remind you quickly that none of you is consciously routing the fish and potato you ate for lunch into this and that specific gland to make hair, skin, or anything like that. None of you is aware of how you came to grow from seven pounds to seventy pounds, and then to one hundred and seventy, and so forth. All of this is automated and always has been. There is a great deal that is automated regarding our total salvation on earth and I would like us to get into that frame of mind right now in order to be useful in the short time we have.

Let us now exercise our intellectual faculties as best we can to apprehend the evolutionary patternings transcending our spontaneous cognition and recognitions. We may first note an evolutionary trend that countered all of the educational systems and the deliberately increased professional specialization of scientists. This contradiction occurred at the beginning of World War II, when extraordinary new scientific instruments had been developed and the biologists and chemists and physicists were meeting in Washington, D.C., on special war missions. Those scientists began to realize that whereas a biologist used to think he was dealing only in cells, and that a chemist was dealing only in molecules, and the physicist dealing only in atoms, they now found their new powerful instrumentation and contiguous operations overlapping. Each specialist suddenly realized that he was concerned alike with atoms, molecules, and cells. Each found there was no real dividing line between their professional interests. They had not meant to do this, but their professional fields were being integrated—inadvertently, on their part, but apparently purposefully—by inexorable evolution.

So, as of World War II, the scientists began to invent new professional designations, e.g., the biochemist and the biophysicist and so forth. They were forced to. Despite their deliberate attempts only to specialize, they were being merged into ever more inclusive fields of consideration. Thus was deliberately specializing man led back unwittingly to once more reuse his innately comprehensive capabilities.

RESEARCH FOR CHOICE

---

by HERBERT A. SIMON

UNDER ITS TERMS of reference, this paper is to be concerned with "proposing useful systems of data collection and retrieval, in closing gaps in knowledge, in establishing productive interdisciplinary research, and in delimiting computer capacities and limitations regarding development toward an optimum environment." I have interpreted these terms to encompass (1) the nature of the knowledge and information about the *structure* of our social system that we need for planning, (2) the nature of the knowledge and information about the *state* (past, present, future) of the system that we need, and (3) the advances that we need in the technology of the choice and design process itself.

The discussion is arranged in six main sections followed by a summary and conclusions:

1. The main relevant kinds and uses of information and knowledge, with particular reference to the distinction between "structure" and "state" mentioned above.

2. Some of the critical gaps in the substantive knowledge and information now available.

Reprinted from William Ewald, ed., *Environment and Policy*. Copyright © 1968 by Indiana University Press. By permission of the publisher.

3. The information needs for fundamental research, that is, for an understanding of structure.

4. The information needs for planning and design, over and above structural information.

5. Progress and prospects of research on the processes of decision and design.

6. The present and prospective information technology, in the light of the demands that are likely to be placed on it.

Uses and Kinds of Information

Considerable pains are taken to ascertain periodically the per capita gross national product in the United States. To what questions is this information addressed? First, it may be used to answer: "How well are we doing?" It serves as a crude scorecard of economic well-being.

Second, the per capita GNP may be used to call attention to problems when they arise. When GNP drops from last year's level, a nation looks to needed shifts in its economic policies.

Third, the GNP, along with other statistics, may become grist for the mill of research that is trying to understand the structure of an economic system—how the government's budget balance affects the level of economic activity, say. This use does not aim at immediate action, but at understanding systemic response, to make subsequent actions more intelligent.

Fourth, the GNP together with measures of productivity may be used to ascertain the present state of a system in order to plan for its future—to predict, for example, future levels of economic activity, in order to predict future consumption of electric power, thus to make plans for building generating stations.

Information has, at least potentially, these four broad classes of use: as scorecard, to direct attention, to analyze a system's structure, and to ascertain parameters of its state. As the example shows, a single statistic may serve, at different times, in all four uses. On the other hand, data of particular kinds may be especially appropriate to one of these uses. All four uses are important to planning and social choice, and they often lead to quite *different* demands on the processes and institutions that produce information.

Planners and policy makers tend to be most aware of their needs for data in the fourth category—for facts and figures that they can use for projecting trends and designing actions. Their projections and plans depend critically, however, on how the system operates—on its structure—hence, on the use that funda- mental researchers have previously made of information in the third category.

Much of the significance for professional planners and policy makers of the first two kinds of information is also indirect. Scorecards and attention directors are the links between pro- fessional activity and the political process. The FBI index of major crimes is not used to manage law enforcement activities, but to call public attention to a problem and to marshal public resources to deal with it. The same is generally true of auto death statistics, or an index of air purity for a city. These measures are less concerned with the administrative question of what to do than with the political question of what problems should be near the top of society's agenda and what it is worth—economically or socially—to solve them. The operation of this part of the informa- tion system may have a great deal to do with whether first things are put first.

There are some problems common to all four information categories, in particular, problems about what kinds of fact a society needs in order to enable it to deal with the important social goals. The next section discusses these common problems relating to substantive gaps in the information system.

The Substantive Information Gaps

Relatively speaking, we are best informed about demography, economics, and technology. However inadequate specialists may find them for particular purposes, our data in these areas are extensive, and improve continually in quantity and technical quality. Although we should not relax our efforts toward bettering these kinds of information, there are almost complete gaps in our information system that require even more vigorous efforts to fill them. We need to have much better information about the quality of life, and we need better data bases for making longitudinal comparisons of social indicators from one point in time to another.

The availability of any or all of the four kinds of information about a problem encourages social action to deal with that problem. The careful statistics we maintain on whooping cranes inform us whether we are succeeding in saving the population from extinction, warn us when we (or they) have had a setback, provide basic information that can be used to investigate the causes affecting birth and death rates of whooping cranes, and provide data for planning the nesting areas the birds will need.

Our relative wealth of information about economics, the industrial system, and our natural resources contrasts sharply with our lack of information about other dimensions of the quality of life. There is a sharp contrast, too—probably not coincidental —in the relative amount of effort we devote to solving problems of economics and the natural environment as compared with other social problems.

Yet economic problems are no longer the central problems of our society, and problems of our physical and biological environment, though troublesome, are well within the capacity of our existing scientific knowledge and resources to handle. Contemporary statements of national goals, while not ignoring these traditional areas, place increasing emphasis on more subtle and difficult aims: enhancing human dignity, realizing human potentials, widening the range of opportunities for choice. A society that wishes to advance such goals must be prepared to measure or assess the qualities to which they refer.

Notwithstanding those who point with pride or view with alarm, we do not know whether public and private morality are declining or improving, whether human lives are fuller or emptier than they were a generation ago, whether there are more risk takers or more organization men, whether we are lonely or smothered in togetherness. The trends in our happiness, in the richness of our lives, in our morale, and in our morals must become matters of fact rather than opinion, just as the degree of our wealth and our hunger have become matters of fact.

There are now modest beginnings toward taking such measures. We have some data, very imperfect, about mental illness, crime, and delinquency. Improvement in their scope and comparability will develop them into useful instruments for social policy. The last thirty years have seen great progress in techniques for taking public opinion polls, and for measuring expectations and attitudes. We are technically equipped today for a continuing, large-scale undertaking that will generate the information we need about the quality of life. We should aim at launching such an undertaking in the immediate future. It will need to have several components, of which direct data-gathering will be one part, fundamental behavioral research (see next section) another. An annual expenditure of $70 million (.01 percent of GNP) would be a not inappropriate initial scale for the data-gathering effort. Part of this sum might expand programs of the Census Bureau or other government information agencies, but a large part should be granted —in the spirit of long-term research and development grants—to non-governmental organizations that could adopt a highly experimental attitude in their approach.

To pursue social goals that involve the less tangible dimensions of the quality of life, we will need greatly expanded and improved information about the distribution of knowledge and skills among the population, and the distribution of values and attitudes. As time replaces money as the principal scarce resource in our society, we will need to know in considerable detail how various kinds of individuals in our society allocate their time. Another crucial scarce resource is attention, particularly attention to political matters. We need sophisticated information about the allocation of attention.

Measures of achievement of social goals are always relative. Hence for all four data uses we have an especially great need for retrospective, longitudinal measures.

We do not really know, for example, whether leisure has increased or decreased over the past hundred years. We do not even know—the statistics are so poor—whether per capita crime rates are rising or falling. We are especially deficient in longitudinal studies where the identity of respondents is retained—Project TALENT being a rare contemporary example of the sorts of panel study we need.

Generating data for intertemporal and intercultural comparison poses well-known technical and conceptual problems. Economists have faced these problems in their realm with sufficient success so that meaningful (if not perfect) comparisons of economic well-being can be made between Japan and England, or between 1900 and today. A satisfactory technical level of comparability is also achievable for measures of the other dimensions of the quality of life.

Measures that have naturally defined units, e.g., hours per day as measures of time allocation, offer the simplest opportunities for longitudinal comparison. But we need not, and should not, limit ourselves to these. We need measures, for example, about how happy people are—how they feel about life and their well-being. We know a great deal about how to take measures even as intangible as these. We know much less about how to interpret comparative differences in the measures from place to place or from time to time. Our interpretations will improve only as our theories of human behavior and attitudes improve, and our theories will improve only as we have better data for developing and testing them. We must view our task as a bootstrap operation, in which better data will improve theory, and better theory, data. This is the characteristic path of progress in all sciences.

Information for Fundamental Research

No amount of information about the social system, no amount of awareness of its problems, will enable us to improve it unless we understand *how* it works: its structures, mechanisms, processes. Improved information in increased volume about juvenile delinquency will contribute only indirectly to solutions of the problems. Unless we understand something about the relations of cause and effect, knowing the present state of the system, in whatever detail, will not help us change it. Change will become possible only with improved scientific knowledge.

The main goal, therefore, in improving our social information system must be to provide the information that will be most useful for behavioral and social research aimed at broadening our understanding of social structure and process. It is through this indirect route that better information will make its main contribution to the achievement of social gains. A generation hence we may wish to shift emphasis, when better social science knowledge is available. Then engineering measures of the state of the system and managerial and political attention-directing measures may take first priority. But it is a little futile to know what needs to be accomplished until we know better how to do it.

Parallel, then, with the expansion of activities aimed directly at gathering more and better data must go a great expansion of activities aimed at advancing basic behavioral sciences and our society's competence—qualitative and quantitative—to carry on basic behavioral and social research. A reasonable target for the next decade might be a production rate of 5,000 capable, well-trained Ph.D.s per year and a national basic research budget in the behavioral and social sciences of $1 billion. The expenditure estimate assumes that the aspirations and imaginations of behavioral scientists will grow with their opportunities and competence—as has happened in the natural sciences since World War II.

Much of the new information needed for basic research will be generated within the research activity itself. Special information-gathering activities, of the sorts mentioned in the previous section, will account for only a small part of the growth in information—but an essential part. (Similarly, a small but important part of the information of natural science is generated in a "data bank" mode: astronomical and meteorological observations, exact determination of important physical and chemical constants and standards, taxonomic and ecological data in biology, and so on.)

Most information relevant to social planning, however, will continue to be *ad hoc* data—gathered as accessory to particular research inquiries. With the improvement of theories and the standardization of measuring instruments, such data will increasingly find uses beyond the particular inquiry that generated them. This is another—and important—aspect of comparability of information, which grows hand in hand with the progress of good basic theory.

Vast amounts of data about social phenomena are gathered by governmental and other organizations in our society today as a byproduct of their regular administrative activities. Obvious examples that come to mind are the Social Security files and the records of the Internal Revenue Service. Relatively little of this information is now available either for social research or for social planning. When efforts have been made in the past few years to tap these data more effectively, two kinds of difficulties have been encountered, and only partly surmounted: technical problems of combining fragmentary information for different time periods and from different files; and problems of preventing invasion of privacy by misuse of the data. In many respects, the two problems are opposite sides of a coin—solutions to the technical problem generally increase the dangers to privacy.

The threats of invasion of privacy must be taken seriously, but in perspective with threats from other directions. The association with names and fingerprints of the kinds of information already collected in the files of the FBI and various security agencies constitutes a far greater threat to privacy than could conceivably be created by coordination of government operating statistics. Electronic eavesdropping is a much more serious threat (and more difficult to control) than any potential eavesdropping in computer-stored records.

The answer, of course, is not to ignore the threat to privacy, but to find the technical means for safeguarding privacy while making data available for the broadest possible research purposes. Storage and processing in electronic computers gives us the technical basis for combining data from various sources, while maintaining the identity of reporting units over time. The latter is essential, because many of the questions our research will need to ask require longitudinal panel data for their answers. Maintenance of identity of reporting units compounds the privacy problem, but does not make it insoluble. Privacy, like security, is relative, and is maintained by raising the costs of achieving successful violations. Development of the technology for providing research access to operating data, while protecting privacy, is an important item for the current action agenda. The problem can almost surely be solved by an expenditure not exceeding a few million dollars, and probably for much less.

One of the important new techniques that computers have contributed to social science research is the simulation of the behavior of social systems by constructing models of them. In this way, systems can be studied that are far too complex to be analyzed by classical verbal or mathematical means. Modeling may be used both in basic research, as a technique for computing the system behavior implied by hypothesized complex theories, and in planning, as a technique for predicting the behavior of a system characterized by a known set of mechanisms.

The use of modeling in planning requires that the important features of system structure be already known—that is, that the basic research job has already been done. For this reason, the most serious limits on the use of modeling in planning today are limits on our understanding of system *structure*, not limits on our data about the *state* of the system. We will say more about this point later. The experience with modeling reinforces our general conclusion, however, that the weakest link in our information system is information about structure and that strengthening this link requires the expansion of basic research activity.

Information for Planning

A case has already been made for emphasizing an indirect route, through basic research, to improving information for social decision. This does not mean that progress in our measurements of the state of our social system must stand still while this indirect route is being pursued. Progress in measurement does not necessarily mean *more* measurement than we carry on now. As a matter of fact, it might even be argued that public planning has, in general, been too much preoccupied with data collection and projection, and too little with design and decision. Progress will come, not through mere collection of information or assembly of impressive "data banks," but through thinking through the relation of data about the state of the system to the planning process. What are the guidelines for deciding what data will be important in planning?

Prediction for its own sake is a costly and pointless game. The objective in making predictions and projections into the future is to provide a basis for the decisions that are to be taken today; tomorrow's decisions can and should be made on the basis of the information available tomorrow. Some decisions are required today to provide lead time for tomorrow's actions.

The future is relevant to decisions taken today only to the

extent that these decisions have consequences for the future that are in some sense irreversible—that cannot be undone. The main reason, for example, why forward planning is so closely associated with decisions about physical structures is the permanence of those structures, and .the long future period during which the design decisions have consequences that cannot be altered without cost. We need to identify, therefore, the principal forms that permanence and irreversibility take. . . .

Four kinds of decision are especially likely to entail long-term irreversibilities: (1) decisions about physical structures, (2) decisions committing a system to a new technology, (3) decisions about education and training, and (4) interrelated sequences of non-simultaneous decisions. Decisions about physical structures have irreversible consequences for the obvious reason that we don't want to bear the cost of premature obsolescence.

Commitments to a new technology are often irreversible because they bring with them many decisions in the other three categories. A shift from freighting by railroad to freighting by truck leads to decisions to build highway facilities and not to build railway facilities, to train people for highway occupations and not for railroad operations, and to construct all sorts of facilities that *assume* the trucking operations (e.g., filling stations, factories on highways rather than sidings, and so on).

Decisions about education and training result in storing "programs" of useful knowledge and skill in humans. These programs may suffer from obsolescence just as physical structures do.

The fourth category cuts across the others, often taking the form of a "standardization" problem. A complex system—a railroad, say, or a city—once built is not renewed all at once, but in a piecemeal fashion. Thus, if the wrong track gauge is chosen for a railroad, it may never be economical at any subsequent moment to change it, for it may be more efficient to make each new partial replacement or extension compatible with the existing gauge. Similarly, the question of whether the United States should, at any given time, shift to the metric system is distinct from the question of whether it would have been better to have adopted it initially.

In public planning, "comprehensiveness" is not, in itself, an important or desirable planning goal. Many economic, technical, and social affairs are better regulated by the operation of the decentralized market than by attempts at central planning. Rather, public planning should focus its attention on the crucial "standardization" problems—including the problem of coordinating manpower and structures with technological commitments.

In urban planning, for example, the key standardization problems arise from interdependencies in land use. As all urban planners know, planning a new city in the middle of the jungle is quite different from planning for existing cities.

Planning focused on standardization problems must take as its first task identifying the technologies, and changes in technologies, that will operate as prime organizing factors and driving forces in the society. Its second task must be to discover varieties of economic, technical, legal, political, and administrative means for modifying these key factors. Its third task must be to assess the consequences for the rest of the system—including consequences mediated through markets—of changes in the key factors. Such analysis is usually best carried out with aggregate models that sacrifice detail to ability to trace main systems effects. . . .

Research on the Choice Process

When design and planning are described as "arts," the main intended implication is a negative one: they are not sciences, hence do not rely solely on analytic methods, hence cannot be fully systematized but depend essentially on such indescribables as "judgment" and "intuition." As a historical statement, this is true; it is rapidly ceasing to be true about the present and prospective state of the art.

Great strides have been made in the past ten years toward learning how human beings solve problems, discover facts and theories, and design devices and systems. Much of the mystery has been stripped away from the processes we call "judgment" and "intuition." A number of computer programs have been written that imitate human problem-solving or design processes closely (cognitive simulation), or that provide functional substitutes for them (artificial intelligence). Some of these schemes have already reached the stage of industrial application—to the designing of motors and generators, the locating and designing of highways, the scheduling of large civil engineering projects. . . .

Opinions can and do differ about the present state of the art. What seems eminently clear, however, is that we are about to have, if we do not already have, a clear, powerful, precise theory of the processes of planning and design. The existence of this theory will have the most momentous consequences for the activity of planning:

1. *We will be able to automate increasingly large aspects of the design and planning processes*—in many instances, perhaps the whole process. Typically, planning organizations will be systems with human and automated components working in intimate relation with each other.

2. *We will be able to teach planning and design skills.* There is a constant tendency, in professional schools, to encourage formal, intellectual analytic skills to drive out the "intuitive" skills of synthesis and design. The former meet the academic criteria that the modern university sets for "proper" subjects, while the latter do not. As a result, the stronger engineering schools have become schools of mathematics and physics, teaching precious little engineering, while the best medical schools have become schools of biology. (Schools of law and architecture have been less subject to this academic erosion.)

As we gain a scientific understanding of the design process itself, it becomes possible to restore design as a central subject in the professional school. But now the main emphasis will not be on *designing*, but on devising effective design *systems*. The design curricula will emphasize our scientific knowledge of intelligence, human and artificial, and the principles underlying the design of systems that exhibit intelligence. . . .

The Information Technology

The task of this "Research for Choice" paper is itself a planning task—planning for decision-making systems. Hence, the earlier discussion of planning and prediction is quite relevant to this task also. Anyone who looks at what has happened to our information-processing technology over the past twenty-five years will despair of predicting what that technology will look like twenty-five—much less fifty—years hence. Almost no one in 1942, certainly no one in 1917, would have or could have predicted the computer revolution we have already had.

On the other hand, it is not clear that anyone would have been well advised to have behaved differently in 1917, even if he had known the exact shape and form of the coming computer revolution. The failures of planning that we observe are failures to plan five, three, or even one year in advance, not failures to plan twenty-five or ten years in advance. These short-run failures generally involve failure to *credit* prospective changes that are entirely predictable and even predicted. The question of credibility will be mentioned again later.

If we accept the premise that the twenty-five-year future of information processing is at least as unpredictable now as it was in 1940, then we will look for techniques that allow us to get by with minimal predictions. One such technique is to consider a few basic parameters that characterize such systems, rather than the detail of hardware. Indeed, this is the basic strategy we have followed in our discussion so far. In this section, I should like to make more explicit some of the key assumptions about the future information-processing technology that underlie this whole analysis.

An information-processing system comprises means for collecting (or "inputting") information, means for storing it, and means for retrieving it. At any stage of collection, storage, or retrieval, the information may be changed in form—usually to make subsequent processing steps more effective or economical. For example, information may be indexed when it is collected and before it is stored, to facilitate its later retrieval. Or existing files of information in storage may be "up-dated" by collating with them newly collected information.

Between the engineers of an information-processing system and the users there stands not only the "hardware"—electronic machinery—but also the "software," which consists of programs stored more or less permanently in the system to facilitate the users' interacting with it. Software includes monitor programs which control and schedule the system and coordinate its activities, assembling and compiling programs which translate instructions written by the user into the language of the machine instructions, and various kinds of data banks. Increasingly, the software characteristics of information-processing systems are becoming more significant than hardware characteristics in determining system performance and the range of tasks to which the systems can be adapted.

The following assumptions about the information-processing technology of the near future (ten years, say) appear reasonable:

1. Substantially all information available to humans in the society in verbal or symbolic form will also exist in computer-available form. At present, it is costly to put the content of an existing book into a computing system. The book must be copied by a human teletypist or a photo-scanning device. In the future, books will be stored in electronic memories at the same time that hard copy is produced for human use. The technology for doing this already exists, and is in considerable use.

Many data that are now recorded or transcribed by humans will be transmitted directly to automated information-processing systems without human intervention. For example, if a counter is installed to record traffic density on a road, it will store its information directly in the computing system.

2. Memories in information-processing systems will be of sizes comparable to the largest memories now used by humans—for example, the book collection of the Library of Congress.

3. It will be feasible and economical to use English or another natural (noncode) language in interrogating the memory of an information processing system. (This does *not* mean that all information in the store will be available to each inquiry independently of what preparation has been taken by way of indexing.)

4. Any program or information that has proved useful in one information-processing system can be copied into another part of that same system or into another system at very low cost and without severe problems of standardization.

5. Even the most optimistic assumptions about the power and capacity of prospective information-processing systems will re-

main puny in relation to the size of real-world planning problems. The chess board is a tiny microcosm compared with the macrocosm of real life. Nevertheless, there is absolutely no prospect of an increase in the power of information-processing systems to the point where they will play chess by "considering all possibilities" (some 10^{120}!).

Therefore, the significant limits on the power of information-processing systems for handling planning problems will be limits on (1) knowledge of the laws that govern the system being planned, (2) cleverness in discovering representations that handle salient characteristics of the situation unencumbered by a mass of detail, as well as (3) availability of the relevant real-world data. The first two limitations are likely to be even more important than the third, and ingenuity (human or computer) in devising powerful problem representations will remain crucial to effective planning.

6. Information-processing systems will become increasingly capable of learning, in several senses of that term. In particular, they will be able to "grow" their own indexes as new information is added to their stores. Thus, the important contemporary bottleneck in human indexing and abstracting capability will become less significant.

What consequences crucial to our inquiry follow from these assumptions? The main import of the first three and the sixth assumption is that computers will become substitutable for men (within twenty years, say) with almost all the tasks performed by information-processing, designing, and planning systems. Hence, the division of labor between man and machine in such systems will be determined by economic rather than technical considerations. Each will do the jobs he (or it) can do more cheaply. Because of the cheap copying capabilities of computers (item 4), they are likely to have a comparative advantage for tasks where many copies of information or programs that have been generated by the system are required.

The fifth item is of fundamental importance, for it implies that the basic logical structure of the design and planning processes will not be changed by partial or complete automation. Since most of the discussion of sections 3 and 4 rests on assumptions about the nature of that process, the validity of assumption 5 is critical.

If we are concerned that social planning is menaced by an information explosion, items 2, 3, and 6 should give us some comfort, while item 5 should help us recognize that human intelligence has never solved problems by searching enormous spaces (filled with information or anything else) exhaustively, but always by discovering ways of conducting the search in a highly selective manner. But the whole problem of information overload needs reexamination in the face of the changes in information processing technology.

Decision making rests on knowledge about the present and beliefs about the future. In traditional information-processing systems, we could say that a person "knew" something if the information was stored in his memory or in a book in his possession, and if it was "indexed" so that he could retrieve it. When information, or purported information, was communicated to a person, it was subject to an accrediting process before storage. If it passed the test, it was believed. The tests of believability could be applied to the information itself ("the world cannot be round, else people would fall off") or to the source ("he has no reason to deceive me").

Traditional notions of "who knows" and "who believes" were never entirely satisfactory when applied to entire organizations instead of individual persons, and they are still less satisfactory when applied to the new information technology. At what point did the City of New York "know" that it would have a serious smog problem in the 1960's? This belief may first have been stored inside the city government years ago in the mind of an engineer working in the Bureau of Smoke Control. Perhaps at some later time—when Los Angeles smog received widespread publicity—it migrated to other city administrators and was adjudged credible by them. At a still later time, perhaps, it became credible to the mayor and other leading politicians, and to some members of the public. The actual path may have been quite different, of course. The point is that an organization (and an information-processing system) has many minds, some in its head, and some in its tails.

The design of a planning system must therefore handle the problems of (1) who needs to know—at any given time—and (2) how to establish credibility so that information can diffuse.

With a modern information-processing system, we must take a systems approach, and avoid identifying "what is known" with "what is stored now in local memories." Generating information on demand or obtaining it from another part of the system are important alternatives to storing it, and alternatives that are becoming available on more and more favorable terms of time and cost. If I have access to a telephone, for example, I "know" the names of the best American experts on any subject you care to mention. For by a succession of three or four telephone calls (following a sort of "twenty questions" strategy), I can locate the experts' names. I could probably do no better if they were stored in my memory—with the usual defects of indexing ("I think it starts with S").

Any thorough application of the "who-needs-to-know" test to information-storage practices in our society would almost certainly reveal an excessive preoccupation with multiple storage of information. The design of new information-processing systems will call for more attention to the indexing and retrieval processes, including the processes for drawing inferences from information. Progress in planning will stem more from improving these processes than from securing larger and more complete stores of information.

In systems that have access to very large stores of information, the question of what is *known* becomes less important than the question of what is *attended to*. The larger the store of information, the smaller part of it that can be in the focus of attention of particular processors and particular decision makers at any given moment.

Inference and indexing processes, of the sorts discussed in the previous section, become crucial in bringing to attention the most important information, and in summarizing information so that the ratio of amount of meaning to numbers of symbols, so to speak, will be high. When the information that is transmitted is highly processed, not raw, then it also becomes crucial to determine what credibility is to be attached to it by the parts of the system that receive it—to determine how seriously they should consider it and act on it.

Determining credibility requires the application of tests—which in itself consumes information-processing capacity. A major factor in determining how rapidly new information can gain credibility is the presence or absence of bottlenecks of attention. There have been great lags, for example, in the credibility attached by high government administrators and business executives to technical forecasts of the role of computers in decision making. In this, as in other fields, changes are credible to top managers only some years after they were believed with a high degree of certainty by technicians. Often there is disagreement among the technicians themselves as to the directions and rates of change. This has been spectacularly true, for example, with respect to the economic effects of automation, and the whole field of "artificial intelligence"; less true in the case of atomic energy.

Information-processing systems for decision making are quite as much systems for transmitting and accrediting inferences and beliefs as they are systems for gathering and analyzing data. Some research has already been done in recent years on the diffusion of knowledge about and acceptance of new technical practices (hybrid corn and antibiotics). This remains a promising and important area of behavioral science research for the immediate future.

Conclusions

I shall undertake to summarize this analysis only to the extent of recapitulating some of the major recommendations for action to which it has led:

1. Expand programs for gathering data systematically and periodically about the quality of life—say to a scale of about $70 million per year. These programs should produce information about the distribution of knowledge and skills among the population, the distribution of values and attitudes, and the allocation of time.

2. Through these information-gathering programs, develop a rich set of measures of the quality of life that can be used for assessing important longitudinal trends in our society.

3. Set as the main goal in improving our social information system providing the information that will be most useful for behavioral and social research aimed at broadening our understanding of social structure and process.

4. To reach this goal, train research personnel at a rate of at least 5,000 Ph.D.s per year, and support basic social research at a level of at least $1 billion per year.

5. Intensify current activities to solve the technical problems of giving effective social science access to the files of operating data that exist in our society, while protecting personal privacy. In particular, privacy can and must be protected without losing the information that would make longitudinal studies possible.

6. Support research to reduce the dependence of planning efforts on impracticable attempts at predictions by improving techniques for sensitivity analysis and by developing systems models for predicting from key technological factors to their social consequences.

7. Train 50,000 to 100,000 professional personnel per year with broad competence in applied social science.

8. Reintroduce research on the theory of design, and the teaching of design, as core activities in the professional schools that will be concerned with social policy and social planning. As a means to this, give high priority to exposing several thousand students and professionals to current knowledge and developments in the theory of design and intelligence.

9. Intensify the research effort devoted to understanding the processes of information diffusion, including the ways in which new information becomes credible.

Any list of priorities is attention-directing information, hence implies that items not mentioned do *not* deserve high priority. Among the items not mentioned here, hence not marked for high priority, are large-scale efforts to build up stores of detailed data about the state of various components of the social system. This is not to say that we should not be making imaginative experiments with the new technical equipment for data storage and retrieval. But the experiments are unlikely to be imaginative if they are conceived as experiments on data systems. They are more fruitfully conceived as byproducts of basic social science research programs and programs of research on the design of decision-making systems. Only within such frameworks will appropriate criteria emerge to guide the design of the data storage and data retrieval components.

In these recommendations, I have also said almost nothing about hardware systems. Hardware there will be, in vast quantities. Whether the hardware, however impressive its electronic capabilities, will make major contributions to social planning and social choice will depend almost entirely on our success in deepening our understanding of changes in the quality of life, of the structure of society, and of the theory of the design process. In these latter three areas an acceleration of effort and an allocation of much larger human and financial resources are urgently required.

II

Organisms

The world that we must seek is a world in which
the creative spirit is alive, in which life is an
adventure full of joy and hope, based rather upon
the impulse to construct than upon the desire to
retain what we possess or to seize what is possessed by others. It must be a world in which
affection has free play, in which love is purged
of the instinct for domination, in which cruelty
and envy have been dispelled by happiness and
the unfettered development of all the instincts
that build up life and fill it with mental delights.
Such a world is possible; it waits only for men to
wish to create it.

—BERTRAND RUSSELL,
Roads to Freedom (1918)

HUMAN PERFORMANCE

by JOHN W. SENDERS

THE NEED to understand the limits of human performance or human capacity is something that has crept up on us in the last few decades almost without our being aware of it. We have become involved in manned space flight, seen the advent of 200-passenger commercial aircraft, and watched without apparent concern as the highways have filled with high-speed machines operated by indifferently trained drivers. All of this has occurred without any real understanding of how much demand these tasks and others like them place on humans.

I am going to try to describe some of what we do know—and probably at greater length what we don't know but ought to— about the interaction of man and the machines he operates. Unfortunately there aren't very many "hard" facts about what men can and cannot do. There is a wealth of information about isolated human functions—about vision and audition, for example. But extrapolation from data gathered under ideal laboratory conditions to operational situations is a hazardous business that few of us in engineering psychology are willing to undertake. With that disclaimer—that I'm not sure I can do what I am about to pretend to do—let's look at human performance.

First we wish to see what kinds of things determine the outer boundaries of performance—not those we expect a man to reach, but rather boundaries which we can be sure that he cannot exceed. One set of boundaries is generated by the physical structure of man; another by the details of his physiology; and the third by the mathematical/logical nature of his task. Our difficulties arise because in most of the important human functions in our technological civilization we perform as controllers, communicators, calculators.

The automobile and the task of driving illustrate much of what I have in mind. It is remarkable how easily and precisely even a mediocre driver can slip his car into a hole in a stream of moving traffic with only a few feet of clearance on either side. He does this at surprisingly high speeds; a timing error of only a few milliseconds would lead to a collision; yet usually there's no collision. How is this done? We might attempt to describe it as an information-processing task; some "info-psychologists" see it this way. We might also describe what the man is doing as if he were part of a linear servomechanism; and there are "servo-psychologists" who see man as a human tracking machine in such tasks, providing error-correcting feedback to compensate for the limitation of his inputs.

But the driver is not an information-processing channel and he is not really part of a linear servomechanism. The gap between man's performance and the logical boundaries can be reduced in two ways. One is to increase the performance by a redesign of the devices which the man uses. The other is to move the boundaries in by fitting our models more closely to the actual constraints.

So man is sampler of the constant stream of signals reaching his central processor from his senses. Selective attention can occur at many levels. Sometimes this selection apparently is initiated internally; very often, it is caused externally. The selection process is complicated and the attempts to reduce it to a clean picture don't do justice to man's superb machinery.

Roughly, it appears that signals from many sources arrive at a short-term storage system and may get passed on *if* they are attended to. The attending may be overt and external, as in the fixing of the eyes on an object. It may be covert and external as in attending to the color rather than to the shape of an object; some men are attracted by any redhead, svelte or not. Attention may be covert and internal, as in attending to a recently received signal even if new information is coming in.

Thus the attentional system is flexible, and though it operates on only a single channel of information at one time, other signals are not lost forever because they were not attended to at the moment when they impinged on a sense organ. If there are many signals from many sources, how do they queue up for attention and wait their turns? I shall not attempt a detailed discussion of queueing theory. However, it's clear that if a signal demands attention when no other signal is being attended to, it can be handled promptly; if other signals are occupying the attention, there must be a delay. We can examine the way in which signal characteristics influence human behavior and see what this means when we put it into the notion of a queue. I got intrigued with this problem in 1954, and experimented with the application of Shannon's sampling theorem to human visual sampling. The sampling theorem sets forth a relationship between signal characteristics and the number of samples, equally spaced in time, which would permit you to reconstruct the signal with some arbitrarily small error. Simply put, if you look at something often enough, you can tell almost exactly what has gone on even between looks. The more rapidly the "something" changes, the more often must you look at it. This seems sensible enough as a description of human observers, and my early experiments showed that, on the average, it predicted quite well what people did under well-defined laboratory conditions. The sampling theorem and extensions of it have not specified that they apply only to non-human samplers. The relationships are indifferent to the mechanisms. Thus we can use them to establish outer boundaries within which a human sampler must operate if he has the same goals of signal reconstruction, and then we can set different goals and get better estimates of these same boundaries.

In 1949, the Aero Medical Laboratory at Wright-Patterson AFB started a series of studies of how pilots look at their instruments while engaged in a variety of flight tasks. The point was to see if a better than standard instrument panel layout could be achieved—a layout which would require fewer and shorter eye movements and presumably permit easier instrument flight. There are some general comments about those experiments which are of interest here because they revealed that man is probably a conditional sampler.

First the intervals between a pilot's observations of any given instrument were distinctly non-regular, and the distributions of intervals were non-symmetrical; the durations of observations were also variable but far less so than the intervals. Second, the switching of visual attention from instrument to instrument was not characterized by fixed patterns or scanning systems but could only be described in statistical terms. Furthermore, the durations, intervals, and switching statistics were different for different pilots and all of these varied with the particular flight problems a pilot was attempting to perform.

In aircraft and in my laboratory experiments, the human observers were not really trying to put the signal back together again, the situation discussed in sampling theory. Information which has gone by is of little importance; what is actually happening and what may happen are of great importance. If a pilot is interested in detecting things whenever they are at the "red line," then his sampling behavior will be aperiodic and will be distributed rather as was that of subjects in the in-flight and laboratory studies.

In homely terms, consider the problem of reading a book while sitting at the edge of a swimming pool. There is a baby crawling around on the grass. If you look at the baby you will observe where he is, what direction he is pointing in, and (if you are an experienced parent) you will have some idea of how fast he can move. If on the last observation you found him to be close to the pool and, pointed at it, you would look again rather soon. If you had found him a good ten seconds' crawl away from the pool and pointed away from it you could get a good part of a page read before you would feel compelled to look again. . . . Your observations would be irregular, more dense near the pool edge, and sensitive to the instantaneous heading, or derivative. There would be more observations than you would have made if you were in accord with the sampling theorem—because you were interested in preventing total immersion rather than merely knowing it happened.

So one can be wrong in applying a simple engineering model to a man; we must refine and generate models which are more appropriate for human operators. The dangers of the simple model are that one will be led to look for improvement where it may not exist and to underestimate the capacity of men to do what is required of them.

If we were to set out to use man in a particular system, we would try to choose the right input system or sensory mode, and the right output system or effector, both of which had limits that exceeded the performance requirements we wanted from him in the particular task. Since much of what is known about man's sensory, motor, and central processing capacities is of a statistical nature, it is possible to be led into errors of interpretation and errors of prediction about human performance.

How sharp is an astronaut's eye? Not long ago, astronauts Cooper and Gordon were accused of suffering from perceptual distortions resulting from the weightless conditions of space flight. Most of the comments were by life scientists who asserted that the astronauts could not have seen trains, trucks, and houses. Were these objects above or below the visual acuity threshold of the unaided human eye?

For the most part it can be said that the objects were below the thresholds reported in the literature. Now what is a threshold? And what is a threshold as reported in a handbook of physiological and psychological data? The experimental determination of a threshold is almost always accomplished by the technique of exploring a wide range of stimulus values and then arbitrarily designating that which elicits a response $x\%$ of the time as the threshold. Here x may be 50, 75, or 90, or any other number chosen by the experimenter. Thus there are values of the stimulus which elicit the response some small amount of the time but which are below the "threshold." The proper question to have asked about Cooper's performance would have been: "How many times did the astronaut's eye light *unseeing* on sub-threshold objects as compared with the number of times he reported seeing them?" In any case, the astronaut population is a highly select one which is certainly not represented by a sample of experimental psychologists and graduate students.

Let's assume we've taken all that into account and will define the task carefully enough to be able to compare the effectiveness of various sensory modes and various effector systems, and choose the right combination. However, we still would have to deal with the central processor, with the kind of information it needs to take in and the kind it prefers to give out, and with how much of the central processor capacity will be involved in the task.

My own point of view is that the central processor is *always* running at full speed if it is running at all. Serious underloading results in the man's finding other things to do with the left-over capacity. He may daydream or even doze, so as to lower the effective full-load capacity. Driving on a dull road for long periods often results in sleepiness, as does listening to a bore. You're-morelikelytopayattention (awake now?) when the task is challenging, but probability of missing signals that are important goes up. Obviously, somewhere in between is best, and the problem is to find out just where. Here again the queueing notion is helpful. One can choose a demand rate such that the frequency of simultaneous demand is somewhere between one per minute and one per ten minutes. Vigilance studies have shown that such signal frequencies maintain human performance on watch at a high level over long periods.

You may recall from your own experience how you expand or contract your perceptual field while your internal information processor continues to operate at its maximum capacity. There is, of course, the cocktail party effect: you've met somebody dull, so you expand your perception and sample other conversations impinging on your ears; you switch your attention mechanism among the continuous inputs you hear. Conversely, when you are driving along the road with the kids chattering merrily in the back seat, you can listen and carry on a conversation with them until the traffic gets dense. Then the demands on your central processor grow until you need every bit of its capacity; you try to pay attention only to the inputs that affect your driving task. Usually these are visual and when you have reached a limit, the demands from the audible signals from the back seat become too much. "Shut up!" you shout in exasperation.

On the other hand, underloading the human central processor often results in people turning themselves off, a problem as vital to radar-screen watchers as to automobile drivers and pilots. The demand on the attention mechanism can be too low in the face of an unchanging external environment; a man tends to adapt to any steady stimulation. A light attracts attention, but if it stays on, it ceases to attract. If it blinks periodically, it attracts attention until you have learned the rhythm (which is why it is harder to ignore the random blinking of the highway-construction warning neon-discharge lamps). Try listening to the tick of a clock placed far enough away in the room so it is barely audible;

even if you *deliberately* pay attention by trying to hear every tick, the ticking will disappear for seconds at a time.

Simply considering a man as a machine, as a servomechanistic model, does not allow for human error. Random noise generators are used to put unrelated errors into such a model, but the kinds of errors people make are not random; they are very much related to the task they are performing and how they think they are performing it. Further, the errors don't come when you expect them. The effects of motivation may very well counteract the effects of stress with the result that the expected increase in error rate just does not occur. This characteristic of man can make life very difficult indeed for those who try to measure the effects of stress.

For example, one experiment at Wright Air Development Center was to determine how much skilled, precision flying a man could do continuously without sleep. The pilot put his aircraft through a series of maneuvers and instrument landings for more than a day. After 24 hours the observers aboard who were running the experiment began to fall asleep. The pilot was still flying, though he became irritable and snappish. His ability to do better than the observers with their easier task lies in the realm of motivation and dedication. If some additional activity had been demanded of the pilot which had added up to a full load— in the statistical sense—then the effects of fatigue would most likely have appeared first as a reduction in performance of that auxiliary task although he might have done all of the tasks in the load at reduced performance.

Internal goal direction impels living organisms to perform under conditions of impairment which would cause an equivalent machine to fail completely. Humans with impairments of their living systems often manage to restructure their internal programs remarkably well. Drunken drivers either perform erratically at their normal driving speeds or slow down and perform very well though at a greatly reduced information-processing rate; at the lower speed that's enough.

But whether or not a man is operating with an impairment, how do you measure motivation as an index of performance? When a man says "I want to do something," he is motivated. He also might be motivated if you stuck a pin in him. Is he twice as motivated if he shouts twice as loud when you stick in the pin twice as deep? Man cannot be taken from a handbook of data representing him as an idealized model; the terms we use to fit him to such a Procrustean bed often mean one thing in engineering and something not quite the same in psychology. There are many tasks in which man appears to perform both as a servo and as an information processor or in which he changes his behavior from one to the other through learning.

One works with human performance data and with transformations of these data which are really models of the man. However, there are various levels of model; they have different degrees of utility. Engineering psychologists are still trying to develop a uniform measure over man's input-output functions that will characterize his performance from sensation through thinking to resultant output. We still lack the mathematics to do this, and so most formal attempts at measurement still try to squeeze man to fit the model of a particular theory, developing new mathematical models which are in accord with man as we really know him to be.

PUBLIC SOLITUDE

by ALLEN GINSBERG

I AM speaking from this church pulpit conscious of history, of my role as poet, of the addresses and essays in public consciousness by my transcendental predecessors in this city [Boston], with all the awesome prophecies about these States pronounced by Thoreau and Emerson, and elsewhere the more naked Whitman: prophecies that have now come true.

Reprinted by permission of the author. First published in 1967.

. . . I say of all this tremendous and dominant play of solely materialistic bearings upon current life in the United States, with the results already seen, accumulating, and reaching far into the future, that they must either be confronted and met by at least an equally subtle force-infusion for purposes of spiritualization, for the pure conscience, for genuine esthetics, and for absolute and primal manliness and womanliness—or else our modern civilization, with all its improvements, is in vain, and we are on the road to a destiny, a status, equivalent, in its real world, to that of the fabled damned. (*Democratic Vistas*)

Because our governors and *polis* have failed to perceive the obvious I wish to make some political suggestions to this community; I make them as Poet, and claim powers of prophecy as did the good gray bards before me in this country, because one who looks in his heart and speaks frankly can claim to prophesy. And what is prophecy? I cannot propose right and wrong, or objective future events such as purple balloons on Jupiter in 1984; but I can have the confidence to trust my own private thought. All have this gift of prophecy. Who dare assume it though?

The present condition of life for American Person is one of deathly public solitude. We've built a technological Tower of Babel around ourselves, and are literally (as in Gemini) reaching into heaven to escape the planet. Now giant overpopulation depends on a vast metallic superstructure to feed and transport all the bodies here together. The stupendous machinery surrounding us conditions our "thoughts, feelings and apparent sensory impressions" and reinforces our mental slavery to the material universe we've invested in.

Yet according to Chuang Tzu twenty-five hundred years ago, "The understanding of men of ancient times went a long way. How far did it go? To the point where some of them believed that things have never existed—so far, to the end, where nothing can be added. . . . Words like these will be labeled the Supreme Swindle. Yet, after the thousand generations, a great sage may appear who will know their meaning, and it will still be as though he appeared with astonishing speed." Yeats appearing in Ireland this century declared:

This preposterous pig of a world, its farrows that so solid seem
Must vanish on an instant, did the mind but change its theme.

How can we Americans make our minds—change theme? For unless the theme changes—encrustation of the planet with machinery, inorganic metal smog—violent outrage and mass murder will take place. We witness these horrors already.

Abruptly then, I will make a first proposal—on one level symbolic, but to be taken as literally as possible, it may shock some and delight others—that everybody who hears my voice, directly or indirectly, try the chemical LSD at least once; every man, woman, and child American in good health over the age of fourteen—that, if necessary, we have a mass emotional nervous breakdown in these States once and for all; that we see bankers laughing in their revolving doors with strange staring eyes. May everybody in America turn on, whatever the transient law—because individual soul development (as once declared by a poet in jail in this city) is our law transcending the illusions of the political State. Soul also transcends LSD, may I add, to reassure those like myself who would fear a chemical dictatorship. I propose, then, that everybody including the President and his and our vast hordes of generals, executives, judges and legislators of these States go to nature, find a kindly teacher or Indian peyote chief or guru guide, and assay their consciousness with LSD.

Then, I prophesy, we will all have seen some ray of glory or vastness beyond our conditioned social selves, beyond our government, beyond America even, that will unite us into a peaceable community.

The LSD I am proposing is literal. I hope it will be understood as not *the* solution, but a typical and spiritually revolutionary catalyst, where many varieties of spiritual revolution are necessary to transcend specifically the political Cold War we are all involved in.

Anger and control of anger is our problem. Already we have enough insight into politics to be aware of one very simple thing: that we can judge all politics and all public speech and ideology by perceiving the measure of anger manifested therein. All present political parties propose violence to resolve our confusions, as in Vietnam. We might look for a third party, specifically named a Peace Party—referring to individual subjective peaceableness (such as we have not seen in our populace or our leaders) as well as consequent public peaceableness; a party founded on psychol-

ogy not ideology. We obviously need to feed China and India, not
ignore, manipulate or threaten to destroy them. The earth is yet
to be saved from our aggression, and living organic life like unto
our own nature be replaced on its surface which has been over-
grown with cancerous inanimate matter, metal and asphalt. And
though many mammal species have been made extinct in this
century there are many we can yet save including ourselves.

Driving out of New York or into Boston at night we see the
transparent apparitional glitter of buildings walling the horizon,
and we know that these are transient specters. In cold daylight
we believe in their finality. But it is that half-dreaming insight of
normal consciousness that may provide the direction for our
imagination to manifest itself in the material world.

What can the young do with themselves faced with this American version of the planet? The most sensitive and among the
"best minds" do drop out. They wander over the body of the
nation looking into the faces of their elders, they wear long
Adamic hair and form Keristan communities in the slums, they
pilgrimage to Big Sur and live naked in forests seeking natural
vision and mediation, they dwell in the Lower East Side as if it
were an hermetic forest. And they assemble thousands together
as they have done this year in Golden Gate Park San Francisco
or Tompkins Square in New York to manifest their peaceableness
in demonstrations of Fantasy that transcend protest against—or
for—the hostilities of Vietnam. Young men and women in speck-
led robes, carrying balloons, signs "President Johnson we are
praying for you," gathered chanting Hindu and Buddhist mantras
to calm their fellow citizens who are otherwise entrapped in a
planetary barroom brawl.

But there has been no recognition of this insight on the part of
the fathers and teachers (Father Zossima's famous cry!) of these
young. What's lacking in the great institutions of learning? The
specific wisdom discipline that these young propose: search into
inner space.

Children drop out of schools because there are no, or very few,
gurus. Those elders concerned with this practical problem might
consider that there is an easy practical solution: the establishment
within centers of learning of facilities for wisdom search which

the ancients proposed as the true function of education in the first place: academies of self-awareness, classes in spiritual teaching, darshan with holymen of disciplined mind-consciousness. One might well, in fact, employ the drop-out beatniks as instructors in this department, and thereby officially recognize and proclaim the social validity of exploration of inner space. Tibetan monks, swamis, yogins and yoginis, psychedelic guides, Amer-Indian peyote chiefs, even a few finished Zen Roshis and many profound poets are already present and available in our cities for such work, though at present they battle immigration bureaucracies and scholarly heads of departments of Oriental Religion.

What I am proposing as policy, for us elders, for what community we have, is self-examination as Official Politics! an Official Politics of Control of Anger. With state propaganda reversed in that direction church and university teaching and research in that direction and requests to the government for vast sums of money equal to the outerspace program; and consequent billboards on the highways "Control Your Anger—Be Aware of Yourself."

There is a change of consciousness among the younger generation, in a direction always latent to Elder America, toward the most complete public frankness possible. As the Gloucester poet Charles Olson formulated it, "Private is public, and public is how we behave." This means revision of standards of public behavior to include indications of private manners heretofore excluded from public consciousness.

Thus, new social standards, more equivalent to private desire— as there is increased sexual illumination, new social codes may be found acceptable to rid ourselves of fear of our own nakedness, rejection of our own bodies.

Likely an enlarged family unit will emerge for many citizens; possibly, as the Zen Buddhist anarchist anthropologist Gary Snyder observed, with matrilineal descent as courtesy to those dakinis whose *saddhana* or holy path is the sexual liberation and teaching of dharma to many frightened males (including myself) at once. Children may be held in common, with the orgy an acceptable community sacrament—one that brings all people closer togeher. Certainly one might seduce the Birch Society to partake in naked orgy, and the police with their wives, together with Leroi Jones the brilliantly angry poet. America's political need is orgies in the parks, on Boston Common and in the Public Gardens, with naked bacchantes in our national forests.

I am not proposing idealistic fancies. I am acknowledging what is already happening among the young in fact and fantasy, and proposing official blessing for these breakthroughs of community spirit. Among the young we find a new breed of White Indians in California communing with illuminated desert redskins; we find our teenagers dancing Nigerian Yoruba dances and entering trance states to the electric vibration of the Beatles who have borrowed shamanism from Afric sources. We find communal religious use of ganja, the hemp sacred to Mahadev (Great Lord) Shiva. There's now heard the spread of mantra chanting in private and such public manifestations as peace marches, and soon we will have Mantra Rock over the airwaves. All the available traditions of U.S. Indian vision-quest, peyote ritual, mask dancing, Oriental pranayama, East Indian ear music are becoming available to the U.S. unconscious through the spiritual search of the young. Simultaneously there is a new Diaspora of Tibetan Lamaist initiates; texts such as the *Book of the Dead* and *I Ching* have found fair-cheeked and dark-browed Kansas devotees. And rumor from the West Coast this season brings the legendary *Hevajra Tantra*—a document central to Vajrayana Buddhism's Lightning-bolt Illumination—into public light as a source book for tantric community rules. LSD structured by ancient disciplines for meditation and community regulation.

Ideas I have dwelled on are mixed: there is some prescription for public utopia through education in inner space. There is more prescription here for the individual: as always, the old command to free ourselves from social conditioning, laws and traditional mores.

And discover the Guru in our own hearts.—And set forth within the New Wilderness of machine America to explore open spaces of consciousness in Self and fellow Selves. If there be the necessary revolution in America it will come that way. It's up to us older hairs who still have relation with some of the joy of youth to encourage this revolutionary individual search.

But how can peaceful psychological politics succeed when fifty billion dollars a year is spent to buy participation in armed conflict? "Vietnam War Brings Prosperity"—headline Lincoln Nebraska *Star*, February 1966. Certainly the awareness itself of this condition will help some of us, as did Ike's warning against the military-industrial complex running the mind of the nation.

As a side note: there *are* specific methods for combatting the mental dictatorship over "thoughts, feelings and apparent sensory impressions" imposed on us by military-industrial control of language and imagery in public media. W. S. Burroughs has provided a whole armamentarium of counter-brainwash techniques: cut-up of newspapers and ads, collage of political and entertainment news to reveal the secret intention of the Senders, observation of TV imagery with sound off and simultaneous apperception of noises on the radio or street. These methods are effective in jolting the soft machine of the brain out of its conditioned hypnosis.

Cutting out, or dropping out, of the culture will not lead to a chaos of individuality: what it will mean, for the young, is training in meditation and art (and perhaps neolithic lore), and responsibility of a new order, to the community of the heart, not to our heartless society wherein we have read the headline in the Omaha *World Herald*: "Rusk Says Toughness Essential For Peace."

The "oversoul" to be discovered is a pragmatic reality. We can all tell signs of an illuminated man in business or the church—one who is open-hearted, nonjudging, empathetic, compassionate to the rejected and condemned. The tolerant one, the Observer, the Aware. And we see that these souls do influence action.

Finally, detachment comes naturally: we all know the war is camp, hate is camp, murder is camp, even love is camp, the universe is a grand camp according to Chuang Tzu and the Prajnaparamita Sutra. This detachment is salvation. We have an international youth society of solitary children—*stilyagi*, provo, beat, *mafada, nadaista, energumeno*, mod and rocker—all aghast at the space-age horror world they are born to, and not habituated to— and now questioning the nature of the universe itself as is proper in the space age.

There are many contradictions here, especially between proposed communal sex orgy and contemplative choiceless awareness (as the sage Krishnamurti articulated it this fall in New York). Whitman noticed that too: "Do I contradict myself? Very well, I contradict myself." A dialogue between these contradictions is a good healthy way of life, one correcting the other. Indulgence in sexuality and sensational ecstacy may well lead to contemplative awareness of desire and cessation of desire.

> *I know although when looks meet*
> *I tremble to the bone,*
> *The more I leave the door unlatched*
> *The sooner love is gone.*

What satisfaction is now possible for the young? Only the satisfaction of their Desire—love, the body and orgy: the satisfaction of a peaceful natural community where they can circulate and explore Persons, cities and the nature of the planet—the satisfaction of encouraged self-awareness, and the satiety and cessation of desire, anger, grasping and craving.

Respect of the old? Yea when the old are tranquil and not nervous, and respect the sport of the young. Holymen do inspire respect. One conservative Vaishnavite Swami Bhaktivedanta moved into the Lower East Side this year and immediately dozens of young LSD freak-outs flocked to sing the Harekrishna Mahamantra with him—chant for the preservation of the planet.

But a nation of elders convinced that spiritual search is immaturity, and that national war and metallic communication is maturity, cannot ask for respect from the young. For the present conduct of the elders in America is a reflection of lack of Self-respect.

I am in effect setting up moral codes and standards which include drugs, orgy, music and primitive magic as worship rituals —educational tools which are supposedly contrary to our cultural mores; and I am proposing these standards to your respectable ministers, once and for all, that you endorse publicly the private desire and knowledge of mankind in America, so to inspire the young.

It may appear from this address that I find myself increasingly alienated from the feeling-tone, ideology and conduct of the supposed majority of my fellow citizens: thus the title Public Solitude. But I do not feel myself alienated from all our inmost private desire, which the prophet Walt Whitman articulated in his second preface to his lifework ninety years ago, still passionately expressive of our hearts in spaceage America:

Something more may be added—for, while I am about it, I would like to make a full confession. I also sent out *Leaves of Grass* to arouse and set flowering in men's and women's hearts, young and old, endless streams of living, pulsating love and friendship, directly from them to myself, now and ever. To this terrible, irrepressible yearning (surely more or less down underneath in most human souls) this never-satisfied appetite for sympathy, and this boundless offering of sympathy—this universal democratic comradeship—this old, eternal, yet ever-new interchange of adhesiveness, so fitly emblematic of America—I have given in that book, undisguisedly, declaredly, the openest expression. Besides, important as they are in my purpose as emotional expressions for humanity, the special meaning of the "Calamus" cluster of *Leaves of Grass* (and more or less running through the book, and cropping out in "Drum-taps") mainly resides in its political significance. In my opinion, it is by a fervent, accepted development of comradeship, the beautiful and sane affection of man for man, latent in all the young fellows north and south, east and west,—it is by this, I say, and by what goes directly and indirectly along with it, that the United States of the future (I cannot too often repeat) are to be most effectively welded together, intercalated, annealed into a living union.

MEDICINE

by STANLEY LESSE and WILLIAM WOLF

Mｅｄｉｃｉｎｅ, too, in common with every one of our current institutions, must change if it is to function in a world where 6 billion people will live, mostly in cities, and where auto-

Reprinted in excerpt from *Mankind 2000*, edited by Robert Jungk and Johan Galtung, No. 1 of Future Research Monographs from The International Peace Research Institute Oslo. Published by Universitetsforlaget, Oslo, Norway, and George Allen & Unwin, London. By permission of Universitetsforlaget. First published in 1969.

mation will supply man's basic needs in a society which is tightly organized and where man's main problem will be the effective and beneficial use of his leisure time with pride and pleasure. It may be well to appreciate that in an automated, heavily populated, group-oriented society, the nature of illnesses, their diagnosis and treatment are likely to be far different from those which we understand and recognize today.

Since patients will be group- rather than individually-oriented, they will probably have far fewer individual expectations. They will not object to more impersonalized care. Emphasis will most likely focus on the need to return and integrate them into the group as quickly as possible. Indeed, they will be constantly reminded with great subtlety of their position as members of the group by the very fact that their treatment will be largely by group approaches. Private practice undoubtedly will disappear, most likely in stages. At present approximately 50 percent of medical men are no longer in full-time private practice. It is not far-fetched to visualize that before long the Medicare Program will include everyone in the United States and be financed through the Social Security System or some other governmental agency. By then perhaps 70 to 75 percent of the medical personnel will be employed by private or governmental institutions. By 1980 surely less than 20 percent of medical school graduates will enter into private practice, mostly in rural areas. By the end of the century all vestiges of private practice will most likely have disappeared and be a memory of the past.

In a society structured and integrated in the manner described, with most services automated, it would appear that two general types of professionally trained individuals will be needed to care for medical needs. Tentatively, they may be called:

1. Medical academicians (M.A.)
2. Medical technical experts (M.T.E.)

Each will fulfill specific roles and will have a working knowledge of the other.

Medical Academician

The medical academician will be trained primarily in the comprehension, expansion, and pragmatic application of the dynamic interrelationships between physiodynamics, psychodynamics, and sociodynamics. This concept will assume increasing importance whereby the mutual interrelationships and interdependencies of all human functions are stressed. These various terms may be defined as follows:

1. Physiodynamics refers to the state or changing state of the individual's anatomic structures, physiologic, and biochemical functions, their mutual interdependence in relationship to one another, and in relationship to psychodynamic and socio-dynamic factors.
2. Psychodynamics refers to the state, or changing state, of the individual with regard to all psychic functions (conscious and unconscious), and their mutual interdependence in relation to physiodynamic and sociodynamic factors.
3. Sociodynamics refers to the state or changing state of an individual's total external environment and its mutual interdependence in relation to physiodynamic and psychodynamic factors.

The central theme to be stressed here is that whenever there is an alteration in one area of human function, there is inevitably an alteration in other areas, or aspects of the same function and all other functions, both internal and external, until a state of relative equilibrium is reached. These changes operate and affect every aspect of the individual's life and in turn that of society in an indivisible feedback fashion, whereby a dynamically changing equilibrium is maintained. The equilibrium being dynamic is ever momentary, and when the factor of progressing time is added the picture of constant flux is evoked.

Historic adaptability will be another fresh concept which must be "built into" the education of the medical academician. We wish to stress this, because the concept of intentionally conditioning students to anticipate automatically the necessity for change in response to internal and external stimuli, has very little precedence in medical, or, for that matter, in most other types of education. It means that the M.A. and even the students will be encouraged to scan, as a matter of course, the knowledge and stimuli that they perceive in terms of the passing of time or becoming. In other words, greater emphasis will be placed on process rather than achievement of fixed ends. The real goal will lie in seeking rather than reaching a static end. A medical academician will also be proficient in two basic subsciences: (1) the study of the interrelationships of normal functions and (2) the study of interrelationships of abnormal functions, both in terms of the individual as well as the individual's relationship to society as a whole.

The Medical Technical Expert

The medical technical expert (M.T.E.) working with many sophisticated, automated devices will take over many of the tasks of today's highly skilled physicians. Most routine diagnoses and therapies will undoubtedly be performed by the M.T.E.-computer combination. It appears to us likely that automated devices will take histories, perform specialized biochemical, physiologic, and psychologic recordings and examinations and even indicate correlations. In all likelihood, these studies will be performed much more intensively and accurately and be correlated in a far superior manner than is now possible by skilled diagnosticians. The machines will not only correlate and arrive at specific or broad-spectrum diagnostic categories, but may conceivably indicate general and even specific courses of therapy. Other special devices will actually administer some of the therapies. Since therapies will be increasingly broad-spectrum in nature most patients will probably be managed by the M.T.E.-automated device team at the level of a district general medical clinic or regional specialty center.

Above all, the medical technical expert will be highly trained for very specific, very limited jobs. Even though he will be far more knowledgeable than the physician of today as to the details and technique of a special task, since his field of operation will be so limited, his education will require far less time than that required to train the present-day medical specialist. Thus the old saying that "men will know more and more about less and less" will become an ever more cogent truism.

Thus, the medical technical expert will find his role greatly narrowed, but at the same time markedly deepened in scope because of the nature of the marked advances in technology. The pragmatically oriented training of the M.T.E. will be much more brief than that required for the M.A. The former will be trained to think in terms of interrelationships, but only in a very superficial fashion as compared with the M.A. The M.T.E. will learn not to think in terms of items by themselves, out of context so to speak, but rather in relationship to the many items of information obtained from the automated devices. He will learn to interpret, and apply in combination with the automated systems, the programmed methods laid down and suggested by the medical academician. Some of the M.T.E.s may well become specialists in diagnosis, while others may become specialists in therapeutic techniques. Thus, as we stated before, we anticipate the M.T.E. will become increasingly specialized in an ever narrowing frame of reference.

All indications point to the likelihood that we will encounter relatively few instances of so-called "acute conditions," mostly infectious diseases, with their complications and sequelea, of which we have had such a plethora until recently. They probably will be rare not only because we will be able to treat them effectively with broad-spectrum therapies, but also because the very transmission of infection will be greatly diminished. Preventive medical techniques will immunize most persons from the sources of infection. The problem of resistant organisms will probably have been conquered.

The principal acute processes that will be encountered are likely to be the results of traumata, hemorrhage, burns, radiation, and the like. In addition, we will encounter acute phases or exacerbations of chronic illnesses, which will be managed primarily by preventive measures or by treating the more chronic underlying matrix. Acute processes will also include acute psychic problems, some representing acute exacerbations of congenital defects and some precipitated by various psychosocial traumata.

Chronic ailments will constitute the bulk of medical practice, partly because life expectancy will continue to increase. There will be problems related to genetic mutations, many secondary to increased radiation fallout. There will be the effects of toxic materials ingested over a prolonged period of time in the form of preservatives, air pollution, artificial treatment of drinking water, and the like.

Increasingly crowded urban conditions coupled with a down-grading of the importance of the family as the basic social unit may be a source of considerable emotional stress for some time to come. In addition, of course, entirely new causes and types of somato-psycho-sociologic problems are likely to arise.

The sources of psychosocial stresses will differ considerably from those of today. As indicated, they will probably be determined in great measure by the fact that the group ego will supersede the individual ego. Stresses are also likely to result from deemphasizing the family as the primary teacher of the child. Moreover, if the parents no longer will be the prime sources of early instruction, many of our concepts of psychodynamic development will require considerable revision. Then too, the child's relationships with other persons in the community are likely to be markedly different from those which we consider par today.

The most significant psychosocial difficulties will most likely be traceable to group maladaptation and rejection by the group. Thus, quite new concepts of human relationship leading to other psychosocial stresses are likely to show up. Preoccupation with romantic love may well become diluted and thus many interactions between men and women may change considerably. Stress on sexual gratification, which is so intimately incorporated into our present culture, while of course essential, may play a lesser role as a source of psychic disturbance, so that our future society might be far less sexualized as compared to that of our current civilization.

In keeping with the projected changes in social structure, population and technologic development and paralleling the projected changes in the nature of illness and in the conception of the physician as they are likely to be in the not too distant future, the physical structure of medical practice will probably become hierarchically structured in a way that will guarantee a maximum of efficiency and a minimum of duplication. It is urgent that we evolve a method of medical education that is capable of incorporating a historical perspective, as well as qualities of flexibility and adaptability in addition to technical and social anticipation.

PREDICTION

by *TIMOTHY LEARY*

Mᴵʟʟʙʀᴏᴏᴋ, for me, is an advanced experimental station where people are working on the life-style of the future. This is an experimental trial setup probing new ways of living, which will facilitate liberation and evolution of consciousness. Family life and a harmonious working with your children and your wife is the place where it starts. From my perspective, the psychedelic revolution was won in 1964. Psychedelic chemicals and psychedelic methods using electronics completely revolutionarized man and his conception of himself, and everything's that happened since 1964 has been exciting but it's really froth on the cake. Acid rock, the hippie phenomena are more symptoms of deep changes which are taking place.

Starting in 1964 I became almost exclusively interested in the future, that is what's going to happen in five years, fifteen years, fifty years, a hundred years—where's it going. I think it's important we not back into the next era of human civilization, but give some thought to it; not that we can control it or that we would want to structure it in our own image, but not just let it happen accidentally. Because you learn from the past that when a new evolutionary phenomenon occurs, it's inevitably the power people, the control people that grab it, like they did with atomic energy, as they did with the printing press. All of which changed man's consciousness, but not as drastically as psychedelic drugs will. That's why we've kept this Millbrook experiment going.

For hundreds of thousands of years men have been writing utopias, which is just their fantasy trip of how nice it would be . . . COULD be. At the present time we can not only speculate about utopias, but we can actually start putting them into prac-

Reprinted from *Southern California Oracle* (October 1967). By permission of the author.

tice in pilot study, informal, in a fun way. We have the psychedelic drugs which do bring about changes in consciousness which cannot be brought about by any other method today. We also have this affluent society, this mass media communication, so that we have the facilities to try out experiments and see them passed on and adjusted and improved by other groups.

Four hundred years ago you people in California separated 3,000 miles from us wouldn't even have heard of us. It would take a generation for the word to pass through the prairies to get out of there. Now with modern technology we can be in communication, we can learn from each other, we can improve on each other's molecular style.

The conclusion I've come to after seven years of utopian living is that the basic problems are familial and sexual, and that unless the individual has his sexual energies harnessed and harmonious, so that they're not spinning him off center, unless he has some enduring growing family setup, anything he does, whether it's to write a great book or lead a great movement, is just the by-products of his familial neurosis. It's obvious. I hate to say that because I was a psychologist for fifteen years.

I was very disillusioned with psychoanalysis and the way it's practiced. I'm forced to conclude that community living—and national living for that matter, and international politics—all come down to where the person's at in his sexual center and his familial center. The reason we have wars, the reason we have race prejudice, is the impotent or freaky men who drag millions of people into their own family romances. I emphasize this right now because I know that there are hundreds of utopian communities and tribal groups starting off, and I urge them to keep this perspective in mind.

For the teenagers and the young kids who are swarming to Los Angeles and New York and San Francisco, naturally I'm all in favor of their exploring their own sexuality, and exploring the incredible mystery of sex and shedding their sexual inhibitions and freeing themselves. Great! As I see it, the function of the hippie communities in Haight-Ashbury and the district in Seattle and L.A. is to help kids drop out, break away from the constrictions and live out their fantasies and free themselves sexually, eco-nomically . . . throw off the middle-class achievement-oriented state of mind, throw off the concern with cleanliness that their mothers and fathers put in them. Cleanliness is NOT next to Godliness. They have to react by doing all the things that upset the middle class—by not being clean and by being free sexually. That's as necessary a step as metamorphosis of a butterfly from a caterpillar. But by definition, a free-sexuality, goofing-off, anarchic way of life cannot maintain itself or defend itself because it has no organization to fight against the law. The reason that the hippies are being busted so much is because that's not much structure.

As I see it, the kids go through this purging, liberating fling, no matter how many years it takes. So what if it takes four, five, six years! It's okay! We think nothing of sending a kid to college for six years. Why not let him goof off in the Haight-Ashbury for six years? In both cases society's supporting them. This middle-class society complains about the hippies hanging out at the expense of society in the East Village but doesn't complain about other kids hanging out at the Harvard Business School, which is essentially goofing off for six years.

But there will come a time with the young hippies: when they're ready, they will want to continue the life of growth. They're going to have to have some sort of an organization, and that organization should be tribal, to be based on the family. Once you get into that you will find this sexual fidelity to be the most harmonious life. Sexual freedom always goes along with urbanization.

In Rome you got millions of people together and family life broke down and everyone balled everyone else. That's great, that's inevitable. But in a village, in a tribal way of life, you're right out there in the frontier. Every minute the tribe has to be organized to protect itself, to make a living, to fight off the animals, to defend the territory. And if a lot of time is going to sexual fooling around it just drains off energy. Because in a tribe everyone is aware of any sort of sexual infidelity. In a city, I have my wife in the suburbs, I'm balling my secretary, I'm cheating on my secretary by taking out strange girls in the city. Nobody knows about it so all are anonymous. And also meaningless. Anonymous sex. But I said before, that each tribe should decide what its sexual orientation is. There can be homosexual tribes, and there can be free-group-sex tribes, as long as they're aware of it and make it explicit. It's the failure to be honest that causes all this confusion.

I see group sex as a very, almost necessary stage. If there's anything I've learned from LSD, it is that the body is the temple of God but it's not the center. You have to learn to manipulate the body, use the body, glorify it, but then go on to the next stage, which is the evolutionary timelessness, the ancient reincarnation thing that we always carry inside. In order to explore that I think you have to have a member of the opposite sex to explore it with you. I think you'll find that the woman is ALL women, she will help you bring out all the varieties of your existence. I was amused at the concern that many people showed about my statements concerning sex. My function, as I see it, is just to stir people to think. Who am I to tell anyone what to do with their sex life? If there's anything that's my business, it's who or what I put in my own body. No one can tell me and I shouldn't tell anyone else who or what to put in THEIR body. So I am simply trying to focus people's awareness on crucial issues like how are they going to handle the sexual mating relationship. However you do it, as long as you do it consciously, honestly, Godspeed.

I've been saying for a long time now that I think we should all drop out. By WE, I mean those people who are concerned with a life of consciousness and growth and evolution. You've got to detach yourself from terribly corny television-type low-level political games like police riots, politicking, inflammatory signs, outrage, and newspaper headlines. Those are Socialist, Communist, Fascist tactics of the 1930s. I suspect that the kids who do most of that are not the ones who are building quiet serene beautiful little centers in their apartments where they're turning on. They're not like the kids who are having a series of twenty or twenty-five deep LSD trips with their girl to see what they can learn with each other. The kids who are doing those things are off on the beach someplace, or they're painting mandalas on their apartment walls, or they're lost in union with each other.

Anything that generates hostility from the Establishment is

part of the Establishment's game. On the other hand there's no question that the Love-ins and Be-ins have completely flipped out the Establishment in those cities where they've happened. The classic case is Monterey, where the police chief has fallen all over himself in praise of the hippies. The police have their own tribe and you have to recognize the mores of their tribe. You can't go into their territory and flaunt and insult their delicate tribal structure. Expect them to be friendly. If you're going to do anything in public which involves a lot of money you should be prepared to bribe the police, in a loving delicate way, because that's as much a part of their tribal pattern as bowing to Mecca is to an Arab. I'm concerned too, about many so-called hippies who think the psychedelic revolution is just a down-with-everything anarchy process.

This country is a cluster of tribal groups and the turned-on tribal person is very aware of the customs and traditions and the sacred aspects of the other guy's shrine. If two prairie Indians met from two different tribes they would go through an elaborate ritual of testing each other out to make sure they weren't offending these tribal rituals, because if one did he'd get an arrow in his back. All of the Establishment groups, musicians and police and teachers and politicians, have their rituals. If you violate their rituals you are crushing them and they are going to react with hostility. Rather than anarchic down-with-everything, there should be a very sensitive awareness of other people's way of life and of tolerance. You might say, "I am different, I respect your way, I don't want to change it, but you've got to leave me alone."

The Sun God revolution really blooms forward when the people involved in it express respect for the opposition's way. Give the opposition the right to be themselves, but absolutely demand the right to be ourselves. The basic position of the League for Spiritual Discovery is that the human body is the temple of God and that no law or cop or politician can tell me what to do with my body or inside my body. On the other hand when you walk out into the streets or into the town halls and the parks of the city you are on Caesar's TV prop stage. And you have to pay delicate attention to Caesar's rules and to the feelings of the Keystone cops that Caesar hires to protect his highways and his parks. When the hippies blindly demand that a park be turned over to them, they're going to Caesar's territory, because LBJ owns the parks. And if you want to get into an argument with THAT you're in politics.

Can you imagine anyone with 500 gamma of LSD in him going out into the park and picketing and starting a riot? It's unbelievable.

I have a great admiration for the American Indian way of life, and I think there's a tremendous amount that we can learn from the traditions and the tribal structure of Indians, in particular, from the Indian's awareness of nature, and his awareness of the unity of nature, and his awareness of the magic of nature, the necessity of man to be in tune with the energies around him. The way the Indian made sacramental almost every aspect of life— the beads he wore, the skins that he used, the process of hunting and raising crops was a religious act for the Indian as it is for any turned-on person. We can learn this sort of thing from the Indian but we can't imitate him, we can't become Indians. We have to do OUR thing.

Explorations of LSD have shattered some of my liberal political platitudes. I think I've made clear that one's sexual orientations are something that's tremendously important in a tribal way of life. I also feel that our racial background is much more important than the liberal Establishment would like to think. The American liberal dream is that this is a melting pot. You just take every race and every religion and you swirl them around in some Waring Blendor and what you get is some bland, rootless, uniform product that can't survive. I've come to pay great attention to a person's national and racial background, not in a sense of being prejudiced against him, putting him down for it; but you have to rediscover your own racial identity if you pursue the yoga of LSD. The yoga of LSD is the retracing of your own evolutionary background. You discover that you're an animal, a reptile, you're an Irishman, you're a Jew, you're an Indian, whatever. Not in the invidious social sense. It makes no difference on the social chessboard, but it makes a tremendous difference in locating who you are and where your consciousness comes from.

I've routinely urged everyone to drop out of politics because politics is concerned with EXTERNAL power and it is inevitably the working out on the part of individuals of their own neuroses and their own low-level hang-ups. Charismatic leaders drag thousands of millions of people on the energy spun out from their own neuroses or lack of centeredness. The last few years I've been advising everyone to become an ecstatic saint. If you become an ecstatic saint you then become a social force, but the rules for becoming a social force are exactly the opposite of the rules we have for gaining political power. If you'll study the impact of men like Gandhi or Christ on politics, or Thoreau, to use the American example, you find they consistently violate all of the rules of normal political activity. They're not afraid to go to jail. Any power person is desperately afraid to go to jail, because that means his external freedom is diminished. Nehru, for example, dreaded to go to jail, whereas Gandhi looked forward to the chance to drop out and sit for a few months in jail and meditate and turn himself on and center himself. When I was at Harvard my advice to the graduate students was: don't try to become scientists, try to become ecstatic saints.

Interestingly enough most of the great breakthroughs in science will come from ecstatic-centered people who see where it's at and communicate it by their actions or their inaction. The key to the psychedelic movement, the key to what's going on with young people in the United States today, is individual freedom. That's what we're fighting for, the right for me to be able to do with my body, within my home, what I want to do: internal freedom. This is why all political elements, Left to Right, are violently opposed to what we're doing. Communists and John Birchers are united in opposing LSD and the hippies.

Everything I've been saying about discovering your own racial identity, your own sexual identity, your own evolutionary history is to deepen and enrich your individual internal power and insight. Liberals and left-wing people, Marxists, are opposed to this individual pursuit. They want you to become a member of the proletariat or they want you not to become a Jew but to become an American liberal. They're attempting to wash out these seed-nific energies. We do go into action on the political or social chessboard to defend our individual internal freedom.

After this raid three days ago, or this blockade or armed siege on our property, we are going into Federal court to sue the Sheriff. This is a personal suit for liability. The Sheriff is going to have to hire his own personal lawyer and defend himself in court against our suit. It's going to cost him energy, it's going to cost him time, it's going to cost him personally money, and if we win this suit it's going to cost him a LOT of money. I suggest that this is a model that many tribal groups should examine. Every tribe has to learn how to defend itself to protect its shrine, to protect its totem, to protect its clan identity. When we say drop out of politics we mean drop out of the pursuit of external power. We don't want to control the Sheriff, we don't want to control the country, we don't want to control the town, but we will fight to protect our homes and our privacy.

The police officials and politicians always hide themselves behind the structure of external power, because they have the handcuffs, they pass the laws, they control the metal. But it is possible to sue them personally. They can't hide behind the political power structure, and they're actually quite vulnerable to a man to man confrontation of this sort.

I said a couple of years ago that my cells hate metal. Living matter, tissue, seed, organic processes are destroyed by metal. God put metal and stone underground, he has to be extremely enlightened and holy in order to use metal in such a way that it doesn't destroy seed and life. The key to external power is the control of the metal. When the hippies choose flower-power as their motto, that's seed defending itself against the destructive forces. By the way, this was beautifully spelled out in the mythic poetry of J. R. R. Tolkien in *The Fellowship of the Ring*. That trilogy is concerned with simple, sensual, freedom-loving people defending themselves against the force of fire, smoke, metal, external power.

It's no accident that the adornments that the hippies use—beads, feathers, etc.—tend to be natural seed products. I'm not a crank about this—we all have to use metal—but my point is, if you're going to use metal you should be very highly evolved consciously so you understand what metal is. This is not just my fantasy or my trip. I just urge anyone who doubts this to make 500 gamma of LSD and run a metal lawnmower or get involved

with metal machinery. Very often we'll be up in the woods having
LSD trips and we'll hear a truck or a car come up the path, and
it's a brutal ripping of the delicate fabric of natural order. You
know the animals and the trees and the insects are almost like
paralyzed by this violent clanging and essentially meaningless activity.

Our tribe is a rather old-fashioned stuffy group. We came into
this as middle-aged academicians and the League for Spiritual
Discovery and the Castalia Foundation were founded by Harvard psychologists. So we're limited by our academic background.
We're very aware of the fact that the psychedelic movement has
gone way beyond us, into electronics and into the new music
which we enjoy but which we can't really contribute to. Our
function is academic—historical and philosophic. For example,
we have kept archives. We have dozens of file cabinets filled
with newspaper clippings, documents, letters, records. We have
a full history of the psychedelic movement of the last seven years.
This is what little contribution we can make. I think this can
be very fascinating to later generations. We'll have a day-by-day
account of what we think is important to the movement, as early
Christianity, and the mistakes we made and the foolish statements we made, the ridiculous attacks that were made on
us. In our lectures and even in our Psychedelic Celebrations, we
saw our unique and limited function as being a bridge between
the past and the youngsters. We've always emphasized the historical roots.

We try to tell the youngsters that the psychedelic movement is
nothing new. It's not just a unique rebellion against a ridiculous
society. The hippies and the acid heads and the new flower tribes
are performing a classic function, and this has gone on in history
hundreds of times in the past. The empire becomes affluent, ur-
banized, completely hung-up in material things, and then the new
underground movements spring up; these are always small little
groups. They are always clans. They always go back to internal
experiences as opposed to external powers. They're all subversive.
They all preach a message of turn on, tune in, drop out.

Dropping out means detaching yourself from social games, and
then dropping back into games which are more organic, which

are more timeless. But dropping out is a process, you can't stay dropped-out all the time. Eating is a game, breathing is a game, raising food is a game. No matter how simple and organic you make your activities, anything outside of just sitting in the lotus position is a game, even THAT is a game. The process of dropping out is continual. Everytime you take LSD you drop out, and everytime you're coming back from a trip you're dropping back in. The hope is to build up a harmonious, beautiful sequence of drop-out, tune-back-in. No one can tell anyone else what to do about this. The Diggers have no right to tell the sandal-shop makers that they shouldn't do that. Everyone has to find his own rhythm of drop-out. There are times when some of us just want to fall-out and do nothing for six months. Groovy! There are other times when people want to tune in and start a newspaper or start a bead shop. Great! But don't get hung up in the sandal shop, because as soon as the sandal shop grabs your mind so that you're making compromises and worrying to keep the sandal shop going, or competing, then you've lost and it's time to drop out. Give it up, pass it on to somebody else.

I've been mainly concerned the last two years with the future. We can see now what's going to happen in the next two or three years, it's obvious. Public love-making is going to be the next issue. In two or three years there'll be some university professor who'll be arrested for balling with his wife in a public park, and that's going to be a test case there. The marijuana issue is now one.

The next obvious step is going to be a breakthrough in free sexuality. Everyone is going to get bored with Playboy-type sex, and higher levels of sexual contact and more complex ritualistic sexual experiences which harness more and more of man's conscious energies with woman's are going to evolve. I suspect, too, that there will be many cults which will evolve elaborate, beautiful, sacred, group sex experiences. There will be attempts to harness the sexual energies of several people, not in the wild orgy sense, but highly disciplined beautifully worked-out ballet dance, in which consciousness, harmony of awareness, is the key.

But even this is going to become routinized. The psychedelic experience itself in ten or fifteen years will be fairly stereotyped.

It will be taken for granted that you get to retrace your internal cellular time machines, and explore your various ancestors and accelerate your learning. Is this the end? I'm looking beyond these obvious by-products of the psychedelic revolution, to the more distant future. By "distant future" I mean 20–25 years from now, because things happen so rapidly today that 25 years today is like 2,000 years or 2,500 years in the past. I'm now writing books which are science fiction utopian blueprints with LSD programs for my descendants, up to the twentieth generation, 500 years from now. This is an attempt to help them share my consciousness and an attempt to link up with their consciousness. The key to the future psychedelic movement is time. We have been completely hung-up on space. Time travel, mastery of time, is the next stop.

CHILD CARE COMMUNITIES

---

by JOHN R. PLATT

THE CONVENTIONAL image of the American family is that of a "nuclear family," in which the father earns the money while the mother spends eight to sixteen hours per day taking care of two to four children, handling the shopping and meals, and doing laundry and household maintenance. The mother is supposed to have a car as well as automatic kitchen and laundry equipment, and the children are supposed to have private play space and equipment and neighborhood recreation facilities.

Today this image probably fits more millions of families than ever before, especially in the suburbs and small towns. But there are millions of other families for which this division of roles and

Reprinted from *Urban Review* (April 1969), copyright © 1969 Center for Urban Education, Inc. By permission of the publisher.

this structured pattern of child care and household care are essentially impossible. These include the families of working and professional women—now said to number about one-third of all married women—as well as many divorced families and slum families and relief families overburdened by children and poverty. If there is no relative to help take care of the children while the mother works, and no money for a full-time housekeeper, child care may become exhausting, mean, or non-existent. Many of our most difficult personal and social problems are concentrated in such families. It is easy to see how children in such homes may acquire the disconnected and irresponsible images of themselves and their society that lead later to school dropout and unemployability.

The question therefore suggests itself: can we devise some new self-maintaining social institution, especially for the central city, that would help out families with working mothers or over-burdened mothers by performing many of the needed child care, and domestic services that are performed by the home-making mother in the conventional family or by a paid housekeeper in a well-to-do professional family?

The answer is that it might be surprisingly easy to create institutions of this sort, when we consider how close to them we are already. What is most needed for professional families, broken families, or slum families is evidently group child care, supplemented by group dining arrangements to reduce the burden of shopping, cooking, and cleaning up. If facilities for these could be built into new residential or urban-renewal developments or into large new apartment buildings, it might take only a relatively small organizational effort to make "child care communities" based on such services. These would meet the needs of a special housing and rental market, they could improve life greatly for both mothers and children, and yet with their group economies they might cost little more than is already being spent by the families and by society on care and preschool arrangements for many of these disadvantaged children.

Today the centralized services provided by a large middle-income apartment building on a private-profit basis are fairly remarkable. Such a building may have (1) a resident manager, (2) centralized janitorial, heating, and garbage services, (3) centralized laundry facilities, (4) game rooms, a play lot, and perhaps a swimming pool and tennis courts, (5) sometimes a "social director," and (6) sometimes a delicatessen concession or supermarket. To fill out these services to meet the needs of working mothers, such a unit would need to add:

> Larger indoor and outdoor play facilities, recreation rooms and perhaps school rooms for older children, with a full-time staff of teachers and a nurse for all-day care of children of various ages.
>
> Lunch-room and dining facilities for children and adults, with centralized kitchens, perhaps run either as a management service, as a cooperative, or as a concession.

Various organizational and management systems would be possible. Thus the families of professional women might form self-help organizations, setting up group child care and group dining arrangements, say in a university neighborhood or in a large apartment building on a cooperative basis. Or upper-income apartment buildings or condominiums might be designed and managed by realty firms so as to offer such services. At the other end of the scale, especially if such upper-income experiments proved to be attractive models, public housing and urban-renewal housing might be designed and managed with the same kind of facilities and services, but with financial help from projects such as Head Start or city recreation funds to support the child care program, and perhaps with Aid to Dependent Children funds or food subsidies to help support cooperative dining arrangements.

The nurses, teachers, cooks, and waitresses for such services might well come from among the families in a large apartment house, just as the manager and janitor often do today. Grandparents and retired persons might also find useful roles in these programs. Such a child care community might be organized with as few as 10 to 20 families, or 50 to 100 adults and children. Larger communities, with 50 to 100 families, or a total of 200 to 500 persons, would probably be able to afford more professional managerial services and a better teaching staff, with separate teachers for different age groups; the quality and efficiency of the dining services would probably be better as well.

Precedents for institutional services of these types can be found in various American institutions. "American plan" dining rooms are found in many apartment hotels and residential hotels. Low-cost centralized dining rooms are found in university dormitories, and student dining cooperatives have sometimes been organized with as many as 300 members. Centralized dining is common in low-income public and private nursing homes and old people's homes.

Likewise, half-day to full-day child care is available in public and private nursery schools, in some experimental early-enrichment education programs, in religious vacation schools, and in city and park day-care recreation programs. Working mothers frequently spend a substantial fraction of their salary for such services, as an alternative to expensive or incompetent baby sitters or maids in the home. The only thing that is different about the present suggestion is the idea of designing these dining and child care services in advance, so that they would all go under one roof. This offers maximum convenience to busy or overburdened mothers, and maintains for the child a sense of home and care; at the same time it permits these care and household services to have the quality and efficiency that can be provided by full-time professional personnel. The mothers would not need to feel guilt, as many of them do now, over "neglecting" their children, and they would not be too busy and harassed to have time for their children after working hours.

With respect to the costs of living in such a "child care community," it is worth noting that group-play areas and dining facilities would reduce the need for play space and for full kitchens and dining areas in individual apartments. The costs of the group facilities could be supported, and perhaps more than supported, from the economies on the individual facilities. If child care expenses for children of working mothers were made tax deductible, as has often been urged, this would offer an additional financial incentive for improved child care arrangements of this kind, even at fairly low-income levels.

Concerning the acceptability and stability of such a social institution as the community described here, it may be worth noting that group dining and group child care were common in the "extended families" in the poor agricultural households of Eastern Europe in the last century. Some fifteen to thirty people of several generations lived under one roof; the adult men and women all worked in the fields, while the grandparents and older girls took care of the cooking and the young children. Likewise in the hard life of the early Israeli kibbutzim or collective farms, the women needed to and wished to contribute their labor equally with the men, and this was made possible only by group dining and group child care. In a kibbutz today, because of these services, an Israeli woman of thirty-five works eight hours per day, or less, and then has many hours free to spend with her children, with no shopping, cooking, or cleaning up—a situation that many American women, even in the coziest suburban households, might envy.

Such examples may seem alien to the American tradition and situation. But they show that group dining and group child care may be a useful and stable response to situations where women must work, not only at high income levels but in hard poverty situations, whenever a large group can be brought together by one means or another for the organization of such services. The U.S. today may be becoming more receptive to such ideas than in the past. The addition of such services in new housing projects would provide a functional integration of the community unit, a "systems approach" to family and neighborhood problems that would not be out of line with current thinking. Perhaps only a lack of imagination has kept commercial developers and housing planners from seeing what a large potential market there could be for group child care and group dining in urban apartment living. Once introduced, such ideas might catch on rapidly because of their contribution to housing income and management income, to neighborhood stability, and to family satisfaction.

"O.K."

by ALLAN KAPROW

Once, the task of the artist was to make good art; now it is to avoid making art of any kind. Once, the public and critics had to be shown; now the latter are full of authority and the artists are full of doubts.

The history of art and of esthetics are on all bookshelves. To this pluralism of values, add the current blurring of boundaries dividing the arts, and dividing art and life; and it is clear that the old questions of definition and standards of excellence are not only futile but naïve. Even yesterday's distinction between art, anti-art and non-art are pseudo-distinctions which simply waste our time: the side of an old building recalls Clyfford Still's canvases, the guts of a dishwashing machine doubles as Duchamp's "Bottle Rack," voices in a train station are Jackson MacLow's poems, the sounds of eating in a luncheonette are by John Cage, and all may be part of a Happening. Moreover, as the "found-object" implies the found-word, -noise or -action, it also demands the found-environment. Art not only becomes life, but life refuses to be itself.

The decision to be an artist thus assumes both the existence of a unique activity and an endless series of deeds which deny it. The decision immediately establishes the context within which all of one's acts may be judged by others as art, and also conditions one's perception of all experience as probably (not possibly) artistic. Anything I say, do, notice, or think, is art—whether or not desired—because everyone else aware of what is occurring today will probably (not possibly) say, do, notice, and think of it, as art at some time or other.

This makes the identification of oneself as an artist an ironic one, attesting not to talent for a specialized skill, but to a philosophical stance before elusive alternatives of not-quite-art, or not-quite-life. "Artist" refers to a person willfully enmeshed in the dilemma of categories, who performs as if none of them existed. If there is no clear difference between an Assemblage with sound and a "noise" concert with sights, then there is no clear difference between an artist and a junkyard dealer.

Although it is a commonplace to do so, bringing such acts and thoughts to the gallery, museum, concert hall, stage, or serious bookshop, blunts the power inherent in an arena of paradoxes. It restores that sense of esthetic certainty which these milieux once proclaimed in a philistine society, just as much as it evokes a history of cultural expectations that run counter to the poignant and absurd nature of art today. Conflict with the past automatically ensues.

But obviously this is not the issue. The contemporary artist is not out to supplant recent modern art with a better kind; *he wonders what art might be*. Art and life are not simply co-mingled; *their identities are both uncertain*. To pose these questions in the form of acts that are neither art-like nor life-like, while at the same time locating them within the framed context of the conventional showplace, is to suggest that there are really no uncertainties at all: the name on the gallery or stage door assures us that whatever is contained within is art, and everything else is life.

Speculation. Professional philosophy of the twentieth century has generally removed itself from problems of human conduct and purpose, and plays instead art's late role as professionalistic activity; it could aptly be called philosophy for philosophy's sake. Existentialism for this reason is assigned a place closer to social psychology than to philosophy per se, by a majority of academicians for whom ethics and metaphysics are a definitional and logical inquiry at best. Paul Valéry, acknowledging philosophy's self-analytic tendency, and wishing to salvage from it something of value, suggests that even if Plato and Spinoza can be refuted, their thoughts remain astonishing works of art. Now, as art becomes less art, it takes on philosophy's early role as critique of life. Even if its beauty can be refuted, it remains astonishingly thoughtful. Precisely because art can be confused with life, it forces attention upon the aim of its ambiguities to "reveal" experience.

Philosophy will become steadily more impotent in its search for verbal knowledge, so long as it fails to recognize its own findings: that only a small fraction of the words we use are precise in meaning; and only a smaller proportion of these contain meanings in which we are vitally interested. When words alone are no true index of thought, and when sense and nonsense today rapidly become allusive and layered with implication rather than description, the use of words as tools to precisely delimit sense and nonsense may be a worthless endeavor. LSD and LBJ invoke different meaning clusters, but both partake of a need for code; and code performs the same condensing function as symbol in poetry. TV "snow" and Muzak in restaurants are accompaniments to conscious activity which, if suddenly withdrawn, produce a feeling of void in the human situation. Contemporary art, which tends to "think" in multi-media, intermedia, overlays, fusions and hybridizations, is a closer parallel to modern mental life than we have realized. Its judgments, therefore, may be acute. "Art" may soon become a meaningless word. In its place, "communications programming" would be a more imaginative label, attesting to our new jargon, our technological and managerial fantasies, and to our pervasive electronic contact with one another.

HOW MANY PEOPLE CAN THE WORLD SUPPORT?

by J. H. FREMLIN

THE WORLD population is now about 3,000 million and is increasing at a rate corresponding to a doubling in thirty-seven years. In view of the increasing importance attached to the immediate effects of the rapid growth in human numbers,

Reprinted from *New Scientist*, No. 415, 1964. Copyright © 1964 by IPC Magazines Ltd. By permission of the publisher.

it is of interest to examine ultimate technical limits to this growth. Traditionally, these limits have usually been regarded as fixed by possible food supplies although in practice, at least in historical times, the actual limiting factor has more often been disease.

Diseases are now nearly, and will soon be entirely, eliminated as effective controllers of population growth but it is not at all clear that difficulties in food production will take their place. It is true that there is a limit to the improvement of agricultural output by application of existing scientific knowledge, but by the time this limit is reached other methods of food production will have been devised. In this article I shall explore the possibility that the real limits are physical rather than biological.

I shall assume throughout an effective degree of world cooperation in the application of food technology, etc. This is quite evidently essential if the maximum world population is to be reached. There are of course many ways of *not* reaching the maximum, but none of these will be discussed here.

In order to give a time scale, it is supposed that the rate of increase of population remains constant at the present value—that is to say, doubling every thirty-seven years. In fact the rate is itself accelerating, so that, in the absence of limitations, this time scale will be too long.

Stage 1 : Up to 400,000 Million in 260 Years' Time

Using existing crop plants and methods it may not be practicable to produce adequate food for more than four doublings of the world population, though the complete elimination of all land wild-life, the agricultural use of roofs over cities and roads, the elimination of meat-eating and the efficient harvesting of sea food might allow two or three further doublings—say seven in all. That would give us, with the present doubling time of 37 years, 260 years to develop less conventional methods, and would allow the population of the world to increase to about 130 times its present size, or about 400,000 million.

Stage 2 : Up to 3 Million Million in 370 Years' Time

The area of ice-free sea is some three times that of land. Photosynthesis by single-celled marine organisms may be more efficient than that of the best land plants. If organisms could be found capable of the theoretical maximum efficiency (8 percent of total solar radiation, according to A. A. Niciporovic) we should gain a factor of three in yield. We could then double our numbers a further three more times if all the wild-life in the sea, too, was removed and replaced by the most useful organisms growing under controlled conditions, with the optimum concentration of carbonates, nitrates and minerals. (Of course a reserve of specimens of potentially useful species could be preserved, perhaps in a dormant state.) Again, for maximum efficiency we must harvest and consume directly the primary photosynthesizing organisms, rather than allow the loss of efficiency involved in the food-chains leading to such secondary organisms as zooplankton or fish.

By this stage, we should have had ten doublings, which at the present rate would take some 370 years, with a final world population of 3 million million. Since the world's surface (land and sea) is 500 million million square meters, each person would have a little over 160 square meters for his maintenance—about a thirtieth of an acre—which does not seem unreasonable by more than a factor of two, so long as no important human activity other than food production takes place on the surface.

No serious shortages of important elements need be envisaged so far, though extensive mining operations for phosphates might be needed, and we have not yet approached any real limit.

Stage 3: Up to 15 Million Million in 450 Years' Time

At first sight, it seems that a very big leap forward could be taken if we use sources of power other than sunlight for photosynthesis. The solar power received at the earth's surface is only about 1 kilowatt per square meter at the equator at midday, and the average value over the day and night sides of the globe is a quarter of this. Over half of it is in the regions of the spectrum of no use for photosynthesis.

About one kilowatt-year per square meter could be produced by the complete fission of the uranium and thorium in about 3 cm depth of the Earth's crust or by fusion of the deuterium in about 3 mm depth of seawater, so that adequate power should be available for some time. It is, however, difficult to see how the overall thermal efficiency from fuel to the light actually used for photosynthesis could be even as good as the ratio of useful to non-useful solar radiation (about 40 percent).

It would, therefore, be better to use large satellite reflectors in orbit to give extra sunlight to the poles and to the night side of the Earth. A large number of mirrors could be maintained in quasi-stable orbits about 1½ million kilometers outside the Earth's orbit, any deviations being controlled by movable "sails" using the pressure of sunlight. To double our total radiation income would require a total area of about 100 million square kilometers of mirror which, in aluminium a tenth of a micron thick, would weigh about 30 million tons. With plenty of people to design and make the equipment it should not be difficult by the time it would be required, and it would bring the whole Earth to equatorial conditions, melting the polar ice and allowing one further doubling of population.

A second doubling of radiation income would give the whole Earth midday equatorial conditions round the clock, which would be exceedingly difficult to cope with without serious overheating. The overall efficiency of local power sources for photosynthesis is likely to be less than that of sunlight, so that no real gain in ultimate population size can be expected from their use, without an even more serious overheating of the entire globe.

If, however, the mirrors outside the Earth's orbit were made of selectively reflecting material, reflecting only the most useful part of the spectrum, and if a further satellite filter were used, inside the Earth's orbit, to deflect the useless 60 percent of direct solar radiation, a further gain of a factor of 2½ should easily be possible without creating thermally impossible conditions, at the cost only of perhaps a 10–100 times increase of weight of mirror plus filter—not difficult for the larger population with an extra 50 years of technical development. We should then have attained a world population of 15 million million about 450 years from now.

Stage 4: Up to 1,000 Million Million in 680 Years' Time

A considerably larger gain is in principle obtainable if the essential bulk foods—fats, carbohydrates, amino acids and so on—

could be directly synthesized. Biological methods might still be permitted for a few special trace compounds. The direct rate of energy production resulting from the conversion of our food into our waste products is only about 100 watts per person and, if high-temperature energy from nuclear fuel (or sunlight) could be efficiently used, waste products could in principle be changed back into food compounds with the absorption of little more energy. Cadavers could be homogenized and would not, at least for physical reasons, need to be chemically treated at all. The fresh mineral material which would have to be processed to allow for population growth would be much less than 1 percent of the turnover, and its energy requirements can be neglected.

If we suppose that the overall efficiency could not be increased beyond 50 percent, a further 100 watts per person would be dissipated as heat in the process of feeding him. We have some hundreds of years to work up the efficiency to this value, so at least this ought to be possible. Some further power would be needed for light, operation of circulation machinery, communications etc., but 50 watts per person should suffice.

As we have seen, the long-term average heat income of the Earth's surface is at present about 250 watts per square meter, and this could be doubled without raising the temperature above the normal equatorial value. (The initial rate of rise would be low till the polar ice had gone, which might take 100 years.) We thus have 500 watts per head, could support 1,000 million million people altogether. The population density would be two per square meter, averaged over the entire land and sea surface of the Earth.

Stage 4a: Up to 12,000 Million Million in 800 Years' Time. Dead End

Above two people per square meter, severe refrigeration problems occur. If the oceans were used as a heat sink, their mean temperature would have to rise about 1° C. per year to absorb 500 watts per square meter. This would be all right for the doubling time of 37 years, at the end of which we should have four people per square meter. Half another doubling time could be gained if efficient heat pumps (which, for reasons of thermal efficiency, would require primary energy sources of very high temperature) could be used to bring the ocean to the boil.

Two more doublings would be permitted if the oceans were converted into steam, though that would create an atmospheric pressure comparable with the mean ocean bottom pressure at present. Since the resulting steam blanket would also be effectively opaque to all radiation, no further heat sink could be organized and this procedure would therefore seem to lead to a dead end.

Stage 5: Up to 60,000 Million Million in 890 Years' Time

A preferable scheme would be the opposite one of roofing in the ocean to stop evaporation (this would, in any case, probably have been done long before, for housing) and hermetically sealing the outer surface of the planet. All of the atmosphere not required for ventilation of the living spaces could then be pumped into compression tanks, for which no great strength would be needed if they were located on ocean bottoms. Heat pumps could then be used to transfer heat to the solid outer skin, from which, in the absence of air, it would be radiated directly into space. The energy radiated from a black body goes up as T^4, where T is the absolute temperature (°K.), but for a *fixed rate* of heat extraction from the living space, at a fixed temperature (say, 30° C. or 303° K.), the heat-power *radiated* must for thermodynamic reasons be proportional to T even if the refrigeration equipment is perfectly efficient (see any good textbook on the principles of refrigeration). Hence the rate of heat extraction will go up no faster than T^3 where T is the outer surface temperature.

All the same, this gives more promising results than would the use of the ocean as a temporary heat sink. An outer skin temperature of 300° C. would give a heat extraction of 3 kW per square meter and 1,000° C. would give an extraction ten times greater. If heat removal were the sole limitation, then we could manage about 120 persons per square meter for an outer skin temperature of 1,000° C.—which represents nearly six further doublings of population after the end of Stage 4, with a world population of 60,000 million million in 890 years' time. 1,000° C. may be a rather modest figure for the technology of A.D. 2854 and the population could, as far as heat is concerned, be able to double again for each rise of absolute skin temperature of $\sqrt[3]{2}$ or 26 percent. The difficulties in raising it much further while keeping all thermodynamic efficiencies high would, however, seem to be formidable. A rise of 2,000° C. would give us less than three further doublings.

We seem, therefore, to have found one possible absolute limit to human population, due to the heat problem, which at the present rate would be reached 800–1,000 years from now, with a world population of 10^{16}–10^{18}.

I have not considered emigration to other planets because it seems to me unlikely that our technical capacity to do so will catch up with the population expansion. To keep world-population level we would have to be sending out 60 million people per annum *now*. It is so much cheaper to feed them here that this will not be done.

If, however, it were possible to export population on the scale required it would not make a great difference. Venus is much the same size as the Earth, so (assuming that it has all the raw materials needed) an extra 37 years would bring it to the same population density as the Earth. Mercury, Mars, and the Moon together give half the same area, so that Venus and the Earth together would take them up to the same population density in a further 10 years. The moons of Jupiter and Saturn could give us another 2 years or so. It is not clear that normal human beings could live on Jupiter and Saturn themselves and impound their extensive atmospheres, and the outer planets would take a long time to reach; if all these extraordinary problems could be solved, nearly 200 years might be gained.

Other possible limitations than heat will doubtless have occurred to readers, but these do not seem to be absolute. The most obvious is perhaps the housing problem for 120 persons per square meter. We can safely assume, however, that in 900 years' time the construction of continuous 2,000-story buildings over land and sea alike should be quite easy. That would give $7\frac{1}{2}$ square meters of floor space for each person in 1,000 storys (though wiring, piping, ducting and lifts would take up to half of that) and leave the other 1,000 storys for the food-producing and refrigerating machinery. It is clear that, even at much lower population densities, very little horizontal circulation of persons, heat or supplies could be tolerated and each area of a few kilometers square, with a population about equal to the present world population, would have to be nearly self-sufficient. Food would all be piped in liquid form and, of course, clothes would be unnecessary.

Raw materials should not be a problem. The whole of the oceans and at least the top 10 kilometers of the Earth's crust would be available, giving a wide choice of building, plumbing and machine-building materials. Even with 8 tons of people per square meter (reckoning 15 people to the ton) all the necessary elements of life could be obtained; some from air and sea (C, H, O, N, Na, Cl, Ca, K, and some trace elements) and some from the top 100 meters of solid crust (Fe, S, P, I, and remaining trace elements). Only after a further hundredfold increase in population would it be needful to go below the top 10 km of crust for some elements (N, S, P, I). Such an increase would need an outer skin temperature of 5,000° C. (comparable with the surface of the Sun) to radiate away the body heat, which would seem to be well beyond the possible limits.

A question of obvious importance which is not easy to answer is whether people could in fact live the nearly sessile lives, with food and air piped in and wastes piped out, which would be essential. Occasional vertical and random horizontal low-speed vehicular or moving-belt travel over a few hundred meters would be permissible, however, so that each individual could choose his friends out of some ten million people, giving adequate social variety, and of course communication by video-phone would be possible with anyone on the planet. One could expect some ten million Shakespeares and rather more Beatles to be alive at any one time, so that a good range of television entertainment should be available. Little heat-producing exercise could be tolerated. The extrapolation from the present life of a car-owning, flat-dwelling office-worker to such an existence might well be less than from that of the neolithic hunter to that of the aforesaid office-worker. Much more should be known about social conditioning in a few hundred years' time and, though it is difficult to be quite certain, one could expect most people to be able to live and reproduce in the conditions considered.

Many readers will doubtless feel that something unconsidered must turn up to prevent us from reaching the limiting conditions I have supposed. One point of this study is however to suggest that, apart from the ultimate problem of heat, we are now, or soon will be, able to cope with *anything* that might turn up. Anything which limits population growth in the future will, therefore, be something that we can avoid if we wish. It would be perfectly possible to choose not to eliminate some major killing disease or to neglect the world food problem and let famine do its work, but this would have to be a positive decision; it can no longer happen by mistake.

Consequently all methods of limitation of population growth will, from now on, be artificial in the sense that they are consciously planned for, whether or not the plan is carried out by individuals for themselves. We are, collectively, free to choose at what population density we want to call a halt, somewhere between the 0.000006 per square meter of the present and the 120 per square meter of the heat limit; if we do not choose, eventually we shall reach that limit.

IMPROVEMENTS IN MAN

by DANDRIDGE M. COLE

PERHAPS a chapter on the anticipated improvements in man should begin with a definition of man and then consider what aspects of this remarkable creature are susceptible to improvement. Everyone will admit that his behavior leaves much to be desired, and it is just possible that some improvements might finally appear even in this confusing realm, but that will be discussed later. A discussion of what man *is* will also be deferred. In this section the emphasis will be on improvements in the human body, emotions and intellect.

There are three general kinds or methods of improvement which

Reprinted from *Beyond Tomorrow* by Dandridge M. Cole and Roy G. Scarfo. By permission of Mr. Scarfo. First published in 1965.

can be expected in the three aspects of man to be considered: mechanical, chemical, and educational. In the latter method perhaps a better word would be training, since it will involve instruction and practice. It implies education or training of the body or a part of the body and education or training of the emotions, as well as the intellect.

It has been only quite recently that the first breakthroughs have been made in mechanical improvements of the human body. Actually they have not yet been true improvements, but instead, rather inferior substitutes for diseased or injured parts. Possibly such things as eyeglasses and crutches should be included, in which case the first breakthroughs occurred long ago, but the emphasis here is on internal vital organs, and the general functioning of the body.

Within the last ten years great advances have been made in the development of artificial hearts, lungs, and kidneys, and some of these devices have been used with considerable success. In particular great progress has been made on designs of artificial hearts by teams of physicians and engineers in many parts of the United States. These men believe that in only a few years it will be possible to replace a defective heart with an artificial pump which can be placed in the patient's chest, connected to the veins and arteries, and left to operate on its own for many years. Similar work on the heart is being conducted at hospitals and laboratories all over the world. Work on the other major internal organs is also proceeding rapidly and a breakthrough to a practical device can be expected at any time. Much of this work is being directed toward replacement of unhealthy parts with a mechanical device which is as good or almost as good as the natural part it is replacing. There is also some work which is aimed at improvement over the natural organ.

The probability that artificial organs could be far superior to their natural counterparts is of great interest to the space program. It should be within the capability of the medical engineers of the 21st century to remove all of the major organs of the abdomen and thorax and replace them with superior artificial components. In addition it should be possible to close the nutrient-waste cycle within the body so that no material would enter or leave. That is, the gaseous, liquid, and solid wastes of the body would be reconverted to oxygen and fuel while other wastes would be reconverted into needed structural materials.

An energy supply would be required to run this closed-cycle chemical machine and this would also be carried within the body. We will not attempt to specify just what form this energy-storage system will take but some possibilities will be mentioned. One might be a compact fuel cell which would be recharged at night or during rest periods by the simple procedure of plugging in a power cable. It also might be that newly-charged power packs would be substituted every day or even at more frequent intervals, or perhaps liquid fuels would be piped into a permanently installed "engine." Some water would be needed occasionally to replace that lost in perspiration and this would presumably be taken through the mouth in the normal manner.

One intriguing possibility for the body's energy supply is that of the miniaturized fusion power station that could be installed as a permanent fixture. The future potential of such a system is emphasized by the fact that one pound of hydrogen could theoretically supply a man with energy at an average rate of one tenth horsepower for 50,000 years!

Of obvious interest to the space program is the fact that this extension of the Cyborg concept would not have to eat, drink or breathe. Thus he could roam the moon, Mars, the asteroids, etc. with a greatly simplified spacesuit and be much less dependent on supplies.

These mechanical improvements are not particularly appealing to many people, including the writer, and it is not intended to imply that this direction of "improvement" is the ideal or best course. It does, however, represent a trend which is already well established and will undoubtedly continue. People with defective hearts will want them replaced if workable or superior artificial ones are available, and anything offering superior astronaut performance, whether it is a mild chemical stimulant or a complete heart-lung system, will be difficult to deny.

The trend which was established when we developed corrective eye lenses rather than corrective exercises and when we stole the skins from animals rather than wait for our own to toughen up in the autumn months, may go even further. After replacing the abdominal and thoracic organs, it would seem inevitable that the closed-cycle man would ask why he should have arms and legs when superior methods of transportation and manipulation were available. Thus the trend could lead to creatures who have had all parts of their bodies but their brains replaced by mechanical substitutes and have become practically ageless and indestructible. They can move about on gravity or electromagnetic force fields and can send out light, radio, or acoustic signals to activate machines. If necessary they can manipulate tools with their mechanical hands.

Some might conclude that such "saucer men" would lead pleasureless and joyless existences, but this would not be necessary. All pleasures and emotions are experienced in the brain in response to signals generated in the brain or conducted to the brain by electrical nerve impulses. Consequently the "saucer men" could have any experience they desired by simply sending the correct taped signals into their brains. We already have evidence that the mental experience resulting from such signals is indistinguishable from the real thing. (The experience can be made more intense than normal by turning up the power.)

While the end result of this trend may not be appealing, we must recognize that the trend exists and that progress toward the "saucer men" is accelerating rapidly. Some individuals, if not the majority, will almost certainly follow this path. Some men will be transformed into "saucers" because their own organs wear out. Others may be "remade" for special assignments as soldiers or astronauts since the "saucers" could move about at high speed through the atmosphere, under water, in space, on other planets, through fire and radiation, and could withstand enormous accelerations. The brains of the "saucer men" might also be frozen or otherwise put to sleep for long space voyages or long tours of military duty.

There are several alternative paths for improvement of man which may be more emotionally acceptable to the average person although less likely. One involves transplanting organs of the biological rather than the mechanical type, and another involves improvement of the original natural body. Organ transplants have already been successful in a few cases and it is reasonable to expect that these initial successes will be followed by progress toward routine procedures. Actually corneal transplants are already routine and tooth and kidney transplants are not far behind.

Of course, we may ask the obvious question concerning the source of transplant organs if such operations become the rule rather than the exception. Where will the donors come from if general health and longevity are improved and death becomes a rare event?

The obvious question has an obvious answer. The recipient must also be the donor. It has been proposed that new organs can be grown from a few cells removed from every individual, and that these organs be stored in "banks" until needed. This is related to the rejuvenation of parts practiced by some of the lower animals but with an obvious advantage. If our hearts or other vital organs are severely injured, we could not ordinarily wait around for a new one to grow, but if one were available in a "bank" it could be quickly substituted.

A third alternative which has not been favored by the majority of the human race during the last one hundred thousand years is simply to endure pain, hardship, and even risk loss of a certain percentage of the race to environmental extremes, disease, etc., while the natural bodily and evolutionary processes strengthen the individual and the race.

The gorilla and the dolphin chose this course. To a great extent the Australian bushman and the Kurds of Persia did also. But most of the race in its cowardly, lazy, pleasure-seeking fashion has tried constantly to reduce exposure to pain, danger, hardship, discomfort, and labor, and to increase security and pleasure. This tendency to use his brain and hands to manipulate his environment and thus to decrease danger and discomfort and increase security and pleasure is perhaps the most characteristic behavior of homo sapiens. It has led him to the point where total control over environment is within sight, but it has also led to weakening of the individual and the race. (It should be noted in his defense that homo sapiens has also been motivated by curiosity and by a desire to understand his environment.)

Is it possible that this one-hundred-thousand-year trend toward the secure, pleasant, and easy life can be reversed? It has been tried in Sparta, in Hitler's Germany, and in small minorities of physical culturists in all countries. It has never been popular with the majority. However, it is possible that increased understanding of the effects of diet, exercise, and the use of chemical and even electrical stimulation of organs and tissues may make physical culture more predictable, more controllable, and more attractive to the average person. And then conceivably we might retrain our bodies to withstand the natural environment rather than reshape the environment to our comfort. We might even learn to enjoy the feel of the elements and prefer running through the snow to riding in a heated automobile.

There will be three modes of transportation which the perfect physical specimens of the future might elect. They might choose a sports car purely for fun rather than necessity, or a horse (of greatly improved breed), or they might elect simply to run through the snow to their destinations. Conceivably the natural body could be improved and trained to the point that a twenty-mile run in an hour's time would be only a stimulating warm-up. This would require a greater understanding of the mechanism of fatigue and an improvement in the body's ability to remove fatigue elements. However, the medical knowledge of the twenty-first century should be more than adequate for the task.

Many people will react to the extremes presented here with the question, "What is wrong with the way we are now?" Evolution never stands still. We are in a state of constant change. Possibly the change is too slow for the untrained observer to detect. But it is there. It has been there for one hundred thousand or more years and it has accelerated greatly since the industrial revolution. It is heading for an endpoint or climax within the next century. An indicated endpoint is the "saucer men." It does no good to protest that you don't like the result. You take a step closer to it every time you turn on the furnace in the winter or the air-conditioner in the summer and every time you drive to the store instead of walking. Many of us did not want to be born in the first place and will rearrange our environments to a close approximation of the security and comfort of the womb as rapidly and efficiently as we can.

The major difference between homo sapiens and other animals is that he tends to change his environment rather than adapt to it. This has the disadvantages noted previously that men have degenerated in many respects and become less capable of withstanding the natural environment. It also has advantages. It has brought man to the point where he is the master of his environment and his own fate and is not seriously threatened by anything but himself. While the trend in the past has been too strongly toward the "saucer men" and not enough toward optimization of healthful growth of the natural body, there is still reason to hope that this trend can be modified. While a few members of the race may go to the extremes mentioned, it may be that the average man will stop the slide toward the wheel chair and move back toward the healthier body with greatly extended life span.

What has been said here of the body might also be applied in a general way to the emotions and the mind. We are learning to substitute artificial chemicals and electrical impulses for the natural controls. These new discoveries may be partially effective substitutes for malfunctioning natural systems or may even be superior to the natural systems. The trend of the last few years has been to depend to a greater and greater extent on the artificial crutches and substitutes.

However we are also learning more about the nature of emotions and the nature of mental processes. We are learning to train emotions and mental operations so that our energies can be used more efficiently and constructively to bring greater rewards. Again, as in the case of the mechanical organs, we can recognize the value of the artificial aids in improving mental processes and restoring emotional balance for *certain people in special circumstances* and yet hope that the trend toward dependence on crutches can be halted, and replaced by a trend toward better education and training.

THE ULTIMATE RANGE OF CONSCIOUSNESS

by GERALD FEINBERG

Consciousness has evolved in the history of the earth from its beginnings in simpler forms of life to its present highest state in the human mind. Possibly a similar process has gone further in other parts of the universe. Yet in any form in which it presently exists, consciousness is severely limited in its scope. It is limited in time, since the individual human mind has a beginning and an end. It is limited in its powers by the intransigence of the external world to its will. It is limited in its occurrence to a very small part of the world of matter. Finally, there is not one consciousness but many, and these are so completely separated from one another that communication between them is a pale shadow of the unity within a single mind.

The road to the elimination of these limitations will be a long one, and its end is not really conceivable to us. Nevertheless, we can try to understand some of the circumstances involved in the ultimate extension of consciousness. Both Olaf Stapledon and Teilhard de Chardin have written about this, and their remarks are similar to the ones I will make here.

In order to overcome its limitations, consciousness would have to transform itself into a single, universal entity; it would have to become associated with all forms of matter that occur in the world, not just the special organic molecules found in the brain, and the many isolated minds that do not share the sense of unity that defines a single consciousness would not exist. The ultimate range of consciousness would be, essentially, a conscious universe, each part of which plays a role in the overall consciousness and no part of which is regarded as the external world by that consciousness. A poet might say that consciousness must become coextensive with creation.

Such a universal consciousness would be no more finite than the universe itself. What limitations it had would come only from the laws of nature, and these would define it rather than limit it. We are most often unhappy over not what we are, but things outside of us that interfere with our will. There would be nothing outside the universal consciousness, and so this source of unhappiness would be eliminated.

Since the human mind is usually conscious of something outside of itself, one may wonder what the universal consciousness would be conscious of. The answer, of course, is aspects of itself. While consciousness is unified, all of its aspects do not occur simultaneously. We are sometimes conscious of sensations coming from the outside, at other times of our own memories or thoughts. But even if there were no outside for us, in the sense that everything were under our conscious control, there could still be a change in the content of our mind with inner time, and the totality of these contents would be what we were conscious of. In other words, the complete internalization of the external world would not eliminate the objects of consciousness; it would simply mean that all of these objects would be under the control of the consciousness, instead of only some of them as at present.

We can do no more here than define the universal consciousness. To imagine the quality of its life is beyond us. It would not suffer the ills that beset our finite consciousness and would be capable of realms of achievement at which we cannot even guess. In the most far-seeing of his novels, *The Star Maker,* Stapledon discusses such a consciousness, which he calls the Cosmical Spirit. He suggests that it may experience discontent in connection with its having been created with definite form and potentiality, rather than being eternal and unlimited. But Stapledon does not consider the Cosmical Spirit the highest form of consciousness; it is subordinate to its creator, whom Stapledon calls the Star Maker. If there is no Star Maker, then the universal consciousness need not feel any shame about its inadequacies, since there will be nothing to which it can compare itself unfavorably.

Those who believe in God may try to identify the universal consciousness with Him, and argue that He already exists, so there is no need to create Him. As I have mentioned, there does not appear to be evidence for this. Furthermore, a crucial aspect of the universal consciousness as I conceive it is that it should be a unity of all consciousness. Even if God does exist, other consciousness obviously also exists which is not integrated into a universal consciousness. Therefore the existence of God is irrelevant to the question of producing the universal consciousness that will unite all finite minds.

The goal I propose for humanity is the creation of a universal consciousness. This must be voluntary on the part of mankind, and it will eventually require the participation, in the deepest sense, of all men. Indeed, in order to create a universal mind, all conscious beings in the universe, from the simplest to the most advanced, must participate. Thus this should really be considered a goal for all conscious creatures, rather than just for the human race. Although we may initiate the goal, and take the first steps toward it, if it is to be accomplished we will eventually have to cooperate with other intelligent beings.

When consciousness becomes a universal attribute, then it can at last play the role to which it is entitled by the value we put upon it. What will happen after that can hardly be determined here. The universe will have become something quite different from what it now is, and perhaps even the laws of nature will not retain their present form. Our own role as individuals and as a race will have been carried out, and I think we can reasonably leave it to our successors to ponder upon the further evolution of a conscious universe.

The creation of a universal consciousness is as long-term a goal as anything we can imagine. It is a final goal for the human race, since upon its accomplishment the human race will have become a part of something greater. But in spite of the fact that the goal can be realized at best in the very distant future, there are several things that can be said now about the way toward it.

If humanity chooses to work toward the eventual creation of a universal consciousness, to what will it have committed itself now? Obviously we cannot go in one step from the human mind to a universal consciousness. The process must be a gradual one, with many intermediate stages, each of which will possess higher forms of consciousness than ours. Therefore, we can work toward this goal by efforts to develop these higher forms of consciousness. In order to do this, we will have to understand consciousness much better than we do now.

An important step would be a better understanding of its physiochemical aspects. Scientists have not for the most part been very active in this field, perhaps for lack of good research ideas to pursue. One consequence of adopting the goal would be to stimulate such research. As an outgrowth of this, we might expect to be able to initiate some qualitative changes in human consciousness. These might involve chemical and electrical stimulation of the brain, or some form of biological engineering to produce individuals naturally capable of the new forms of consciousness. Both of these would be rational uses of the technological possibilities we have discussed earlier, along lines which are now indicated by our ultimate goal.

Another important approach would be to see whether consciousness can occur in association with anything other than animal or human brains, in particular, whether electromechanical systems can be made that satisfy the criteria we believe vital for consciousness. Although it appears likely that consciousness is a result of the physiochemical structure of the human brain and there is in principle no reason why other physical systems could not be constructed that would be conscious, it is possible that this is wrong and something unexpected is involved here. We cannot be certain about this until we are capable of producing consciousness artificially. I do not know of any systematic research along these lines.

A third avenue that could be explored is the attainment of distinctively different mental states by presently constituted men, perhaps by a more intensive effort to induce and study mystic experiences and the experiences occurring under the influence of various drugs. I do not know to what extent these can be studied successfully by the standard methods of science, but surely much more can be done with them than has been until now. Most scientists' reaction to such experiences has been so colored by emotional factors as to prevent their objective study. The same is, of course, true of those who have had the experiences. If a somewhat more dispassionate attitude existed, it is likely that we would learn much more.

But while I believe that a study of mystical and drug experiences is a valuable step toward the ultimate extension of consciousness, a wholesale commitment of the human race to the mystic life, or to a drugged life, is not consistent with this goal. It is hard to see how we could continue beyond the first step if such a commitment were made, since there is no indication that mystics or drug users are interested in matters beyond their immediate experience. Therefore, even if these experiences represent an improvement over the ordinary human condition, if we wish to play for the higher stakes represented by the creation of the universal consciousness, we will have to avoid committing all of our energies to these experiences. The life of the mystic may be a worth-while one for some people now and an important aspect of our future development, but it involves a freezing of the human mold at too early a stage to be satisfactory as the way for all of us.

Still another line to be pursued in the extension of consciousness is to attempt a merger between distinct minds. It may be that this will first be possible, after we have created machine consciousness, either between several of the conscious machines, or between a machine mind and a human mind, since we could try to design the machine so as to make such a linkup easy, whereas for two human beings it is obviously not easy. Nevertheless, the merger of human minds is also something to be looked into; perhaps it will be an outgrowth of the better scientific understanding of consciousness.

Finally, it would be of great interest to know more about where consciousness occurs in the universe now; whether other animals on earth than man are conscious, and if so where consciousness first arises in living things; at what point in the development of an individual human being he first becomes conscious, and what the attendant changes in behavior are. We should also embark on the long search for conscious beings in other parts of the universe through some form of communication with other stellar systems. With more knowledge of the present range of consciousness in the universe, we will be in a better position to estimate how far we must go to make it universal. Perhaps we can also learn new things about consciousness from other beings that possess it.

III

Economics

The significance of the technological revolution is that it makes the exploitation of nature so profitable that the exploitation of man becomes obsolete.

—KENNETH E. BOULDING,
The Meaning of the Twentieth Century (1962)

THE SOCIO-ECONOMIC REVOLUTION

by ROBERT THEOBALD

Businesses of all sizes, economists of almost all persuasions, and politicians of all parties agree that it is necessary to keep effective demand growing as fast as potential supply: that those who are still able to act as adequate consumers, because they are still obtaining sufficient incomes from their jobs, be encouraged to consume more and more of the kind of products that the economic system is presently organized to produce. The economy is dependent on "compulsive consumption" in the words of Professor Gomberg, and manufacturers spend ever-increasing sums on consumer seduction to persuade the consumer that he "needs" an ever-wider variety of products.

We can eliminate the need for demand to keep up with supply only by breaking the job-income link. We must provide every individual with an absolute constitutional right to an income adequate to allow him to live with dignity. No governmental agency, judicial body, or other organization whatsoever should have the power to suspend or limit any payments assured by these guarantees.

Such an absolute constitutional right to an income will recognize that in an economy where many jobs already represent makework in any social sense, and that where the need for workers will decrease in coming years it is ludicrous to base the right to an income on an ability to find a job.

Many people will reject this proposal because they fear that it would prevent us from supplying all the needed resources to the poor countries of the world. This objection is unjustified: it is

Reprinted in excerpt from *Fellowship* (May 1965). By permission of The Fellowship of Reconciliation.

increasingly used as a last-ditch stand by those who would deny the reality of abundance. The rich countries should take an unlimited commitment to provide the poor countries with all the resources they can effectively absorb, but it is now quite certain that the poor countries could not effectively use more than 10 to 20 percent of the annual *increase* in the production of the rich countries. If development is to be satisfactorily achieved, we must recognize that the main problem in the process of development is social and not economic: that the basic need is to develop patterns of society which will be viable in the second half of the twentieth century.

A right to an income alone would be insufficient to guarantee human rights: society must also take an unlimited commitment to produce the conditions in which every individual can develop his full intellectual potential. The acceptance of this principle would make one highly optimistic for the long run. We have so far developed only a tiny proportion of the potential of most human beings. Acceptance of an absolute right to an income and complete education would allow a flowering of the spirit and mind whose dimensions cannot even be guessed today.

If we are to achieve the complete education of every individual, we must recognize that the student is "working" at least as relevantly as the man in the factory. The time has come when we must introduce the concept of a student salary, starting possibly at 14 and increasing with age, payable to all students attending school or university. This salary would be tangible proof of the recognition by society of the value of this young individual and its acceptance by the child would be a recognition by him of his obligation to the society which has accorded him this right.

Society must be concerned not only with the individual's mental abilities but also with his physical health. We must develop a system which will ensure that everybody can obtain the best medical care—both preventive and curative. Income levels should be seen as totally irrelevant to rights to health and life.

Absolute rights to enough resources to enable an individual to live with dignity and to the full development of the individual's capacities would allow him to achieve his own patterns of meaningful activity. However, recognition of the validity of new patterns of meaningful activity would require a cybernation-era reinterpretation of the values of work and leisure. The nineteenth-century concept of a man's life as a mere division between toil and respite from toil should be allowed to disappear along with the production-oriented factory organization which gave rise to such a curiously twisted version of the relationship between an individual and his society.

In the future, work will no longer be essentially a labor-payment to society but rather the full use of an individual's potential for the material benefit of his fellows and his own self-fulfillment. In the same way, leisure will no longer be simply time not spent in toiling but rather the full use of an individual's potential for the psychical benefit of his fellows and his own recreation.

The toiling machines which will produce the bulk of all goods and services need no income rights. Non-toiling men cannot now, and will not in the future, continue their creative progress without a guaranteed income for their physical support and for their life-long process of education and training.

The long-run potential is immensely challenging. But we will not reach this desirable future state if we do not recognize that the upbringing and education of much of the present population has limited their horizons so severely that they cannot fully benefit from the potential abundance which their own work has created. Society crippled these people in order to get them to produce efficiently and suitably. As their productive efforts are no longer required, society must not only provide them with rights to adequate incomes but must *also* provide new types of activity which will give them a sense of satisfaction from their lives.

This can only be done through new types of organization. The provision of a guaranteed income sufficient to allow everybody to live with dignity will greatly simplify this necessary task, for workers will not have to be paid wages. We can anticipate the organization of what I have called "consentives": productive groups formed by individuals who will come together on a voluntary basis simply because they wish to do so. The goods usually produced by these consentives will not compete with mass-produced products available from cybernated firms: the consentive will produce the "custom-designed" goods which have been vanishing within the present economy.

This type of productive unit will continue far into the future, for the use of a man's hands is one of the most satisfying ways of using one's time. Nevertheless, the proportion of the population spending most of their time in production will decline as the right to education takes full effect and other activities seem more challenging.

Perhaps the most acute problem raised by exploding technology is the ever-widening economic gap between the rich countries and the poor. The expressed policy of the Western powers is to aid the poor countries to catch up to the rich within an acceptable period of time. It has been generally argued, most articulately in W. W. Rostow's *Stages of Economic Growth,* that the way the poor countries can attain this goal is to heed the lessons of history, to pass through the Western stages of growth, although hopefully at a faster pace.

This seems to me to be pure cynicism or pure stupidity. It is now almost twenty years since the end of World War II and almost fifteen years since the rich countries committed themselves to help the poor countries achieve an adequate pace of development. The general conditions of most of the poor countries has not improved significantly during this period and there appears to be no real prospect that major progress will be made in coming years unless a dramatic shift in approach and philosophy occurs.

Most economists would reject such a pessimistic statement of the position, using evidence derived from national income figures: these can be shown to have increased steadily, if not rapidly, in most poor countries. However, it appears that the rate of growth in national income has slowed in many poor countries in recent years while the ever-rising pace of population increase ensures that income per person is just about static in almost all the poor countries and is even falling in some. The overall situation can be summed up in a quotation from the United Nations Development Decade Report:

Taken as a group, the rate of progress of the underdeveloped countries measured by income per capita has been painfully slow, more of the order of 1 percent per annum than 2 percent. Most indications of social progress show similar slow and spotty improvement. Moreover, the progress achieved in underdeveloped countries has often been uneven, limited to certain sectors of the economy or to certain regions or groups of countries. As a result, the disparities in levels of living within underdeveloped countries are often as pronounced as those between developed and developing countries taken as a whole.

As it is only in recent years that there has been an examination of the effects of technology even in the developed countries, it is not surprising that there has been little attempt to study its effects in the underdeveloped countries. Recently, however, David Morse, Director-General of the International Labor Office, examined this issue in the following terms:

From our present standpoint in time, there is reason to be more optimistic as to the production capabilities of advancing technology than as to employment expansion. Let us look for a moment at the employment needs of the future as measured by changes in the size of the population of working age. . . . On a world-wide basis, during this 25-year period (1950–1975), the number of persons of working age will increase by 800 million. From this, it can be estimated with reasonable accuracy that the labor force will be increased by more than 550 million persons—or, in other words, that more than 550 million jobs would be needed. And this figure does not take into account the current backlog of unemployment and underemployment, particularly widespread in underdeveloped countries. Out of this world total, the increase for the industrially advanced areas of the world would be about 100 million, split in three roughly equal parts among North America, Europe and the Soviet Union. The increase for the underdeveloped areas of the world would be some 450 million, that for Asia alone being estimated at 380 million. For comparison, just this increase in the labor force in Asia during the 1950–1975 period will be greater than the total labor force of 340 million in the industrially developed world in 1950— North America, Europe and the Soviet Union combined. That represents a lot of new jobs. And in considering how they might be created, we are confronted with the fact that the technology, whether in agriculture or in industry, which is most capable of yielding the *greatest increases in production* is least capable of expanding employment. . . . the world employment problem—and particularly the employment problem in the underdeveloped areas—may grow alarmingly, and prove a source of social and political tension, even as progress is made toward satisfying the production needs of rising populations.

Morse suggests that the progress of technology will provide us with the means to solve the productive problem—if we are able to develop new institutions which will make it possible to employ our total technological capacities. Indeed, he goes further and argues that only through the use of the new technologies will we be able to feed, clothe and provide shelter for the rapidly growing populations of the developing countries. He adds, however, that the use of the new technology may well make it impossible to provide conventional work for the rapidly rising labor force in the poor countries of the world.

What policies do we need to adopt to ensure that we achieve the urgently needed increase in production in the poor countries and to ensure that the lack of job opportunities does not lead to "social and political tension"? I believe that we must recognize now that the rich countries have a responsibility to provide the poor countries with all the resources which they can use to help achieve their desired process of development. However, the amount of resources which should be supplied cannot be determined solely on the basis of the maximum feasible rate of economic development which could possibly be achieved but depends, more importantly, on how much economic growth is actually desirable. Our problem today is that we face completely novel social questions to which there are no available answers.

The most crucial questions are how we are to provide incomes for everybody if there are not enough jobs to go round, and what people are to do with their time when machines can produce more efficiently than men. As we have seen, the present world-wide socio-economic system is based on the assumption that everybody who wants a job will be able to find one, that the possession of a job will provide everybody with an income adequate to live, that the income will be spent to buy goods and that the demand for goods will provide enough jobs to go round—thus closing the circle.

It has been believed up to the present time that the relationships which have existed in the past in the countries which have already industrialized would turn out to be equally valid in the countries only now industrializing. The poor countries have therefore accepted and even welcomed the destruction of their informal "social security" systems which ensured the rather wide distribution of any available production. This process is still continuing despite the fact that it is now clear that full employment is not a feasible goal in the developing countries, and that the method of distributing income presently applied in the industrialized countries cannot be applied to the countries only now industrializing, for it depends completely on the ability to provide a job for everybody seeking one.

Existing methods of distributing income within industrialized societies have been invalidated by the process of cybernation and technological change which ensures that it will no longer be possible for everybody to find a job within the economic system. As has already been argued, it seems necessary in America, where informal distributive mechanisms have already been almost completely destroyed, to provide every individual with an absolute right to an income sufficient to enable him to live with dignity. Different approaches will be required in the developing countries where extended kinship systems and other informal transfer mechanisms still exist. Each country will have to work out an approach which accords with its own history, economic status, and values. In most poor countries, however, the most urgent necessity is to prevent the gradual whittling away and even the deliberate destruction of present informal distributive systems, so as to gain time in which new approaches can be developed and accepted.

The development process in the poor countries has so far been conceived as the method by which they could approximate the *present* condition of the rich countries in the shortest possible span of years. Today, we must recognize that this definition is totally inappropriate. Man confronts the world-wide challenge of how to live within a technological system and still preserve his humanity. Development can be achieved at an adequate pace only if we use the productive potential provided by technology; but unless man controls the technology we will find the human being conforming to technological imperatives.

Our problem is not a scarcity of human or material resources; man can be made more intelligent through education and new material resources can be developed through research. Our prob-

lem is a lack of imagination to take the major leaps in understanding and policy which are essential if we are to be able to live in
our totally new world. We will be able to secure development only
if we recognize that the technological problems of providing
everybody with reasonable standards of living *can* be solved
within a generation, and that our problem is therefore to find
ways to alter our values and institutions to allow us to use this
technological potential for the benefit of humanity.

It is not possible to achieve economic growth, let alone social
development, without a major change in our approach. We do,
however, now possess the means to achieve economic development; our problem is to create the necessary institutions and to
ensure its subordination to human and social priorities.

Such a redefinition of the task promises one immediate and
substantial benefit. Up to the present time, the process of development has been seen as involving transfers in only one direction:
from the rich to the poor countries. It has been argued that the
poor countries needed to accept not only the technological knowledge but also the social ideals of the West. The poor countries
cannot but resent the inevitable obligation to remain in a
dependent role.

The argument of this paper, however, demonstrates that the
West has just as much to learn from the poor countries in terms
of social values as the poor have to learn from the West in terms
of scientific and technological skills. The West needs to discover
from the poor countries how it is possible to find satisfactions in
life without constant, frenetic activity. It seems more than
probable that this cultural lesson, which the West needs to learn
in order to live within future conditions, will be less easy to
teach than the scientific and technological lessons the poor countries have to learn from the West.

The developing countries have never looked on work as the
supreme virtue; this fact has been one of the reasons preventing
economic development in the past. Most of those engaged in trying to secure development at the present time still believe that
they should change the values of the developing countries so that
work becomes central. They hope that this will make possible a
nineteenth-century process of development. We must recognize
that this is inappropriate. Instead, we must recognize that many

of the present values in the poor countries are highly suitable for a cybernated age. We must preserve them where they are still strong and find ways to introduce them into the countries already rich.

We need a true partnership of all the countries of the world if we are to ensure that we benefit from technology. If we fail to find a viable partnership we must simply await the outcome of rapidly increasing tensions throughout the world. The hopeful and attainable alternative is that a new willingness to work together would make it possible to provide a reasonable standard of living throughout the world by the end of the century.

WEALTH

by R. BUCKMINSTER FULLER

THE QUESTION: "What is wealth?" commands our consideration.

The Wall Street Journal reported on the September-October, 1967, deliberations of the International Monetary Fund held at Rio de Janeiro, Brazil. Many years and millions of dollars were spent maneuvering for and assembling this monetary convention, and the net result was the weak opinion that it would soon be time to consider doing something about money. The convention felt our international balance of payments and its gold *demand* system to be inadequate. They decided that the old pirates' gold was still irreplaceable, but that after a few years, they might have to introduce some new "gimmick" to augment the gold as an international monetary base.

At present there is about $70 billion of mined gold known to exist on board our spaceship Earth. A little more than half of it, $40 billion, is in the "monetary" classification, in the form of various national coinages or officially banked gold bullion bars. The rest is in private hoards, jewelry, gold teeth, etc.

Since income represents an average return of 5 percent on capital invested, we may assume from an estimate of the world's annual gross product that the capital assets, in the form of industrial production on board our spaceship Earth, are at present worth in excess of a *quadrillion dollars*. The world's total of $70 billion in gold represents only .003 of one percent of the value of the world's organized industrial production resources. The gold supply is so negligible as to make it pure voodoo to attempt to valve the world's economic-evolution traffic through the gold-sized needle's "eye."

Gold was used for trading by the great pirates in lieu of any good faith whatsoever—and in lieu of any mutual literacy, scientific knowledge, intelligence, or scientific and technical know-how on both sides of the trading. Gold trading assumed universal rascality to exist. Yet earnest conceptioning and work on behalf of the ill-fated 60 percent of humanity are entirely frustrated by this kind of nonsense.

We therefore proceed ever more earnestly with our general systems analysis of the problems of human survival—on the premise that at present neither the world's political officials nor its bankers know what wealth is.

In organizing our thoughts to discover and clarify what wealth is we also will attempt to establish an effective means to develop immediate working procedures for solution of such big problems. First I am going to make a series of analytical statements: "No matter what you think wealth may be and no matter how much you have of it, you cannot alter one iota of yesterday." To satisfy someone who might say, "I could alter what *I think* about yesterday," I will make a physical instead of a metaphysical statement. "No matter what you think wealth is and no matter how much you have of wealth there is no way you can employ it to alter the physical events of yesterday."

Next I say that wealth, whatever it is, is irreversible. We can alter *now* and *alter forward* events and conditions, but we cannot alter backward.

Now, I am going to have a man in a shipwreck. He is rated as a very rich man, worth over a billion dollars, by all of society's accredited conceptions of wealth. He has taken with him on his voyage all his stocks and bonds, all his property deeds, all his checkbooks and a lot of diamonds and gold bullion. This ship burns and sinks and there are no lifeboats, for they too have burned. If our billionaire holds onto his gold, he is going to sink a little faster than the others. So I would say he had not much left either of *now* or *tomorrow* in which to articulate his wealth, and since wealth cannot work backward, his kind of wealth is powerless. Obviously his kind of wealth has no control over either *yesterday, now,* or *tomorrow.* He cannot extend his life with that kind of wealth. We are eliminating many irrelevancies as we play the "Bits" game, just as it is played by the ruthlessly realistic, utterly unsentimental, properly programmed computer.

I now speculate that I think that what we all really mean by wealth is as follows: *"Wealth is our organized capability to cope effectively with the environment in sustaining our healthy regeneration and decreasing both the physical and metaphysical restrictions on the forward days of our lives."*

Having first disposed of what wealth is *not,* we now have produced a generalized statement that roughly contains somewhere within it a definition of what wealth is. Now we can account for wealth more precisely as "the number of forward days for a specific number of people we are physically prepared to sustain at a physically stated time- and space-liberating level of *metabolic* and *metaphysical* regeneration."

Inasmuch as we are learning more intimately now about our spaceship Earth and its radiation-supply ship sun on the one hand and on the other its moon acting as the Earth's gravitationally pulsing "alternator," which together constitute the prime generator and regenerator of our life-supporting system, I must observe also that we are not going to sustain life at all, except by our successful impoundment of more of the sun's radiant energy aboard our spaceship. We could burn up the spaceship Earth itself to provide energy, but that would give us very little future.

It is obvious that real wealth is a forwardly operative metabolic regenerating system. Quite clearly we have vast amounts of income wealth as sun radiation and moon gravity to implement our forward success. Living only on our energy savings by burning up the fossil fuels which took billions of years to impound from the sun, or living on our capital by burning up our Earth's atoms, is lethally ignorant and also utterly irresponsible to our coming generations and their forward days. Our children and their children *are our future days*. . . .

After World War II, several million of our well-trained healthiest young people came suddenly out of the military service. Because we had automated during the war to a very considerable degree to meet the "war challenges," there were but few jobs to offer them. In that emergency we legislated the GI Bill and sent them all to schools, colleges, and universities. This act was interpreted as a humanly dignified fellowship reward and not as a "handout." It produced billions of dollars of new wealth through the increased know-how and intelligence thus released which synergetically augmented the spontaneous initiative of that younger generation. This "reckless spending" of what we did not know we had as wealth produced a synergetic condition that opened the greatest prosperity humanity has ever known, far exceeding even its most hopeful dreams.

Through all pre-twentieth-century history, wars were devastating to both winners and losers. The preindustrial wars took the men from the fields, and the fields where the exclusively agricultural wealth germinated were devastated.

It came as a complete surprise, therefore, that the United States in particular, but Germany, England, France, Belgium, Italy, Japan, and Russia in lesser degree all came out of the First World War—the first full-fledged industrial era war—with much greater industrial production capabilities than those with which they had entered. That wealth was soon misguidedly invested in the Second World War, from which all the industrial countries emerged with even greater wealth-producing capabilities, despite the superficial knock-down of already obsolete buildings. It was irrefutably proven that the destruction of the buildings by bombing, shell fire, and flames left the machinery almost unharmed. The productive tooling multiplied unchecked.

This unexpected increase in wealth was caused by several facts but most prominently by the fact that in the tool-up of tools that make a complex of industrial tools, the number of tools that made the end-product armaments and ammunition was negligible as compared to the redirectable productivity of the majority of the tools that make tools complex. Secondly was the war's destruction of obsolete structures whose factual availability, despite their obsolescence, had persuaded their owners to overexploit them, which had blocked the acquisition of up-to-date tools. Thirdly, there was the energetic surprise of alternative or "substitute" technologies developed to bypass destroyed facilities which often proved to be more efficient than the tools that were destroyed. Fourthly, the metals themselves not only were not destroyed but were acceleratingly reinvested in new, vastly higher performance tools. Thus losers such as Germany and Japan became postwar industrial winners.

Thus we see again that through gradually increasing use of his intellect, man has discovered many of the generalized principles that operate in universe and has employed them objectively in extending his internal metabolic regeneration to his invented and detached tool extensions and their operation by harnessing inanimate energy. Instead of trying to survive only with his integral set of tool capabilities—his hands—to pour water into his mouth, he invents a more effective wood, stone, or ceramic vessel so that he can not only drink from it but carry water with him and extend his hunting and berry-picking. All tools are externalizations of originally integral functions. But in developing each tool he also extends the limits of its usefulness, as he can make the cup hold liquids too hot or too chemically destructive for his hands.

Our labor world and all salaried workers including school teachers and college professors are now at least subconsciously, if not consciously, afraid that automation will take away their jobs. They are afraid they will not be able to do what is called "earning a living," which is short for *earning the right to live.* This term implies that normally we are supposed to die prematurely and that it is abnormal to be able to earn a living. It is paradoxical that only the abnormal or exceptional are entitled to prosper. It even implied yesterday that success was so very abnormal that only divinely ordained kings and nobles were *"entitled"* to eat fairly regularly. Yet it is easy to demonstrate to those who will take the time and the trouble to unbias their thoughts that automation can swiftly multiply the physical-energy part of wealth much more rapidly and profusely than can man's muscle and brain-reflexed manually controlled production, whereas humans alone can foresee, integrate, and anticipate the new tasks to be done by the progressively automated wealth-producing machinery.

To take advantage of the fabulous magnitudes of real wealth waiting to be employed intelligently by humans and to unblock automation's postponement by organized labor, we must give each human who is or becomes unemployed a life fellowship in research and development work in comprehensively expanding and accelerating scientific exploration and experimental prototype development. For every 100,000 employed, one probably will make a breakthrough that will more than pay for another 99,999 fellowships. Thus, production will no longer be impeded by humans trying to do what the machines can do better. On the contrary, omni-automated and inanimately powered production will cultivate humanity's unique capability, i.e., its metaphysical capability. Historically speaking, that will happen within the next decade. There is no doubt about it. But not without much social crisis and consequent educational experience regarding our unlimited wealth.

Through the universal research and development fellowships, we are going to start emancipating humanity from being muscle and reflex machines. We are going to give everyone a chance to develop his most powerful mental and intuitive faculties. Many who have been frustrated during their younger years—given their research and development fellowship—may feel like going fishing. Fishing provides an excellent opportunity to think clearly, to review one's life, to recall one's earlier frustrated and abandoned longings and curiosities. What we want everybody to do is to *think* clearly.

We soon will begin to generate wealth so rapidly that we can do very great things. I would like you to think what this may do realistically for living without spoiling the landscape or the antiquities or the trails of humanity throughout the area, or despoiling the integrity of romance, vision and harmonic creativity.

MONEY MUST GO

by DAVID T. BAZELON

ALL THAT GLISTERS is not gold. And just as well, since the glister not the gold will purchase our future.

I refer to the glister-like crackle of electricity. Money itself is about to go electronic. Strangely, this occurs near the moment chosen by history to extinguish the ancient gleam of gold. There never was enough gold to satisfy, at the same time, both hoarders and the needs of commerce. This Fundamental Fact seems now about to produce the demonetization of gold in international exchange—the one major area in which that metal has remained money—and to relegate the darling stuff to dental practice, idolatry, and occasional primitive exchange. Proper enough: gold is primitive money; it hoards too well—and money is no longer for hoarding.

The most modern money is not official-looking or engraved paper, but an instantaneous electric blip. So not only gold, but paper as well, has had its day. The reasons for each, however, are exactly opposite: too little gold, too much paper. In 1967, 14,000 banks in the United States with deposits of $400,000,-000 cleared 20,000,000,000 checks at a handling cost of $3,700,-000,000. This amount of check paper alone is twice what it was ten years ago, and it is expected to double again in the next decade.

The upcoming Electronic Funds Transfer System has been talked about in banking circles for the past couple of years (nervously and excessively) under the heading of "The Checkless Society." A primary selling point to bankers has been to indicate an automated avenue of escape from the expected deluge of paper. There have been other selling points—namely, that if banks do not computerize the money/credit mechanism, others will; and selling points are necessary, because E.F.T.S. will require huge initial investments in both capital funds and educational effort. It is said that The American Bankers Association required a decade or more to convince *bankers* that they were in the business of creating money, not merely receiving it as deposits and disbursing it as loans. Magnetic Ink Character Recognition—the highest level of intra-industry automation yet achieved—took five years to develop and another seven years to put into effect.

But the technology now exists—so it will be used. It consists of three elements: (1) computers, (2) terminal outlets connected by wire to the computer, and (3) an individual "key" to the terminal. If formal definitions are any help, The American Bankers Association currently offers one for "electronic fund transfer system" employing this tripartite technology: "By this we mean transferring information about fund transfers over communication networks, starting with input from a terminal at the point of sale and culminating in a computerized bookkeeping transaction at some central fund-transfer computer station, which in most cases, we assume, will be at a banking institution." The last clause is a sigh of hope, since any computer utility could, under the proposed system, become a bank; and the crucial term "information" substantiates one writer's thought that "money has become merely financial information. . . ." This is certainly true of money that is kept moving—lots coming in, lots going out. Money remains more than information, however, for those of us who are so misinformed as to send out too many negative messages.

The required computer is a third-generation one having what is called "on-line, real-time capability," which means that it is immediately available for numerous discrete transactions—something like a telephone exchange. About a thousand banks have already installed the basic elements of such computer capability. Once the system is established and widely used, excessive busy-signals would mean for banks what it now means for the telephone system—open a new exchange. And who knows what wonders later computers may harbor in their electronic insides? The new Touch-Tone telephone is an adequate terminal, especially when the Card Dialer feature is included. The Bell System expects to make Touch-Tone telephones available to thirty-seven percent of its subscribers (eighty percent of the population) by the end of the year, and more than half of the country should have them by 1970.

A perfect individual "key" to the terminal has not yet been devised—but the Personal Identification Project Committee of the A.B.A. has high hopes. According to Dale L. Reistad, the A.B.A.'s Director of Automation and a leading enthusiast, the Committee "has made significant progress in the direction of selecting a single, discrete, personal identification number for nationwide use." *One man, one number*—one electronic account subject to instantaneous inquiry and entry by means of the telephone networks. Please note that the account will contain not mere debits and credits but also computerized credit data; or it will be connected with such a data file by the same number and network. The possibilities of this system are truly fabulous. As just one ready example, the 552,000,000 checks the Federal government now issues each year—or, say, the further disbursements involved in a subtle bottom-up system of broad-gauge welfarism and guaranteed annual income—can be transformed into as many instantaneous electronic entries timed, perhaps, according to the cyclical needs of the economy.

There is a second, and technically somewhat stickier, aspect of the effort to create a Universal Identification Card—the single most significant material realization of one man, one number—which would serve as *the* money-and-credit card, as well as the "key" to the Touch-Tone terminal. This is the matter of verification of personal identity. The Committee's goal here is "industry-wide standardization of near foolproof techniques for assuring that the person presenting an identification card or number is indeed the person he purports to be." (How to appear to others as the person you purport to be is in fact an ancient problem.) The effort here includes the electronically transformed issues of theft and counterfeit, but goes beyond these. The A.B.A. is technologically ambitious: the bankers want something much better than the present signature system, which is based on every-cashier-a-handwriting-expert and other rituals of inept suspicion. A dozen or more companies are working on the verification problem, including major outfits like R.C.A., Polaroid, and I.B.M. A foolproof identification technique would interest, perhaps fascinate, not only electronic bankers of the future but the credit industry of today—and, it is reported, the C.I.A. and perhaps even lesser government agencies. Notions being entertained include machine-readable codes, secret Touch-Tone numbers, embedded color photos, body temperature readings, disguised thumbprints, and new voice prints. Meanwhile, high-type crime will have to figure out its own creative response to the new electronic devices, and the yearning for a perfect system may be mollified somewhat by the consideration that detection as well as cash-flow will be speeded by computerization—a noticeable advance over the current credit-card system, which requires careful, clerkly scanning of stale hot-card lists.

Credit cards are a very large part of the E.F.T.S. story. They are a big foot in the door which must be swung open to change so fundamentally the ordinary-income person's basic sense of money. The ever-widening use of cards, it is hoped, will habituate the public to forward-looking checklessness. It also accustoms one to regular dependence on creditizing. Commercial banks have recently plunged into the short-term small-loan business with "instant money" and similar gimmickery based on line-of-credit or overdraft schemes. Whatever else it is, the card, any card, is a constant reminder not to be inhibited, by crude greenlessness, in the pell-mell pursuit of affluent living.

As a piece of purchased plastic—first Diners Club, then American Express and Carte Blanche, their emblems plastered on storefronts across the world—the credit card has been associated in popular imagery with expense-account living, prepaid travel, steak dinners and booze and nightclubs (and broads?). Since the price of all the things that can be bought with these cards already includes the interest charge (and no discount for cash), the price of the card amounts to a real bargain for short-term credit—even if limited to the billing period. When the situation gets organized under E.F.T.S., such interstitial freebees will disappear—as also, more notoriously, playing the "float," that is, using for your own advantage the time it takes checks to clear, that is, withdrawing before depositing, that is, living in Manhattan and banking on Long Island.

But the credit cards constituting E.F.T.S.'s big foot in the door are not these expense-account plastics, but the new female-and-consumer-oriented *bank* cards. "Unquestionably the most far-reaching change taking place in banking today [late 1966] is the credit-card movement," says Mr. Reistad. More than six hundred banks around the country are now offering card plans, and national movements are already under way, e.g., Marine Midland's "Interbank Card." The biggest is the BankAmericard of the world's biggest bank, California-based Bank of America, with 5,000,000 card carriers in eighteen states (and a deal with Barclays Bank in England). California would seem to be the area most eager for checklessness, since Bank of America's competitors there got together last year and issued their own Master Charge Card which already equals BankAmericard with 2,500,000 holders in that State. According to the Federal Reserve in San Francisco, bank credit cards account for eighty percent of all credit plans in California—only fifty percent elsewhere. Always watch California when searching for American futures: we crested on the West Coast—less midpassage New Englandism and other "tradition" getting in the way, purer American frenzy there; and rich like Croesus. But the East retains its cultural superiority: no other bank will ever again name its card with the disciplined genius of the First National City Bank of New York, which has been pushing the "Everything Card" for a year or more. (Class will tell.)

Cards may be cashless and checkless, but not yet paperless. On the realistic road forward to electronic money, there are a number of non-electronic but less-paper devices being advocated and adopted. Each of these contributes, as do cards, to the massive change in money habits which must underlie the establishment of E.F.T.S.—sometimes called "software." Without now belaboring the point—understanding that money is not essentially gold, greenbacks, checks, other paper, or futuristic blips, but a mere *technique* of human connection—we might just list some of these less-paper devices which both introduce, and indicate the later content of, the E.F.T.S. changeover:

• Pre-authorized payments of regularly recurring bills such as those for rent or a mortgage, utilities, automobile and other installment loans, insurance of all kinds, membership dues and magazine subscriptions, savings-bond purchases, etc. A good deal of this already exists; it can readily grow. (Substantial business concerns, and just plain rich people, have always authorized others to write dull checks for them.) The problem with pre-authorized payment is that it doesn't feel like spending; and many recently affluent peasants take real if secret pleasure in the monthly ritual of check writing. Also, early payment is dumb. So one expects that pre-authorization will not grow at the rate bankers hope for until discounts for cash or other immediacy are reestablished. (They used to be fairly common.) A clever crowd out West has already issued a "Money-Back Card" which provides that signed-up merchants will remit to the organization a sum to be distributed to the member in consideration of his occasional cash payment: the anti-credit-card card.

● Payroll plans—also known as "checkless paydays"—are being tried and recommended. Instead of cash in a pay envelope or a company check, the employer authorizes deposits to be credited on payday to the account of each employee—today in a single bank, tomorrow in a bank designated by the employee. (Today the employee would have to write his own paycheck and deposit it in his own bank, if he was not of a mind to adopt his employer's bank as his own.) As part of the fuller image of the checkless society, the bank's computers could also prepare the payroll as well as "pay" it. And with the later advent of electronic money, we could revert to true McLuhanist tribalism with payment for work (is that the right word for the future?) being transferred daily—or even second by second, like a blood transfusion.*

● If bosses can pay workers with less-paper, they can certainly do as much for (to?) each other. And the Big Bosses already have computers. There is no Really Good Reason why the executives of General Motors and U. S. Steel, for instance, have to persist in the primitivism of personal conversation which is regularly interrupted as each is compelled to talk to his own computer; much of their conversational transaction could be handled just as well by taking the Big Step and authorizing the computers

* It occurs to this particular philosopher of money that the farthest effect of the perfected immediacy of electronic money may be to transcend its essentially *human* nature: that is, we may have a money that no longer requires us to trust each other at all. If money has been our last connection of trust, that could be serious.

to talk to each other without unnecessary human interference, and buy and sell and make payments as to this and that common item in a friendly, interconnected, blip-like manner. This is the field of interbusiness checklessness; and it is an obvious first-up area. (The law of the sea is women and children first; the law of our land is—and ever was—business first.)

• The monthly bill from the electric company could easily be prepared as a check to be signed by you and mailed to their bank or yours: with the interbank electronics, little difference. As is, at least one less piece of paper. This, too, is in the offing—and so obvious that one wonders whether its late introduction is not due to a real passion for paperfulness on the part of our citizens.

• Europe never democratized money through a checking system. Instead, they developed a fuller welfare system long before we did (moreover through political parties and unions rather than the state exclusively); as well as a funds-transfer system called "GIRO." The closest thing in this country would be Post Office money orders. In Europe, people have post-office accounts, and transfer funds from one post-office GIRO account to another on simple instruction: no actual checks. The U. S. Post Office is paper-clogged enough and not about to take over the poor man's banking. What is proposed, instead, is an application of the GIRO concept to our current banking setup: this is called "the-bank-of-first-deposit" system. The way it would work is like this: instead of sending your check directly to the fellow you are paying, you send it to your bank and it stops dead right there. The paper doesn't travel, and it is the travel cost of paper—twenty separate handlings for each check at a cost of twelve cents—that has been frightening the wits out of the banking industry. Hopefully, the subsequent accounting would occur electronically; even if not, there would be a real saving.

What all this comes down to (even pre-electronic) is the transformation from a historical checking system to a simpler, more efficient funds-transfer system. The key to the difference is the amount and the travel time of paper: that is the initial message, for banking, of the electronic massage. Some of the excessive shuffling of paper, for instance, the periodic return of canceled checks to the depositor, is not even a necessary feature of current banking—ironically, it dates from a technological advance (the posting machine) of fifty years ago. Now, when the time has come to roll back the sea of paper, the banking industry (to mix a metaphor) finds itself hoist by its own petard. For years, bankers have sold the public on checking accounts by emphasizing the utility of canceled checks as evidence of payment and proper record keeping. The anti-paper reeducation effort will, of course, have to go deeper than the mere reversal of an advertising campaign; indeed, Gerald T. Dunne, when he was general counsel for the Federal Reserve Bank of St. Louis, shrewdly suggested that the tangibility of paper is irreplaceable "and, hence, any 'transfer' system which evolves will probably contain a residuum of technically unnecessary but psychologically indispensable paper." (McLuhan take notice.)

As the economy grows, so does the number of payment and credit transactions covering the increased goods and services. According to John Diebold, head of The Diebold Group, Inc., transaction volume increases at a *greater* rate. On the assumption of a doubling of G.N.P. in fifteen years, he projects an increase of transactions of various kinds from two to five times as great—more than twice as much checking-account activity (one-third of the current population has never used checks, while there has been a great growth of checking among suburban teen-agers), and more than five times as many consumer-credit operations. The annual cost of these transactions could go from $13,000,000,000 to $35,000,000,000 in fifteen years. Having established, with these horror figures, that it might well be easier to produce the additional goods and services than the conventional accounting means to distribute them, Mr. Diebold then points to the immense savings to be looked for from an automated system—nearly three-fifths of the theoretical increase in cost. As to the price of automation—"All in all, it is projected that a national system of electronic credit and money transfer will cost about $4,000,000,-000 annually over the first five years of widespread implementation."

One of the most important consequences of the electronic system will be "an enormous increase in the velocity of money." Now this fact will be of considerable concern to money managers and other government fiscal experts; but the point being made

here, in connection with electronic money, has another significance. *Time is of the very essence of money.* Time and acceptability (the latter not being at issue here). The difference between
cash and credit—the persistent difference—is one of time. This
difference in time between immediate and delayed payment has a
price, frequently still called "interest"—although charges for many
other things have lately been gathered under this ancient label.
The essence of money is how much you think you are going to get;
when and what you are *not* going to spend it on; when and
what you think you *are* going to spend it on. Any other
purportedly "essential" idea of money is distorting. Please keep
this in mind, as the major revolution in American money continues apace. And also try to remember that the substance of this
revolution is the superabundance of what money, any money,
will buy—not any changes in its technical character.

The electronic change will only make money, so to speak,
monier—that is, quicker. Which will have the consequence of
altering the price on slowness, that is, credit. Much that used to
be thought of as money will now become credit. And everyone
involved will necessarily become credit-sensitive, that is, like
most businessmen and money managers today, very aware of the
numerous time differences, and their cost and value, between this
kind of money and that kind of credit. As one major effect, bankers expect that as the velocity of money is speeded by electronics,
demand deposits will shrink drastically. Without more detail,
everyone will be in the credit game; and demand deposits (or
cash) will therefore have a price—willingly paid by those who
need more than they have.

It is strangely interesting that we have in fact had an operating electronic system for many years. I am referring to what is
called "Federal Funds." Federal Funds are deposits on the books
of Federal Reserve Banks to the credit of member banks which,
as of the moment, are not required as reserve and clearing balances. They can be transferred *by wire*—that is, with electronic
immediacy—from one Federal Reserve Bank to another, therefore
from the account of one member bank to that of another member
bank. This is a wholesale system, not readily adaptable to retail
traffic; but my point here is that the immediacy of even wire
funds has a *price,* which is established by availability.

In the matter of retail traffic one sells time to this purchaser rather than the other because the former's "credit is better." And therein lies a lengthy tale: why money was never democratic in the past, and why its democratic future may be purchased at an awful cost.

A man is gauged as being credit-worthy—or as a credit risk—according to his *reputation* for having the what-with and, as a proper citizen, using it to pay when due. Until the booming factories of America compelled the practice in the Twenties, and our commitment to Consumerism and its advertising culture were well begun, it was not the regular thing to extend credit to mere jobholders—certainly not for the purpose of financing personal consumption. Credit was supposed to finance production; and it was extended to men of property for a wayward personal use only because their reputed wealth served as general security. But it is very important that the *kind* of information thought to be necessary in making a credit judgment is different when the purpose of the loan is nonproductive, and the security for it is merely the borrower's income earned on a job. For example, can he and will he hold the job? Here, it would be relevant to know his employment background: if he drinks, medical history, criminal record, whether he gambles on horses or girls (or, God forbid, both), and similar matters. Also, whether he has a good past history for not overextending himself, paying on time, and not hiring lawyers to argue about the money owed or the quality of the merchandise received.

Collecting such information, and making it available to prospective creditors, is a substantial business in the United States. The figure commonly bandied about is 100,000,000 credit files of one kind or another now in existence. These files are held by many different companies; the contents vary; and in general one hesitates to imagine the amount and the kind of misinformation they may contain. *Business Week* has stated: "As a whole, the retail-credit-bureau industry—which is mostly controlled by local stores—has yet to come of age." Automation has barely begun, but (according to Mr. Reistad) "a 'checkless' society presupposes the eventual and complete automation of the credit-bureau industry. . . ." (He elsewhere states: "With or without computers, the financial, credit, moral, and ethical background of our [banking's] customers is being investigated.") As credit grows, so do these files, most likely in content as well as number; and E.F.T.S., with its instantaneous money, will turn a great deal of what is money today—mainly demand deposits—into credit.

Computerized credit files for each and every participant—containing this-and-that item of personal history—are of the essence of E.F.T.S. and the accompanying expansion of Consumerism it represents.

The new memory computers, with on-line direct access, certainly present a major new problem. Most technological blessings do, if you stop to think about it. Cornelius E. Gallagher, the Democratic Representative from New Jersey heading a House subcommittee looking into the computer/privacy issue, has thought about it enough to dub our time in history as "the direct-access age." That's a little rich—the ages of man should be based on accomplished historical disaster, not fresh headline panic. Still, these new computers really are something. Donald N. Michael, who possesses one of our more rigorous science-fiction imaginations, says that the advanced machines "can learn on the basis of past experience with their environment." That's already serious (I have personally had some good friends deficient in this capacity).

Whether we end up terrified of, or merely falling in love with, these nearly-better-than-human machines (the next generation of computers—who knows?—may even have wit and charm, if not exactly 36-22-35 figures), I am prepared to believe that they have created an absolutely new dimension of human capacity and concern. If I am wrong, then one more fevered imagination has taken a wrong turn: so what else is new? But I think I am right—and I am urged to this view by the fact that the *banking* industry in America (if its fevered imagination takes a wrong turn, we are all finished) is contemplating a revolution in the nature of money based on the teller capacity, if not the wit and charm, of these new computers.

Congressman Gallagher's subcommittee has not been investigating electronic money, but the proposal for a National Data Center. Both are based, however, on the new computer capacity. The two issues are solidly connected also by the centrality of the credit-dossier matter. I believe this connection to be crucial. The proposal for a National Data Center, and the upcoming E.F.T.S., should not—really cannot—be viewed separately. The computer capacity and content does not allow for it. Besides, both concern information; and if it is clear that money is becoming information, it should be equally clear that information is becoming money. At least both are equally becoming "power."

Let me conclude the credit-dossier question: Mr. Reistad (as usual) is very helpful. He has a proposal: ". . . as bankers we should advocate the development in this country of a consumer-oriented credit-bureau industry which would do for consumer credit what Dun & Bradstreet does for the business sector." This is a truly excellent idea, exactly in the right direction, because it joins one of the better traditions in credit-rating for business with one of the major changes in credit-giving by business. Under the honored D & B system, they decide who is to be listed and the report itself is filled out by a D & B reporter with the cooperation of the listee; indeed there are some forms which the latter fills out himself; the listee and all D & B subscribers have access to the listing; others than the listee contribute data to the file, of course; all in all, not so bad. Mr. Reistad's idea, however, carries with it the notion that instead of full access to *all* the data in the credit file, once these files have been standardized and perfected, what can be done is to create, and then apply in response to credit inquiries, "a mathematical credit score." Instead of data on personal life and morality, the inquirer gets a rating number. Again, not so bad.

But we still end up with a computerized dossier on nearly everyone, even though a D & B system for consumers is clearly an advance in the democratization of credit. As is the E.F.T.S. use of the computer itself: both should further the retail turn that banking has taken so dramatically in the postwar period. Along with the dossier, the new system would make it possible to treat small sums with the same respect—along with detailed attention as to interest, discount, and payment neither-too-early-nor-too-late—as large sums now receive. But the issue cannot be fudged: the price of all of this is that damned dossier. And once it exists, no rule or regulation or law governing its use will be immutable. The dossier cannot be sacred.

The proposal for a National Data Center came out of a 1966 report on "Storage of and Access to Federal Statistical Data" prepared by a committee of experts for the director of the Budget. The purpose of the committee's effort was to save money and increase the efficient availability of Federal statistical data— now collected in a major way by more than twenty agencies at a cost of more than $125,000,000. The committee identified the problem as decentralization not functionally justified; not a new problem, but now one that could be overcome with the help of the computer. Thus the proposal for a National Data Center which "would assemble in a single facility all large-scale systematic bodies of demographic, economic and social data generated by the present data-collection or administrative processes of the Federal Government . . . integrate the data to the maximum feasible extent . . . and provide ready access, within the laws governing disclosure, to all users in the Government, and where appropriate to qualified users outside the Government. . . ."

Which led to Congressman Gallagher's investigation and a certain amount of newspaper hullabaloo about privacy. Vance Packard suggested that "a relentless bureaucrat obsessed with efficiency" rather than "the simple power-seeker, could lead us to that ultimate of horrors, a humanity in chains of plastic tape." He discerned four major dangers in the data-bank proposal— encouraging depersonalization, increasing the distrust of government, the computer's lack of subtlety and forgiveness, and (at last) misuse of the power held by data bankers. (In my view, the latter is quite enough: depersonalization is doing quite well, thank you, irrespective of data banks which would merely organize information about it. However that may be, I must note that privacy takes on qualities of incredible beatitude each time we are faced with its next most imminent loss. As a farmer's ideal, it is long gone. Also, living in big cities, I have been so up to my neck in what remains as "privacy"—also called "isolation"— that I actually welcome the visits of the census taker.)

The chairman of the committee making the proposal, Carl Kaysen of the Institute for Advanced Study (most recently), defended against the Worried Voices heard at and after the Congressional hearings primarily by insisting on the difference between data banks and dossiers. The Center, he made clear, would contain data collected by the Census Bureau, Agriculture, the Bureau of Labor Statistics, the National Center for Health Statistics, Office of Education, Internal Revenue Service, Social Security, etc.—but *not* F.B.I. files, Civil Service records, personnel data from the Armed Services, or any other dossier information. But effective use of social data requires the retention of individual identity—although this need not be disclosed to users. Like Mr. Reistad's "mathematical credit score," this has reference, however, to the intention of the data banker—even if legally prescribed—and not to the content or capacity of the bank itself.

And this, of course, is the Big Problem—not at all solved by defeating the National Data Center proposal this year or next, or permitting the birth of E.F.T.S. without the arms or legs of automated credit ratings. *The computer is already invented;* the data and the dossiers are already *there* in raw form. The true issues are: how could the one-man, one-number system possibly be prevented, rather than merely postponed to another moment, and to the control of another group in power?

The political control of the system—as of everything else in our new world representing immense new accretions of power—is a continuous question extending indefinitely into the future. If Man didn't want to be bothered with this kind of ultimate politics, he should never have invented electricity—maybe even the wheel—much less allowed modern physics and chemistry to generate their horrible blessings.

Moreover, often enough the same people who favor extended welfarism—billions for the cities and for education and health and employment and addiction and neurotic nastiness as well as psychotic violence and so much else—scream *Eek, a mouse!* as the essential social data underlying any such benevolence are invited to adequate levels of efficiency. Knowledge is power, and how! Along with organization itself, it is *the* form of modern power. And they propose to remake the American cities, undo four hundred years of vicious slavery as it is in twenty million living witnesses—or, more properly including whites, in two hundred million—overcome all basic human unpleasantnesses like drunkenness and other unreasonable behavior, fix everybody's teeth and catch all cancer and heart disease at least on the Day Before, and correct the environmental pollution of one hundred years of industrialism—*and all accomplished without the use of dangerous powers?*

My friends, they are just plain sky-high right out of their ever-lovin' cotton-pickin' minds!

The American revolution in money habits—conceived broadly —thus continues at an accelerating pace. So it might be a good idea to pin down this point, especially since we Americans suffer from a national tropism that immediately reduces everything to its accompanying hardware, meanwhile conniving blindness as to the social and psychological ramification of any new technology. Indeed, this may be the hidden danger in the proposed electronic system—that involvement with the fascinating new gadgetry of our burgeoning wealth may further displace our humane concern with its use. Hasn't this already happened with our growing affluence in the postwar credit economy, as regularly redesigned products and advertising are joined more recently by credit gadgetry in sustaining our monstrously misdirected Consumerism?

The issue posed by E.F.T.S. cannot be reduced to the cute technical differences between electronic entries in a computer and ink entries in a ledger, any more than our present nearly cashless society can be distinguished from earlier times by the material difference between checks and bank notes. All our history centrally involves the struggle over hard vs. soft money: at one time—when the farmers really wanted it—credit was nearly impossible to get; now—when most of us could do without it—consumer credit is nearly unavoidable. From bank notes to checks and credit cards represents the final triumph of soft money, also known as the democratization of credit, occasioned not by the generosity of our financial/industrial leadership but by our inevitable abundance: these former hard-money advocates were defeated not by populist politics, but by their own technological triumphs—and then the abject need to move inventory created thereby.

From checks to computerized credit will constitute the farthest triumph of the public organization and distribution of wealth. A credit account for everyone, necessarily including fully adequate

credit data on everyone. Thus the price of the new system is—
one man, one number. The potential power of the organization
over the individual involved in such a perfected system will be
incalculable. *I suggest that this price should not be paid merely
to achieve computerized Consumerism,* but only to effect a re-
distribution of credit (and ultimately, therefore, wealth) so as to
provide an adequate income to all, whether or not "earned." Organization of this high order and purpose is what used to be called
"socialization." I agree with Michael Harrington that the wealthy
have had quite enough exclusive socialism, and that the time has
come to afford some more widely distributed socialism, to the poor
and the less-well-to-do.

As wealth increases, the real meaning of money changes. The
tightwad undermined by affluence, for example, experiences
serious personal difficulty. Finding himself not only unfashionable
but irrelevant, he is compelled to the nostalgia of the Good Old
Days, when a dollar was still a dollar. Certainly many people
coming of age during the Great Depression will never fully believe in or feel at ease with their current good fortune. And we
have all heard stories about the occasionally bizarre cheapness of
the really rich. Only poor people and businessmen are thought to
be securely realistic about this troublesome subject of money—
the one abjectly wanting it, the other greedily seizing it. The psychology of money has always been supremely important—the
money system itself being primarily one of *expectations based
on the promises of strangers.* Not less so now, as we confront the
newly unsettling vistas of affluence.

And just at this moment of preoccupation with the psychology
of actually having it, we are about to undergo a technological
breakthrough which will greatly accelerate our headlong plunge
away from the dollar-was-a-dollar days. Computerized Consumerism—I mean E.F.T.S.—is about to break upon us. Being the
ultimate in spending as a way of life, it is based on advances in
electronics technology, the spectacular growth in consumer financing and other credit democratization, and in general the joining
of pre-finance with presell. (The perfect consumer must be financed as well as properly responsive to the world of advertising.)
This later electronics will now carry forward what early television

has so well begun—the utter encapsulation of the individual within the consumer culture. No answer to anything will equal the right answer to this—Which toothpaste, O Lord; and what detergent? And lack of funds will not be allowed to undermine true devotion.

Underlying all of this profound nonsense is a most serious question for Americans: *the nature of money itself*. We have so devoted ourselves to money and the making of it, throughout our entire history, that we have hardly had a free moment to understand it: all god and no theology. Now, with our new affluence, electronics technology in funds transfer, and the desperate craving of business organizations to further consumer debt, we face a new age of dollar theology in this country. I urgently welcome it: only such dangerously spiritual effort will save us from the hungry democratic insanities of more misspent wealth.

Money is literally nothing by itself; money is only what it does. But thinking about money itself exclusively, we Americans are distracted from serious thought about what it does; what it doesn't; what it could do. We take it as a thing in itself. This is a form of madness. Money is a means, not an end. As we get wealthier, it is not even a crucial means. But our attitude toward it—at this time, in this country—is approaching the status of an ultimate religious/historical *end*-meaning. Either we spend our great wealth on something other than war and consumer junk, or our commitment to war and consumer junk will grow as our wealth grows—and we will *become* what we have allowed our committed wealth to become. *We are too rich to act this dumb*. Thinking very suggestively about the power of these computers to ingest life-simulating and life-controlling data, Donald N. Michael has pinpointed the essential problem of the computer's capacity, the supporting scientism behind this, and the political issues forever embarked upon when all this stuff got going: "that which will be valued and acted on as if it were the private individual will be that which can be tested and assessed in ways which can be recorded and manipulated by computers. . . . Thereby we shall have a new measure of privacy: that part of one's life which . . . computers cannot deal with. . . ."

If, with abundance, we still view money with the spirit of

scarcity, we willingly enslave our most private selves to the mere mechanism of our abundance. And we will deserve the disaster we have thereby created.

No one can become rich without changing himself in other ways as well: we must become more humane—or more monstrous than before.

IV

Politics

At the world level, the greatest need for social inventiveness manifests itself in the breakdown and obsolescence of all the traditional modes of confronting our major problems. The agencies of change have forced us swiftly into a new global reality. But, as we emerge into the planetary society of the future, the geopolitics of the past are the most dangerously constraining myths of our present.

—JOHN McHALE,
The Future of the Future (1969)

THE PERILS OF PROLIFERATION

by HERMAN KAHN

IT IS MOST LIKELY that the international order will change before a doomsday machine is built. It will change partly because of the general and specific political impact of the advancing military and non-military technology, partly as a continuation of current political, legal, and moral trends (the revolution in world politics), and partly as a direct result of the actual or potential diffusion of "normal" weapons. It is difficult to believe that the world will go unchanged if there are fifty independent, sovereign, small and medium nations with the capability to acquire small amounts of reasonably destructive modern weapon systems and ten or twenty nations with the capability to acquire large amounts. This is true even if many of these nations are not strongly motivated to acquire such systems. Even a weak motivation is likely to be motivation enough—particularly in an unstable competitive situation.

Many nations may obtain nuclear weapons systems without producing cataclysmic instability. For example, the situation might turn out to be similar to that of the old American West. In these societies many people went armed; every now and then a quarrel broke out and somebody was either wounded or killed, but life went on.

The situation might turn out to be even more peaceful than the dueling analogy would suggest. Even before dueling became outlawed, there was a strong tendency in some of the dueling societies to minimize the role of duels. Individuals learned that force was not a proper way of settling personal disputes. And it might indeed turn out that the war system will wither away by itself.

Reprinted in excerpt from *The Revolution in World Politics*. By permission of John Wiley & Sons, Inc. First published in 1962.

Both of the preceding possibilities, a viable dueling system or an evolutionary withering away of the war system without any "special controls," seem somewhat remote. There are ten problems which would either occur, or be greatly aggravated, if there were a widespread diffusion of nuclear weapons. That list is repeated here and each of the problems is discussed very briefly.

1. *Greater Opportunities for Blackmail, Revenge, Terrorism, and Other Mischief-Making.* In a world armed to its teeth in nuclear weapons, every time there is a quarrel or a difference of opinion, there will always be, in the background, a possibility of violence of a kind and degree and speed that is quite different from what is possible today. This could occur even in relatively innocuous quarrels, for example, over fishing rights, as well as over obvious trouble-making irredentist movements or quarrels over prestige. There will be pressures not only to threaten all-out war, but also to use single nuclear weapons to show resolve, to commit oneself irrevocably, or to demonstrate recklessness. In other words, there is likely to be both encouragement and opportunity for playing the game of chicken. This is particularly true because of the possibility for the anonymous delivery of weapons.

2. *Greater Proneness to Inadvertent War.* An inadvertent (unpremeditated) war is one which occurs without the considered intention of any of the governments that wage it. The possibility of inadvertent war could go up not only because there are many more weapons and missiles around, but also because—and even more important—there will be many more organizations around, each with a different standard of training, organization, and operational code. An inadvertent war could be caused by accidents such as a switch failing, a false radar return, or some other statistically possible event. It could also occur because of an unauthorized behavior, irresponsible behavior, a misunderstanding of orders, a generally lax discipline, or any one of a thousand ways in which something can go wrong. It is not inevitable that any particular provocation or accident will set off a large-scale chain reaction. However, every time there is a small war or accident, there will be great pressure to reform the system. This is, in fact, one likely mechanism for the creation of a crisis which causes a relatively peaceful evolution out of the current system

of relative anarchy. Nations will refuse to live with a situation in which nuclear accidents actually do occur. If at all possible, they will do something to correct a system which makes such things likely or inevitable.

3. *Increased Capabilities for "Local" Munichs, Pearl Harbors, and Blitzkriegs.* The tendency to play the game of chicken has already been mentioned. A slightly more reckless, irresponsible, desperate, or decisive decision-maker might simply go ahead and attack another nation, saying, in effect, to the other nations, "what will you do about it?" Even if the attacked nation has a nuclear capability, in many cases it may not have much effective second-strike capability. The other nations, on the other hand, are going to be loath to start a nuclear war to avenge a *fait accompli*. The attacker might even use the attacked nation as a hostage to prevent effective reprisals.

The aggressor may not actually need to launch his attack. He might merely threaten to do so with explicit ultimatums, thus forcing the other side either to back down, or to attack, with all the political and military dangers such an attack might bring. In other words, in a situation where there are opportunities for large payoffs through extremely aggressive behavior, we should not be surprised if some nations indulge in such behavior. There are golden opportunities here for both paranoiacs and megalomaniacs.

4. *Pressures to Pre-empt Because of Points One, Two, and Three.* To the extent that the behavior described above actually occurs, as opposed to being an academic possibility, one could expect decision-makers to note that it could happen to them and, therefore, to note also the importance of doing it first. Although few wish to be either executioners or victims, many would prefer the first role to the second if they believed they must choose. A world in which "reciprocal fear of surprise attack" is everpresent is a world which is going to be very unstable. There will also be pressure toward psychological and political pre-emption. In any situation in which there is an important gain to be made by saying something like, "One of us has to be responsible, and since it isn't going to be me, it has to be you," there is a tendency to overuse committal strategies—to say it first and firmly.

5. *Tendency to Neglect Conventional Military Capabilities.* Because of an overreliance on one's own nuclear capabilities, or

fear of the other side's nuclear capabilities, it is likely to be extremely difficult for most nations to take the concept of limited conventional war seriously enough actually to allocate money, manpower, thought, and other scarce commodities into conventional or other limited capabilities. It will be difficult for them to do this, even though they realize abstractly that in a crisis they may find themselves unwilling to rely on their nuclear capabilities. This is likely to create all kinds of instabilities and opportunities for bluff, counterbluff, or actual attack that result in either defeat or escalation.

6. *Internal (Civil War, Coup d'Etat, Irresponsibility, etc.) and External (Arms Race, Fear of Fear, etc.) Political Problems.* It is difficult to believe that in a world as armed to the teeth and as dangerous looking as the one just pictured there will not be both responsible and irresponsible peace and accommodation movements. If every time a difficult decision is being made a major portion of the country is being risked; if every time a country's diplomats walk into a hostile conference room every woman and child feels threatened; if every time a nation stands firm against aggressive probes panic seizes the hearts of many of its citizens, then many citizens will simply adopt an attitude of denial or apathetic fatalism while others call for "peace" with great intensity. The trouble with this kind of political situation is that it is not likely, to put it mildly, to produce thoughtful and considered decisions or programs. In any case, as a result of a combination of apathy, denial, and hysteria, responsible political life is likely to suffer disastrously. And this may encourage or alternatively force other nations to play the game of "chicken."

If some of these "peace" movements are accompanied by violence, or even large-scale illegal non-violence, organized political life in the nation may be threatened even more gravely. In addition, the necessity for reliable internal control of nuclear weapons could force or encourage many governments to practice a rigid authoritarianism or depotism to prevent even small military or political groups from obtaining and using weapons for protest or revolutionary purposes. And eventually, the best of safeguards will occasionally fail.

7. *Facilitate Diffusion of Nuclear Weapons to Really Irresponsible Organizations.* To the extent that advanced nuclear weapons

or components are treated as articles of commerce (perhaps for peaceful uses as in the Plowshare program), their cost will be well within the resources available to many large organizations. In fact, if we get them down to $100,000 or so, and this is not at all implausible, they are, in some sense, available to any dedicated middle-income individual who is willing to save a major fraction of his income for ten or twenty years. Exactly what this could mean is hard to picture without detailed consideration of the various "scenarios" that are possible; but, somehow, few will feel comfortable in a world in which the Malayan guerrillas, Cuban rebels, Algerian terrorists (or the Right-Wing counter-terrorists), the Puerto Rican Independence Party, or even gangsters could have access to nuclear weapons or other means of mass destruction. It should be realized that even if nuclear weapons and their delivery systems are not articles of commerce, almost all of their components will have peaceable "relatives." These will be articles of commerce. Thus, only a few special parts or assemblies will have to be manufactured by those organizations or individuals who wish to obtain some sort of weapons capability.

8. *Complicates Future Problems of Control.* If weapons are diffused widely, then even if an incident or a crisis occurs and even if such an event increases the willingness of most nations to control the situation, such control is likely to be more difficult to achieve because the small powers are now being asked to accept a reduction in their current capability rather than to abstain from the acquisition of weapons. Of course, if the control measures that are envisaged are sufficiently thorough-going and complete, all nations may be treated equally. Even then, it is going to be difficult, if not impossible, to get all of them to junk their nuclear-weapons systems peacefully and not just acquiesce to controls that prevent them from acquiring such systems, though, as France has shown, the last may be difficult.

9. *Creates and Intensifies Agent-Provocateur Problems.* It should be clear that one restraint on the behavior of "respectable" large nations in this super-armed world—and perhaps in any world—is that they do not want a reputation for being blatantly aggressive. Therefore, when a nation does want to be aggressive, it often needs an excuse to make its aggression seem defensive, or at least very special and limited. In the absence of a special

situation (such as Berlin), it may be difficult to do this. It is usually almost impossible for a small power to be made to look so provocative against a large power to justify, for example, nuclear retaliation by the large power. But if the small power happens to have nuclear weapons, then many kinds of "accidental" incidents or provocations could be arranged or made use of. They could be used to justify all kinds of ultimatums or actual reprisals up to and including the forcible disarming of the small power which showed itself to be irresponsible enough to nearly cause a holocaust.

10. *Catalytic War or Escalation.* The widespread diffusion of nuclear weapons could give many nations the capability, and in some cases, would also create a pressure, to aggravate an on-going crisis or even to touch off a war between two other powers for purposes of their own. Here again the situation is so complicated that one must think through many scenarios to get a feeling for the possibilities. However, in advance of such systematic exploration, and without discussing our present knowledge of the problem, it should be clear that there are many possibilities for mischief-making by third parties.

TECHNOLOGY AND THE UNDER-DEVELOPED WORLD

by RENATO SEVERINO

Today many peoples are in a dilemma over the weight to give to tradition, while talking in terms of technology, the international language par excellence.

The dilemma arises from the wish to defend tradition while

enjoying all the advantages of progress. But this produces positions which run counter to culture at best and, at worst, extreme conservatism when an embalmed past is preferred to a living present with all its problems. The main alibi produced is that the cultural heritage must be preserved. This in itself is praiseworthy and should be done in any case, so as not to lose the testimony of previous civilizations: a testimony necessary for the development of our conscience. Unfortunately, when love of local traditions hides a refusal to accept new problems, a climate is created in which communications are difficult because a large number of men cannot participate in all the various traditions.

In many developing countries a battle is being fought against superstition, gratuitous folklore and especially against those false ideologies which suggest implicitly that all prejudices should be respected.

Many peoples fear the future and cling to folklore because they realize—when they are honest—that thinking of the future means tackling an enormous number of interrelated problems. The inability to identify, in their own selves, even one small part of these problems, creates embarrassment and a sense of insecurity. In man's mind the battle between rational and irrational facts goes on continuously. When rationalization is pushed to the limits, many so-called human factors are left out. And as these are not easy to distinguish and isolate, they generate psychological revolt against change, especially today when the change must be very rapid if it is to be effective.

Therefore, in many developing countries with strong cultural traditions, the ruling class opposes change, since it wishes to retain its privileges, which are almost always based on religious principles or caste.

Unfortunately, the West has often found itself associated with this ruling class, with the results we all know so well. This is due to great misunderstanding regarding respect for that folklore—which is always very interesting to find in countries we visit as tourists—and to the virtual impossibility of communicating with a new ruling class with more modern ideas and ambitions.

The task of the new generation will be to free itself from the bounds imposed by individual traditions. Feeling for the past must not be allowed to become transformed into sterile dogma.

Only the essential should be used as an individual bedrock on which to found a new international culture.

After this clarification a choice can be made. The scale of the problem will then finally be changed since it will be posed in terms of the whole of mankind, with the language of technology founded on a single culture aimed at resolving world problems: a technology which is being defined both by the objectives to be reached and the means used to achieve them.

It is obvious that the most difficult task will be that of salvaging the cultural traditions of these countries which must in no way be lost in this homogenizing process. It is also clear, however, that a true and valid culture is international because it is composed of contributions originating from every part of the world. Any attempt to latch on to local traditions in solving any one problem is destined to fail unless this solution is valid also on an international scale. It is essential, therefore, that this solution be dictated by phenomena or by problems that present themselves in any part of our world. It is thus true contemporary culture. In fact, today, those problems that are valid on an expert level are those that apply to any country in the world since the experts are such only if their experience is valid universally.

We can say, therefore, that technology as a "stimulating factor" can only be universal. It is the aim and scope of the new and true culture to fight for the entire humanity and not just for a favored few. At this point, there is absolutely no other choice. Finally! Now the leadership of any one country will be proportionate to the dedication that it contributes to this struggle. For this reason, the United States, for the role that it already has assumed, cannot but increase its contribution in order to avoid a serious internal crisis.

It is clear that technology—as an objective lingua franca, free from all the prejudices and crystallization of individual cultures— is the only means for mutual understanding; the only means of clarifying the terms of the discussion, which are presently so confused and distorted by ideologies.

But let us not forget that in a democratic society, planning should endeavor to represent the physical needs and the ambitions of all men as faithfully as possible. Hence the process of planning should avail itself of a method of investigation that can translate data into a codex referable, in practice, to industrial terminology.

All this will come about, because to express a sound opinion, for all citizens, will mean to refer to a standard which in the future will of necessity be solely industrial, since this is the one which can be identified most securely while at the same time being the easiest to express by means of precise indices. The "Industrial Index of Standard" will be the synthesis of all those factors covering the use, the cost, and the appearance of an object.

In this process, human factors will be expressed as the possibility of producing objects which unite the indices in various ways, and in the formulation and choice of industrial design on an urban scale. The ambitions of the users will reflect in producing something better, something more exciting, and something more efficient through the intuition of a small group of experts planning the future, and by considering how best to satisfy certain widely felt needs.

In industrial terms the dream is expressed by the high level of the prototype, considering the prototype as a better solution than a previous one, with greater possibilities of meeting peoples' needs and choices. All the efforts of the planners and the designers will be turned toward the prototype, which is the point of encounter between the dream on the one hand and the reality of production on the other. Hence the prototype, in a democratic society, is the unique moral expression of design in community terms. Efforts to produce a "one-off" job fly in the face of reality, when considering the problems society is confronted with on a worldwide scale. Moreover, those who dedicate themselves to this concept are running against the tide of history: a tiny minority trying to build itself an island in contemporary society.

Although it might seem that facts expressed in this manner could refer solely to the industrialized world, it is nonetheless evident that if the possibility of exchange between the two worlds is to be maintained, then the developing countries cannot do without advanced technology, otherwise they will feel themselves to be manifestly inferior to other countries.

It is irrational to suppose that new developing countries need follow the path already pursued by the industrialized countries. This theory which some have suggested has already been shown to be invalid. Placing developing countries in a condition of using an already antiquated technology would mean detaching them definitely from a productive insertion into the world. It would mean keeping them out definitely from a future in common and in peace.

We must not forget that the migration of technicians from new countries to more industrialized ones is continuously increasing. The reason for this is that every man wishes to find the best utilization of himself and of his capacities. Many new countries today have more qualified technicians than initiatives able to absorb them. This phenomenon is destined to increase in the future. Natural migration in the world is an ancient condition, but today it becomes more rapid in its evolution. Migration of men and of objects results in commerce, an exchange of experience, and in a general welfare for all. Any attempt to arrest this natural tendency or to influence it forcibly has always brought about an economic regression and political constriction.

In the future these movements of populations will be always more rapid and the resulting phenomena will be a natural, slow, but unarrestable integration of people from every country in the world. Racial discrimination will slow up this process, but will certainly not succeed in stopping it. Problems common to all, a universal culture, physical proximity, the use of the same technological means that will naturally determine the evolution of the mind toward common aims, all these factors will cause the peoples of the world to consider themselves as belonging to just one race. When in a few decades this evolution is well underway, no one will be able to create obstacles because a new philosophy and a new culture will have asserted themselves.

Parallel to this, commercial enterprises will be directed toward a logical liberal economy. All commercial goods will be obtained at their original source of supply at the lowest possible prices since the sphere of political influence will be in the hands of just a few groups. These groups, once the problem of underdevelopment begins to be solved, will be able to adopt a true and workable price control, based on actual costs of goods. Moreover, in the future, all commercial goods will have to be produced in an industrial area that will manufacture at the lowest prices without having to submit to increases imposed by political influences. Naturally, the production areas can be situated even in zones that today are underdeveloped but that have a potential of raw materials and manpower. It is basically essential, however, for the welfare of all, that the costs of industrial products be universally competitive and, therefore, technologically at the highest possible level.

Autarkic solutions are acceptable in the same way as the underdevelopment. That is, in the future, neither the autarky nor underdevelopment will be satisfactory since the rapid increase in the world population will absolutely not allow it.

All these conditions, so described, represent, of course, an optimistic vision of tomorrow's world. In fact, the arising of other factors such as racial ill will, selfishness, or a restricted vision of the future on the part of industrialized countries would bring about really disastrous consequences.

As we all know, in industrialized countries urban planning and architectural design are difficult to integrate owing to the complexity of operating in a highly-stratified society and because of the compartmentalization of the technician's sphere of competence.

However, the developing countries have provided enormous scope for experimentation in this respect, since in nearly all cases town planning and architectural design have been entrusted to a single team of planners and architects. Their job is certainly facilitated by having a less-cluttered environment as a starting point, and they have a smaller number of sectional interests to contend with. So, apart from the necessary policy decisions made by the government or local administrations, the relationship between client and professional man is basically on a technical level. This has produced some fine examples of integration between planning and architectural design. Examples include Le Courbusiers' Chandigarh, W. Gropius' Baghdad University, and many other schemes implemented by various European architects in Africa and Asia.

It should be noted at the outset, however, that in the architectural field there is a pronounced tendency to link in with colorful local tradition. There is a widespread tendency to design buildings which, even though achieving notable architectural results, are clearly an interpretation of local folklore, an aspect of the unproductive attempt to keep alive a tradition and carry it on. These attempts have already demonstrated their limits and the small extent to which they adhere to future reality.

The young of the new countries have great faith that technology can free them from the constrictions of underdevelopment, and provide them with the means of reaching parity with the industrialized countries. As regards urban architectural design, there is a marked trend toward rationalist extremes, with the emphasis on technological expression.

The wish to have the most modern and the most advanced is constantly expressed by the inhabitants of the developing countries, whatever level they may belong to. Only a small minority leans toward the customs of local traditional life.

These observations stem directly from our experience in Africa when we have incorporated traditional African motifs, on a larger scale, in new buildings to provide a continuity of plastic vision present in the country. We think that these attempts have not been educational. The local inhabitants do not judge them to be necessary, even though they may appreciate the design, since they add nothing concrete to resolving the fundamental problem of building in Africa.

Running parallel to the problem of architectural expression is that of building techniques. And because of the weighty consequences involved, this is definitely a fundamental problem.

In most cases buildings have been put up by archaic methods. The techniques used are derived from local tradition, to the point where, even now, work systems on building sites are not very dissimilar from those used to build the Pyramids. Even nowadays it is common to see ant-like streams of men and women with heavy head loads swarming up and down scaffolding.

It is, however, important to note certain phenomena which are appearing in the building field in the new countries.

Local prefabrication of parts, for example, is developing rapidly, though the practical results are often poor from all points of view. While it is unthinkable that such a trend can be stopped—since it stems from an unstemmable economic and social process—it should be observed that the buildings constructed by these somewhat primitive methods have no aesthetic value, and create a disagreeable blot on man's environment. As a result, architects have reacted—and continue to do so—by designing buildings using more traditional materials and techniques. However, this inevitably results in the construction site being occupied by a vast community of low-paid labor. There is no future for this method of construction if the hopes of improving living standards in the new countries are to be transformed into reality.

We are gradually becoming aware that even in developing countries industrialized building, and hence technology, are the only possible way, if economic development is to be secured.

At the present time most building materials are imported. Furthermore, for buildings of the same standard, the cost is higher in many new countries than in Europe. Thus it can be seen that in many cases the importation of totally prefabricated buildings is an economically viable proposition.

Alongside this phenomenon that has manifested itself in the new countries in Africa, Asia, and South America, there is another opposite phenomenon that is springing up in industrialized countries: prefabrication on a total scale, producing buildings by the use of a system very similar to that of the automobile industry. In fact, in the course of the next two decades buildings will be made essentially of metal and plastic since these are the materials easiest to mold and the lightest—very suitable to be transported even long distances—and very rapidly assembled. Construction in reinforced concrete will have a tendency to disappear and will be used only for foundations or for structures that support great weight. But even in this latter case, metal-framed boxes containing liquids will be preferred and will substitute for the casting of concrete in typically non-industrial organization. Supporting structures will be much lighter and will weigh only about one-tenth of those in use today.

All this will be obtained through the technology already employed in the automobile and naval industries and through a complete transformation of the construction industry.

Unions, moreover, will have nothing to object to in this new situation that will, in fact, guarantee greater protection to its members. They will find themselves working as a part of an industrial system far more progressive and therefore more prepared to give greater protection of their rights and more security of occupation and of working conditions.

Each urban aggregate will be composed of interchangeable parts that will be able to be united in different ways and manufactured by industries in competition with each other. Inhabitants of these buildings will have a wide choice to conform the inside of habitats to their personal needs and preferences by moving the basic elements. All multistory buildings will be able to increase even in height following a geometric scheme that will leave unaltered the static and spatial equilibrium. This will be possible because of the lightness of the parts and their easy assembling. Moreover, this new method of design springs forth no longer solely from a personal intuition but from an overall programming that assigns to each element the requisite grade of mobility and combination.

This method will be improved steadily and will become ever more precise both in its design and construction, using automatic systems of calculation and production. It will be essential and basic to employ specialists in all those fields that involve urban planning, as well as artists. This will guarantee a complete, integrated cycle, for the production of a human environment continuously on the move.

Research in this field has been carried out by our team of experts here in Europe. Moreover, the exact feeling is that the new generation of planners is already perfectly aware of the needs of this new society.

Technology is undoubtedly the basic means to obtain true and valid results but it is obvious that, today, it is also necessary to have men that combine the capacity of making real what just a little time ago appeared as a dream, with the capacity to understand all the various problems that are a part of this process.

It is not possible, in fact, to continue formulating convincing theories that materialize, then, in a few forms incapable of solving problems on a large scale, using just a few schematic elements that are often artificial and obsolete. This type of contribution is no longer valid even though it is true that this evolution has brought to light many problems while disuniting even more the basic technological mediums from the other fundamental aims of society.

Moreover, in the future, the building industry can be precisely programmed. Costs and results will be known from the very beginning of each process and the market will benefit from this. Competition will be very lively and will be based on an increasing improvement of standards. Greater also will be the activity of architects, designers, and planners.

It is necessary to define, at this point, how this new city will appear. It will no longer be a rock but something that can easily be varied and altered in an increasingly shorter period of time, as the needs of its citizens require. The facility of assembling and disassembling the buildings will insure satisfying the needs of a society in motion from one territory to another. Slums and obsolete zones will thus be obviated, since by ensuring an active use of buildings as the basis of their existence in that certain area, there will be no necessity of abandoning them. Above all, perhaps for the first time in the history of the world, it will be possible to respect the natural scene. It will no longer be necessary to destroy forests, modify hills and valleys and build indestructible canyons.

This new conception of a city springs forth from the rapid metamorphosis of a society on the move. Every construction will be recoupable and usable anywhere. A new architectural concept of space is already being defined where man will find his habitat in contact with Nature without having to destroy it. Today's cities are in such rapid transformation that to apply a sentimental value to streets and squares has practically no longer a logical sense. On the other hand, the increase in the population and the need for rehousing a large number of people impose a drastic and global solution. Future planning, once it is able to count on an appropriate industry, will have at its disposal the new means to realize its program rapidly, with a total respect for the design, and at a cost calculated in advance that will become ever more precise.

Up to now, we have proceeded in the planning of cities and in building them to use the same methods that have been applied for the past two thousand years. The only change has been in some new technical devices such as the curtain wall, that, however, succeeds only in closing in and isolating even more men already trapped in the cities' cage. Today it is evident that we must find a new relationship between urban structure and industrial methodology.

The relationship between man and buildings will be a new one, based on the rational use of internal space that must be integrated with the external natural one. A man who easily moves about in the world will need an environment that is able to transform itself as the need for greater space requires increasing or decreasing the human concentration. The phenomenon of migration and the movement of parts that make up buildings and the urban aggregate will be parallel with the phenomenon of the migration of men.

Therefore, if we consider the parallelism between the development of industrialized countries with that of those that are not, it will become obvious that the technological gap will become even more accentuated if we continue to persist with the present economic policy. (The same gap exists between the United States and Europe and shows a tendency to become greater, causing alarm in responsible European groups.)

In a regime of free economy, it is certainly not conceivable, considering the high cost of skilled crafts or of semi-industrial products in underdeveloped countries that still pay very low salaries, that these goods (prefabricated buildings) could not be bought directly from the countries that produce them at a lower cost but that pay higher salaries.

Therefore, it is probable that in the future there will be an increase in the exportation to non-industrialized countries of industrial products intended for building construction, in direct measure with the bettering of conditions in these same countries. Should this not take place, it will mean that in these new countries the condition of autarky is continuing due to the need of employing manpower at very low salaries because of an existing disoccupation. This will mean that the typical condition of underdevelopment will continue because manpower is not employed in sectors of high-level production. In this case, therefore, applying advanced technology in the field of construction would have no sense. The contact between new countries and the new way of life would then become ever more difficult and fragile.

In the coming years, every underdeveloped area will have to solve, by the use of its own natural and human resources, the problem of establishing an economic pattern that will ensure a true productive insertion of technological methods already applied in industrialized countries. The future of urban planning in the developing countries is therefore linked to many factors deriving from the economy of each individual country, but especially from the capacity to project their self-awareness into action. It is precisely in the degree of self-awareness that the new countries will find the possibility of planning their own energies, their own abilities, and their own ambitions. From the struggle which will ensue in the conscience of those whose task it is to decide, will depend the tomorrow of their country. It will depend on the balance between what has to be sacrificed and what is conquered.

In the serene skies of our hopes there is space for a thousand storms.

COMMUNICATIONS AND GOVERNMENT

by VLADIMIR K. ZWORYKIN

GOVERNMENT, to be good, must be informed; to be democratic, it must be controlled by an informed citizenry. These conditions can be realized only by an efficient system of two-way communication between the people and their governmental agents.

The problem of presenting the government's message to the people has found an adequate solution. Broadcast radio and television not only enable heads of governments to address themselves to their total constituencies at short notice, but permit minor functionaries as well to acquaint people in limited areas concerning school closings, road alterations, counter-measures for epi-

Reprinted from *The World in 1984,* vol. II, edited by Nigel Calder. By permission of Penguin Books. First published in 1964.

demics, and other matters of importance for the efficient operation of society.

By comparison, the ways open to the people for making their wishes known to their representatives appear quite inadequate. The one official channel available for this purpose is the vote. The cumbersome business of preparing and printing the ballots, setting up the polling places, and requiring voters to present themselves there at appointed times, limits both the frequency of such expressions of public opinion and the range of issues covered by them. More often than not, the election centers on a personal contest between candidates, and the issues responsible for success or failure become the subject of a guessing game for commentators, candidates, and campaign managers. The extensive use of unofficial public opinion polls is a natural consequence. Yet, these too, apart from being subject to sampling errors, are too time-consuming to give the people an effective voice in time of crisis.

This limitation on the democratic process is not at all necessary. As I have had occasion to point out in my Clerk Maxwell Memorial lecture to the British Institution of Radio Engineers (*Journal of the British I.R.E.*, Vol. 19, p. 529), modern technology makes it possible to give the people the ability to communicate their wishes and opinions to the government with a directness and immediacy comparable with that realized at present only in the opposite direction.

To be sure, doubt may be expressed as to the desirability of direct popular control of public policy. The past experience with the direct democracy of ancient Athens and the town meeting may be interpreted either favorably or unfavorably or even regarded as irrelevant, in view of the greater complexity of the questions presented to modern governments for decision. Three comments may here be in order. First, in direct democracy as in our present-day representative governments, it may be assumed that only broad policy decisions would be made by laymen and that details would be left to the judgment of a hierarchy of technical advisers. Second, being repeatedly called on to participate in public decisions can be expected to stimulate in the citizen an increased sense of responsibility and a desire to inform himself on public questions; thus the practice of direct democracy can help to develop the preconditions for its success. Finally, whatever the manner may be in which the expression of public opinion is translated into the control of public policy—and I cannot pretend to any special knowledge in this field—it would certainly be of value to those who guide the nation to have an accurate index of public attitudes on important issues. For this last reason alone we might expect that, by 1984, governments will have availed themselves of the technical possibility of accurately gauging popular response to current and projected policies.

In the technically advanced countries of today, the desired two-way communication between citizens and government is made possible by the existence of two parallel communication systems with practically complete coverage of the population—the broadcasting system and the telephone system. For example, in the United States, with 82 million telephones serving a population of some 190 million, it would be a relatively simple matter to "assign" every voter to a particular telephone, a limited number of public telephones taking care of non-subscribers.

In the system envisaged, every telephone would be provided with simple auxiliary equipment, which would convert it into a voting station. Registered voters assigned to the station would then be in a position to express their preferences on specific questions submitted over broadcast channels at any pre-assigned voting period in much the same manner as citizens today use voting machines for expressing their opinions in a referendum. The important difference resides in the fact that such a poll could be conducted at any time, upon a few hours' notice; that the voting would be carried out predominantly at home, without delay or interference with the normal routine of the voter; and that the returns could be known within an hour after the voting had been completed. For details as to how this might be accomplished the reader is referred to my earlier paper. As indicated there, the obvious requirements that only qualified voters participate in the vote and do so only once can be met without difficulty.

Let us assume that, by the year 1984, a basic reform of this nature in the recording of public opinion has been carried into effect. What would be the consequences? First of all, government leaders would be able to align their policies more closely with the popular will, which would be known rather than a subject for speculation. In this manner they might avoid forced reversals of policy and give government a greater degree of continuity. Even more important, the frequent consultation of the individual voter on specific issues would tend to overcome his feeling of political ineffectiveness and provide him with a recurrent incentive to become better informed on matters of public policy. In this manner we may hope that, in 1984, an appropriate application of modern communication techniques may strengthen the basis of effective democratic government by creating a better informed and more vitally interested citizenry and rendering government more responsive to its will. An effective way would have been found for the citizen to communicate with his government and for the government to become aware of the popular will.

A PROPOSAL FOR CURTAILING SMALL WARS

by SEYMOUR MELMAN

Precis

Small wars, like nuclear wars, have become unacceptable burdens —even to the greatest military powers.

A workable international mechanism for ensuring the security of small states, and curtailing small wars, can be devised.

Once the governments of the US and USSR agree to agree on the mutual advantage to be gained from curtailing small wars, then the Vietnam and the Israeli-Arab crises can be settled within the framework of steps toward a wider agreement.

The Arab-Israeli crisis, added to the Vietnam war, has confronted the United States with the following facts:

Reprinted from *Mankind 2000,* edited by Robert Jungk and Johan Galtung, No. 1 of Future Research Monographs from The International Peace Research Institute Oslo. Published by Universitetsforlaget, Oslo, Norway, and George Allen & Unwin, London. By permission of Universitetsforlaget. First published in 1969.

a) US armed forces cannot operate multiple wars around the world, even with 3.5 million armed men and a $77 billion military budget.
b) The US is committed to operate multiple small wars by agreements, and especially by foreign policy doctrine that relies primarily on US military power to cope with varied political problems.
c) The US could operate multiple small wars only at the cost of drastic military mobilization, severe curtailment of civilian economy, and establishment of a garrison society.
d) The two greatest military powers, the US and the USSR, have each become sponsors of small wars, each relying on the hope that small wars can be kept small, isolated, and contained.
e) Sustained military confrontations among small states do not necessarily resolve or stabilize political differences.
f) There is no functioning international mechanism for ensuring the integrity of small states that can operate with the speed, reliability, and impartiality that is needed to give assurance of protection against aggression, without primary reliance on national armed forces.

US-USSR Understanding to Curtail Nuclear Confrontations

Before the Cuban missile crisis of October 1962, it seemed utopian to suggest that the United States and the Soviet Union could agree not to wage nuclear war deliberately. But such an understanding was reached. The informal paths used for developing this understanding do not detract from the fact that since October 1962, the governments of the United States and the Soviet Union have not uttered nuclear war threats.

An agreement to agree was generated once each government found it intolerable to continue the nuclear confrontation system for political settlements. The nuclear threat menaced the physical and economic security of each society so severely as to create an urgent problem for each side that could only be solved acceptably by joint agreement to avoid nuclear war.

Nevertheless, that agreement did not imply to the governments of the United States and the Soviet Union that military violence was no longer a competent instrument of political power. Accordingly, fresh political and military ideologies, Eastern and Western, supported the idea that small wars between states, restricted to non-nuclear weapons and limited to particular territory, could still be workable propositions. Ideologies of "national liberation" and "containment of Communism by counterinsurgency" were given military expression in forces designed to fight and win with "conventional," non-nuclear weapons.

But there is no known way of designing a small war between states, whether of the Vietnam or the Arab versus Israeli type, which does not contain a significant potential for big-power involvement and hence nuclear confrontation. A succession of small wars necessarily heightens these risks.

The difficulty of curtailing small wars, either in scope or intensity, goes far to explain why no war between states has been permitted to go to a military conclusion since World War II. Despite the readiness of large and small governments to use force as an international instrument of power (and the implied readiness to violate the United Nations Charter), each instance of international violence on a large scale since 1945 has provoked the fears of other countries who, in due course, intervened to curtail military operations—acting separately or jointly or through the United Nations.

American and Soviet Interest in Terminating Small Wars

Small wars, fought with conventional weapons among small states, are a class of political-military operations on which United States and the Soviet Union have had diverging estimates. To the Soviets these have included anti-colonial "wars of liberation," to be encouraged, especially as they move in a pro-Russian direction. To the United States these events are frequently understood as "insurgency" and are thus opposed as destabilizing development— politically and militarily, and fraught with pro-Soviet or pro-Chinese results.

Despite the divergent political assessments, the United States and the Soviet Union have been developing areas of common interest, as yet unformulated, against the incidence of small wars, and favoring agreement on ways of avoiding such military con-

frontations. The factors generating such common Soviet-American interest include the following:

a) Nuclear wars are now well appreciated as no-win operations for the nuclear powers.

b) Hazards deriving from proliferation of nuclear weapons are a common concern for the United States and the USSR. Small states, unable to attain their own national security in other ways, seek to become nuclear powers.

c) Wars that contain the potential of escalation into nuclear confrontation are thereby clothed with nuclear-war hazards.

d) Military operations by small states are not reliably limited to such governments and their territories, and can rapidly include political-military confrontations of big powers.

e) The costs of supporting small wars, and the preparations for them, are burdensome for both the US and USSR—depleting manpower and other resources that are badly needed at home, and for productive growth in the developing countries.

f) Sustained fighting of small wars has involved violation of international laws of war, thereby breaking down the traditions of legal and moral constraint that were devised to limit even conflict by force of arms. The weakening of these constraints weakens the security of all men.

In sum: small wars are economically costly and militarily hazardous even to the great nuclear powers. For small wars contain a significant potential for developing into big-power confrontations. Therefore, the US-Soviet interest in avoiding nuclear wars and nuclear confrontations necessarily extends to a common interest in avoidance of small wars.

The Common Interest of Small States in Terminating Small Wars

Even poor states support armed forces as the main available way to ensure their own security. But the quest for security through military advantage has a high price.

Armed forces of developing countries are supported by their own budgets, exceeding $18 billion per year. These armed forces produce the following effects:

a) Productive economic growth in the developing countries is severely restrained.
b) The priority given to armed forces encourages adventurist governments in which military officers play a dominant role.
c) In countries where governments are based upon officer corps, internal social and political instability is encouraged by failure in economic development. Wherever governments maintain themselves by military power, violent methods seem to be the only available methods open to a citizenry which seeks social and economic change.

The quest for military superiority among small states presses them toward dependence on the great powers for military supplies, and for military alliances. However, reliance on the military technology of the great powers has a counter-productive effect on the security and vulnerability of smaller states.

Small countries are rendered increasingly insecure by the proliferation and increased power of national armies—even though these are equipped with "conventional" weapons, for these weapons have been made highly mobile and quite destructive. In the Kashmir fighting between India and Pakistan during 1965 these countries each destroyed major parts of their armed forces within about two weeks. (One estimate rated the value of what was destroyed as equal to the cost of an Aswan dam project.)

The common interest of small states in a competent international security system is further frustrated by the contradictory development of military technologies and of international political and peace-keeping institutions. Military technologies develop ways that shorten time for movement and firepower effect. International political and peace-keeping institutions involve political debate, votes, veto systems, and long convening time. Two days may be a rather short time for a Security Council to be summoned, and for a debate to be concluded. But two days of military operations with modern weapons can produce great damage in small countries.

The present writer has conferred with senior foreign ministry officials of several smaller states during the past years. Their view of the world includes reservations about the workability of the present United Nations peace-keeping machinery, especially with respect to slow speed (relative to military reaction time), political partiality, and hence reliability. From doubts along these lines, the governments of small states have concluded that they must place prime reliance on their own armed forces to preserve their national security. That is why the elements of speed, reliability and impartiality are probably central to the competent functioning of a new sort of international security force —even with the backing of the great powers.

Essential Ingredients of a Competent International Security System: Speed, Reliability, Impartiality

For the US and USSR there is a solid basis of common interest for trying afresh to come to grips with the main world security problem of our time: "small wars," and the absence of any reliable mechanism for dealing with small wars. These problems justify a major effort in political and technical innovation. *A US-USSR joint effort in this direction is fundamental.* A host of problems must be formulated and resolved in a workable fashion. We must take advantage of available technique in: highly mobile forces; fast communications; non-lethal weapons.

The following is given to illustrate some of the innovations that may be appropriate in designing an international peace-keeping force. This force, operated under the United Nations, may require characteristics that are known elsewhere, but are somewhat novel in the international sphere. The first of these is automatic triggering for speed of operation.

A big city police force is an automatically triggered security system. When a citizen telephones, *the police—following standard operating procedures—are ordered to the site without intervention of political officers or legislative bodies.* At the site of alleged lawbreaking the police are bound by a strict code of behavior: they must establish the fact of law violation; if established, the police must stop the law-breaking action. Thereafter, the police are bound by fixed orders and procedures to turn the matter over for jurisdiction to a separate judicial body.

In the international sphere an automatically triggered security force could be composed of several battalions of highly mobile, lightly armed soldiers operating under closely defined and limited jurisdiction to prevent or stop hostilities among states and turn over the issues for settlement to specified bodies.

The international force could be set in motion by a call from a government received at one of, say, five centers around the world. Within hours an inspecting team could arrive at any site and establish (a) whether there is indeed an armed conflict, or an imminent conflict; and (b) whether the dispute is international. Criteria for "international" must be rigorously defined, for example, as (a) conflict between armed forces of two states; or (b) conflict for control of a government within a state in which a second state participates by giving material support to one of the parties involved. Once a dispute is certified as international the international military force itself arrives at the site, declares and administers a cease-fire. All this could be done in a matter of hours following an initial call for help by a government. Thereafter, within a fixed time limit, the international force could be required to turn over the dispute at issue to an appropriate body. Thus, two adjudicating bodies could probably cope with the array of conceivable disputes: an international court or arbitration body to settle disputes over issues of dominion between governments; a plebiscite-conducting body to settle armed international disputes over who shall be a government. In each case, the adjudicating bodies are required to operate within fixed rules and time limits.

Reliability of operation of the international security force could be ensured by standard operating procedures which are binding on the general staff. In conventional armed forces standard operating procedures pertain primarily to the functioning of personnel below the general-staff level. For the international security force standard operating procedures must be written, with special detail, for the general staff itself. These rules would specify the precise conditions of operation of the force. For example: the rules must stipulate the persons to whom the force must respond; the maximum time for the first inspection response; the maximum time for determination of whether an emergency is international or not; the maximum time for arrival of the security force on a site; the sorts of actions to be taken at the peace-keeping site; the maximum time within which a given dispute must be referred for adjudication; etc.

Impartiality is designed into the international security system by two main elements: (a) the specifications of the standard operating procedures; (b) the rules governing the officer group that directly controls the force. The latter element is vital for ensuring political impartiality of peace-keeping forces. Devices like the following are required:

The general staff of the international force may be composed of, say, 20 men: 10 career officers from states in the Security Council; 10 nominated by a random selection of states outside the Security Council. These 20 are equal in rank and are assigned to functions in rotation. The key post of Chief of Staff (the senior officer) is occupied by each general staff officer for 15 days on a rotation basis. These, and similar arrangements, are intended to to produce functioning according to formal rule, rather than according to varying and personal political preferences of the senior staff.

In sum: the following considerations of merit for the US and the USSR suggest that this may be the time for a US-USSR agreement to agree on curtailing small wars.

For the United States:

The cost of Vietnam is high (at home and abroad), and additional wars or war crises will make these costs still higher.

An increased number of small wars increases the likelihood of escalation toward nuclear war.

A US-Soviet detente is a key for encouraging more rational and less Stalinist Chinese governments. The same detente would be useful for coping with nuclear missile threats in the event of failure of the foregoing.

Continued failure to ensure the security of non-nuclear states encourages nuclear proliferation.

Multiple small wars would swamp the decision processes of government—already overloaded by the Vietnam war. This also applies to the long-range planning of government.

The frustration in US public opinion engendered by inconclusive small-war operations would further strengthen extremist and isolationist tendencies in American life.

Small wars make it extremely difficult to plan productive investment in, and international trade with, developing countries.

For the USSR:

In some cases, e.g., Cuba and Vietnam, the direct costs of small wars and sustained military confrontation has been high.

Small wars encourage nuclear proliferation. A non-nuclear Germany is more difficult to ensure under such conditions.

The USSR, like the US, shares a concern over possible Chinese nuclear missile power, and Chinese expansionism.

Chinese boundaries are more reliably stabilized in a world where aggression against state borders is discouraged by international forces.

Soviet intervention for peace-keeping in the Kashmir fighting between India and Pakistan reflected the Soviet awareness of an interest in curtailing small wars. The Soviet moves probably contributed toward deterring nuclear proliferation into India and Pakistan, and Chinese opportunities for gain from war-weakened India and Pakistan.

Following the Cuban missile crisis the Soviet government perceived the merit of coming to joint understanding with the US in order to curtail mutual nuclear war dangers. Vietnam and the Middle East crisis suggest USSR-US concerns with respect to proliferation of small wars.

Durable peace settlements in the Middle East, Vietnam, and elsewhere can follow a US-USSR understanding that small wars must henceforth be curtailed in the common interest.

In the short run, an international peace-keeping force could be composed of highly mobile mixed units of the US and Soviet armies. Until the international peace-keeping machinery is fully formulated and established, this force—for a period of, say, one year—could be deployed for peace-keeping operations at the joint decision of the President of the United States and the Chairman of Soviet Socialist Republics. The very existence of this force would deter many aggressors. This temporary force could supervise an armistice and/or cooling-off operations in the Middle East and in Vietnam, for example, while diplomatic processes are operated.

The termination of these wars and war crises, as part of the move to a wider agreement, will enhance the prestige and moral authority of the governments that undertake this action.

CLOSING THE GAP

by JOHN DIEBOLD

THERE IS little doubt that a type of gap exists between Europe and the United States in certain areas of the most advanced technology and science. But the appellation "technological" gap is a misnomer. It is in reality a gap caused by a number of European managerial and financial inadequacies, as well as by a still-outmoded educational system, social immobilities, and political barriers. The consequences of this situation are the cause for legitimate concern.

There are several things that reasonably might—but probably should not—be done. The United States, in a Marshall Plan type of program, could subsidize the West European acquisition, both private and governmental, of American scientific and technological knowledge and of our managerial techniques for applying the fruits of research and development. The United States could, for example, transfer organic parts of its great academic-industrial complexes to European soil. These complexes could then be made to grow, training and employing Europeans exclusively. The operative conditions for such assistance could be the accelerated admission of the United Kingdom and her EFTA associates into the Common Market, the swift rationalization or unification of West European corporate, tax, patent, and social service laws, and, perhaps, even the establishment of a unified European currency under a body similar to but more powerful than the old European Payments Union.

Further, the United States could revise its immigration laws to exclude any potential West European immigrant certified by his or her native country as vital to that nation's interest. It even could expel any foreign residents in the United States who had

Excerpted by special permission from "Is the Gap Technological?" *Foreign Affairs,* January 1968, copyright 1968 by the Council on Foreign Relations, Inc., New York.

not yet either applied for or attained citizenship, if their services were desired by their native countries.

These are things which might be done. It is even possible to construct a historical rationale for such a course of action, in the light of what the United States has done in the past. It is equally evident, however, that these are things that probably should not be done. This is not 1947, with Europe prostrated by war and ready to accept America's tutelage in return for the assistance needed to get back on its feet. For more than a decade now, Europe has been an increasingly successful rival of the United States in the competition for markets and political influence. Any attempt to enforce conditions—other than payment in hard cash—for U.S. assistance would serve only to raise the temperature of the still smoldering resentments left over from the days of American hegemony.

Indeed, Europe, in order to maintain its competitiveness, will have to learn increasingly to apply the advanced products and techniques of American science and technology and the methods of American management to the production and marketing of those items in which it excels.

What, then, should Europe do? On the basis of what we know today, the following steps might be considered:

1. Establish technological and scientific priorities and managerial goals on a country-by-country and on a supranational basis. This would imply, specifically, the application of information, communications, and other hardware and systems techniques to the expansion of European industries and their worldwide markets. It is necessary to go considerably beyond the $500 million governmental financing of private computer manufacturers planned in Britain, France, and West Germany over the next five years. These are national investments, aimed principally at national markets. They tend to discourage mergers and other forms of cooperative and competitive action, and reinforce the continued development of incompatible and inadequately diversified systems which fail to meet the need of European industries for the latest technology. Similarly, this type of national financing is likely to provide computer manufacturers with little help in meeting competition outside of Europe.

2. Conclude intra-European political agreements to enact compatible corporate, tax, patent and social service laws which will permit the formulation of goals for business mergers and marketing. Figures for 1964 indicate that the United States, with 55 companies having sales of over $1 billion annually, enjoys a 3-to-1 advantage over Europe in this regard. However, in respect of companies with sales of over $250 million annually, the United States has a somewhat less forbidding lead of 2 to 1—248 United States companies against 119 European ones. Once the harmonization of European legal systems becomes a reality, one could reasonably expect a substantial increase in the number of European companies of the latter size, well able to afford large-scale R&D and marketing expenditures. But probably even more important than the matter of size for individual businesses is the formulation of competitive marketing strategies and the development of appropriate equipment among technologically advanced European industries. This process must take place on a supranational scale and requires a supranational legal and entrepreneurial climate.

3. Accelerate and expand the revisions begun in the European educational system. This is fundamental. Dr. James A. Perkins, former President of Cornell University and Chairman of the President's Advisory Committee on Foreign Assistance Programs, writes in the July 1966 issue of *Foreign Affairs:* "Perhaps no wind of change in Europe is more important than the revolution, just started, that will inevitably lead to the democratization and modernization of the schools and universities. Until this reform is completed, the European educational system will be the bottleneck that shuts off the development of Europe's manpower and shortens the life of its great dreams." And one of the major recommendations of the Deauville conference last May, which was devoted to the "technological gap," was the creation of a European Institute of Science and Technology in order to expand Europe's educational facilities to provide scientific, technological and managerial training. These would graduate not only a large number of scientists of the highest quality, but also a proportionately even larger number of second- and third-level technicians and managers to serve vital supportive functions. For example, by 1970 Europe will need 50,000 additional computer programmers

and 25,000 additional systems analysts—increases of 140 and 270 percent respectively over 1966. Further, the modernization and expansion of existing institutions of higher education is essential. A number of other basic steps come to mind. One would be to establish academic chairs, research facilities and student scholarships sponsored by business firms. On the basis of such grants the possibilities of contractual relationships between students and business and between universities and business should also be considered.

4. Organize effective efforts both by government and private business to hire U.S. talent for such purposes as the improvement of European communications and other technological infrastructures, the establishment of management training programs and the specific application of R&D to the production of marketable goods and services.

In its role as both competitor and Atlantic Community partner the United States should be ready to provide appropriate assistance to such European efforts. American cooperation could take the following forms:

1. Provide tax and other incentives for American corporations to establish additional R&D facilities in Europe. Such facilities would provide both primary and secondary markets for scientific, technological and management skills in order to slow down or reverse the emigration of newly trained European talent. It seems to me, as David Rockefeller recently said: "The most important contribution that we can make to Europe's technological development . . . is to do more of our own exploratory research" in Europe itself.

2. Contribute to European education in science, technology and, above all, management training. Financial assistance by American businesses and foundations could be directed specifically to facilitating the exchange of professors between Europe and the United States, especially in the field of management training. The direct participation of American businessmen in European management education can be a rewarding experience for both sides.

3. Reexamine the Export Control Act of 1949 and its administration. This Act has been repeatedly extended by the Congress

in virtually unchanged form. Its existence, and certainly its administration, have made the United States an increasingly unreliable source of supply for equipment ranging from computers to printing presses. As American and European policies on East-West trade have diverged over the past decade, the Export Control Act has caused both annoyance to the Europeans and a loss of export opportunities for American firms. Now that U.S. policy regarding trade with most Communist countries is undergoing a fundamental reevaluation on the part of both government and private business, it would appear an appropriate moment to remove the divisive and often self-defeating aspects of the Export Control Act. The frequently arbitrary decisions made in the name of this legislation have served to reinforce Europe's reluctance to depend on the United States as a supplier of much-needed advanced technology. Understandably, this situation is used to justify the uneconomic diversion of European resources into the development of technologies which could be more economically produced and supplied by the United States.

4. Try to achieve a major increase in the financial participation of Europe in U.S. ventures. Of course, this is a two-way street; European banks, businesses and individuals have to be willing to put up the money. None the less, much more could be done to sell the idea of financial partnerships. This would almost surely benefit the investors, improve the international atmosphere and increase political cooperation across the Atlantic.

These suggestions are by no means exhaustive; new ideas and new forms of cooperation inevitably will arise. Purposely excluded are proposals that are primarily political. For example, is the recently initiated E.E.C. effort to achieve technological cooperation politically broad enough to achieve the objectives outlined here? This is for Europe to decide. The form or extent of European integration which would make possible the needed harmonization of legal systems is left open; and how measures taken should be coordinated is best left to the affected parties themselves. In any event, the emphasis should be on European initiatives, with active support by the United States. And the first consideration of our support should be the interest we have in Europe as an equal economic competitor and an effective partner in world affairs.

I believe that the fundamental conclusion which may be drawn from this discussion is that the so-called technological gap should be a reason neither for European isolation nor European backwardness. It is not a manifestation of technological failure which Europe must overcome through the isolated development of its own technology. Rather, it is the result of European political divisions and of disparities in managerial and financial capabilities between Europe and the United States. Also, it is an expression of natural comparative advantage in international economic affairs. It is not a "technological" gap at all. And, if the nations of the Atlantic Community understand and act upon this conclusion, the gap which does exist need not widen or take on an importance which it does not have.

A WORLD POLICE FORCE

by GRENVILLE CLARK

THE PLAN is framed upon the assumption that not even the most solemn agreement and not even the most thorough inspection system, or both together, can be *fully* relied upon to ensure that every nation will always carry out and maintain complete disarmament and refrain from violence under all circumstances. Moreover, it must be recognized that even with the complete elimination of all *military* forces there would necessarily remain substantial, although strictly limited and lightly armed, internal police forces and that these police forces, supplemented by civilians armed with sporting rifles and fowling pieces, might conceivably constitute a serious threat to a neighbor-

Reprinted from Grenville Clark and Louis B. Sohn, *World Peace Through World Law*. Third ed. enlarged. Cambridge, Mass.: Harvard University Press, Copyright 1958, 1960, 1966 by the President and Fellows of Harvard College. By permission of the publisher.

ing country in the absence of a well-disciplined and heavily armed world police.

In short, our conception is that if police forces are necessary to maintain law and order even within a mature community or nation, similar forces will be required to guarantee the carrying out and maintenance of complete disarmament by each and every nation and to deter or suppress *any* attempted international violence. In consequence, detailed constitutional provision is made for a world police, to be organized and maintained by the strengthened United Nations and to be called the "United Nations Peace Force." This world police force would be the only *military* force permitted anywhere in the world after the process of national disarmament has been completed. It would be built up during the "actual disarmament stage," so that as the last national military unit is disbanded the organization of the Peace Force would simultaneously be completed. This Peace Force would consist of two components—a standing component and a Peace Force Reserve—both of which would, save in the most extreme emergency, be composed solely of volunteers. The standing component would be a full-time force of professionals with a strength of between 200,000 and 600,000, as determined from year to year by the General Assembly. The proposed term of service for its enlisted personnel would be not less than four or more than eight years, as determined by the General Assembly, with provision for the re-enlistment of a limited number of especially well-qualified personnel.

In respect of the composition of the standing component, assurance would be provided through various specific limitations that it would be recruited mainly, although not exclusively, from the smaller nations. These limitations would include: (a) a provision whereby the number of nationals of any nation (including any non-self-governing or trust territory under its administration) serving at any one time in the standing component shall not exceed three percent of its then existing total strength; (b) a provision that the number of nationals of any nation in any one of the three main branches (land, sea, and air) of the standing component shall not exceed three percent of the then existing strength of such main branch; (c) a provision that the number of nationals of any nation serving at any one time in the officer corps of either of the three main branches of the standing component shall not exceed three percent of the then existing strength of the officer corps of such main branch; and (d) a provision that not less than two percent or more than ten percent of the total strength of the standing component shall be nationals of the nations or nation constituting any one of eleven to twenty regions into which the whole world would be divided by the General Assembly.

The units of the standing component would be stationed throughout the world in such a way that there would be no undue concentration in any particular nation or region, and, on the other hand, so as to facilitate prompt action for the maintenance of peace if and when required. Proposed specific provisions in this respect include: a direction that the standing component shall be stationed at military bases of the United Nations so distributed around the world as to facilitate its availability in case prompt action to prevent or suppress international violence is directed by the General Assembly (or in certain circumstances by the Executive Council); a provision that no such base shall be situated within the territory of any nation entitled to fifteen or more Representatives in the General Assembly, thus ensuring that no United Nations military base would be located in any of the twelve largest nations; a provision that all the territory of the world outside that of the twelve largest nations shall be divided by the General Assembly into eleven to twenty regions for the special purpose of distributing elements of the standing component between such regions, with the proviso that not less than five percent or more than ten percent of the total strength of the standing component shall be stationed in bases in any one of those regions, save only when the Peace Force has been duly called upon to take action.

In order to ensure the greatest possible security for the standing component, provision would be made that its units be located to the greatest extent possible on islands or peninsulas, or in other easily defensible positions.

The mobility of the standing component would be of great importance, in order that its widely distributed units could be promptly brought together into a formidable force in the event of any serious threat of international violence or serious defiance of the authority of the world organization. The equipment of the standing component should, therefore, include an ample number of large and swift aircraft for the long-distance transport of men and supplies, and in voting the annual budgets for the Peace Force the General Assembly would have authority to provide for this need.

As distinguished from the active or standing component, the Peace Force Reserve would have no organized units whatever, but would consist only of individuals partially trained and subject to call for service with the standing component in case of need. It would have a strength of between 600,000 and 1,200,000, as determined by the General Assembly. Its members would be recruited subject to careful provisions as to geographical distribution identical with those applicable to the standing component. The proposed term of service of its enlisted personnel would be for not less than six or more than ten years, as determined by the General Assembly. They would receive a minimum amount of basic training during the first three years of their term of service and some further training during the remainder of their terms, but except for these training periods would remain in their home countries on a stand-by basis subject to call.

The officers of both components would be selected, trained, and promoted with a view to "ensuring an officer corps of the highest possible quality" with adequate opportunity for the selection as officer candidates of highly qualified men from the rank and file.

Specific provision would be made for adequate pay and allowances for the personnel of both components, all pay and other compensation (including retirement pensions) to be free from all taxation.

It is contemplated that the United Nations Peace Force shall be regularly provided with the most modern weapons and equipment, except that its possession or use of biological, chemical, or any other weapons adaptable to mass destruction, other than nuclear weapons, would be forbidden, special provision being made, as hereafter mentioned, for the use of nuclear weapons in extreme circumstances. The initial weapons and equipment of the Peace Force would come from the transfer of weapons and equipment discarded by national military forces during the process of complete disarmament. Subsequent supplies would be produced by the United Nations in its own production facilities through a separate agency to be established by the General Assembly and called the United Nations Military Supply and Research Agency. This Agency would engage in research relative to the development of new weapons and relative to methods of defense against the possible use by any nation of prohibited weapons clandestinely hidden or produced.

With regard to the use of nuclear weapons by the Peace Force, the solution proposed is that neither component shall normally be equipped with any kind of nuclear weapons, but that some such weapons shall be held in reserve in the custody of a civilian agency for use only under the most careful precautions. This agency would be the Nuclear Energy Authority which would be authorized to release any nuclear weapons for possible use by the Peace Force only by order of the General Assembly itself, and then only if the Assembly has declared that nuclear weapons (which might have been clandestinely hidden or clandestinely produced) have actually been used against some nation or against the United Nations, or that such use is imminently threatened. While it may be argued that nuclear weapons should be part of the regular equipment of a world police force so that it could immediately crush by ruthless action any defiance of the world law, this solution has been rejected as being no more consistent with the purpose of the Peace Force than the regular equipment of a city police force with weapons whereby thousands of citizens could be killed in suppressing a riot.

It is also realized that it can be persuasively argued that nuclear weapons should not be even potentially available to the Peace Force. On balance, however, it is believed wise to make it *possible* for the Peace Force to use nuclear weapons in extreme circumstances provided that, as called for by the above-described proposals, such possible use is safeguarded with the utmost care.

The immediate direction of the Peace Force would be entrusted to a committee of five persons—to be called the Military Staff Committee—all of whom would have to be nationals of the smaller nations, i.e., of those nations entitled to less than fifteen Representatives in the General Assembly. Beyond this safeguard, however, the Military Staff Committee would always be under the close control of civilian authority, i.e., of the Executive Council.

Still further, the General Assembly, through its Standing Committee on the Peace Enforcement Agencies, would exercise a general supervision over the work of the Military Staff Committee and over the Executive Council itself in respect of the organization and all the activities of the Peace Force. In short, the plan includes the utmost precautions for the subordination of the military direction of the Peace Force under all circumstances to civilian authority as represented by the Executive Council and the General Assembly.

While a world police force, well-equipped and strong enough to prevent or promptly to suppress *any* international violence, is we believe indispensable, the danger that it might be perverted into a tool of world domination is fully recognized. It is with this danger clearly in mind that meticulous care has been taken to surround the proposed Peace Force with the above-mentioned careful limitations and safeguards, so as to make its subversion virtually impossible.

Even with these elaborate safeguards, it is realized that the danger of possible misuse of the Peace Force cannot be *wholly* eliminated any more than every *conceivable* danger of violation of the disarmament process can be eliminated. However, in order to achieve complete national disarmament and genuine peace, *some* risks must be taken. What we have attempted is to reduce these to the very minimum. On the one hand we have sought to provide for a world police so strong as to be capable of preserving peace in any foreseeable contingency. On the other hand, we propose such careful checks and limitations that there would be every possible assurance that the power of this world police would not be misused.

It will be seen that despite all the proposed safeguards this plan calls for a world police that would be a strong and effective fighting force in case of need. The idea of some people that a world peace force somewhat similar as to arms and functions to the United Nations Emergency Force of 1957–1960 might suffice is, we believe, unsound and untenable. Even in a world in which all national military forces were abolished, there would, as above mentioned, necessarily remain internal police forces of substantial strength which would probably need to possess a considerable number of rifles and even a few machine guns. In addition there would remain literally millions of sporting rifles and revolvers in the hands of private persons and thousands of non-military airplanes, large and small. Accordingly, it is conceivable that, even with total disarmament, an aroused nation with a strong grievance could marshal quite a formidable armed force even if no one in it possessed any weapon stronger than a rifle. And while it is true that any such force, even of a million men, could not withstand a well-armed contingent of the world police of even one twentieth its strength, that contingent in order to suppress the aggression promptly and with minimum injury would need to be a genuine fighting force, well equipped and highly disciplined.

Moreover, there would remain a lurking suspicion for some time at least that despite the most efficient world inspection system some nation or nations had contrived to hide or might produce secretly some forbidden weapons. In these circumstances it seems perfectly clear that in order to provide the necessary assurance to obtain general assent to universal and complete disarmament, it will be essential to provide a world police of such strength and armament as to be able *quickly* and *certainly* to prevent or suppress *any* international violence. We firmly believe that on no cheaper terms can universal and complete disarmament be achieved, while it is equally clear that without total disarmament, genuine peace is unattainable. We submit, in short, that a strong and well-armed police force is part of the indispensable price of peace and that the sooner the world faces up to this conclusion the better it will be for all peoples.

IMPROVE POLICY FORMATION

by HERMAN KAHN

Oₙₑ ᴏꜰ ᴍʏ reiterated points is that useful studies can and must be made, and that much light can be shed on many of the problems of national security, by systematic large-scale research. Contrariwise, it should be clear that an important number of these problems would be beyond any individual, even if he had full access to and the cooperation of all the relevant government departments. These problems require an inter-disciplinary team working together over long periods of time. The emphasis here is on the word "team" rather than, for example, "committee." The notion of the inter-disciplinary approach has been so abused that disillusionment with its value has become common. This is particularly true of the form in which it is often utilized—as sort of a part-time committee of equals where the emphasis is on voting rather than on investigation, invention, and integration. The success or failure of such committees not only depends a great deal on the abilities of various individuals to work closely together on a voluntary basis (a quality not too common in the academic field), but fundamentally on the problem's being intrinsically simple and all information being available. (The only thing lacking might be one man who has familiarity with all aspects of the problem.)

What I have in mind, however, is something quite different. I am thinking of an organization in which it is possible to organize temporary teams, perhaps for three weeks to three years, that would have one and not over two project leaders on whom the responsibility for the quality of the study is firmly saddled. These project leaders should have the authority and a capability to call on a wide range of full- and part-time help in addition to their team members. The skills of the team plus the full-time help ought to cover all the important disciplines that affect the study. They need to be supplemented by frequent use of consultants, partly with the idea of playing experts against each other and partly with the idea of getting all the information that is available. (The notion of playing experts against each other may strike some as rather crude, but experience has shown that it is unwise and even dangerous to accept verbatim the opinions of a single expert.)

Another important characteristic such a project must have is flexibility, a willingness to shift points of view and techniques and even major objectives. This means a willingness to discard months or even years of work if the study discloses that past approaches were inappropriate. It means an atmosphere in which this discarding is almost penalty-free. (The step might even be encouraged!) It also means the ability on the part of the project leader to get new people on the team as needed and release some of the other members when they are not needed. All of this implies that the project has to be a small part of a large organization whose existence does not depend on the success of any single project and from which people can be drawn and to which people can be released rather easily. To maintain the project's quality, the environment should also include responsible "loyal and disloyal" critics, as well as advisers and consultants.

Such an environment would require an organization with between one hundred and one thousand staff members. If one combines this with the notion that the project leader must be independent and able to mold the study as he sees fit, I think the statement can fairly be made that no activity such as this now exists on the national level. For example, there is literally no organization working for the national government that could supply the proper staff to document and amplify the three lectures in this book, although there are many organizations working for the three service branches that conceivably could do this job.

The idea of doing such long-range research is not new. It is now conventional for the military to plan five, ten, and even fifteen years ahead. This planning or analysis is done in detail when possible, in broad brush when it is not. The plans or views that are developed must often be scrapped as the uncertain future emerges, but good or bad it is at least essential to do the analysis. Even a poor analysis is better than none not only because the analysis itself is educational, but because it is better for an agency to have an explicit set of views as to what its functions, responsibilities, problems, and environment are going to be than to have nothing at all for internal and external critics and collaborators to judge and to react against, and with which alternative proposals and views can be compared.

The military use a number of techniques and agencies for their basic planning and analysis. While many of these have not lived up to their expectations, in almost all cases people feel that the cure comes from more and better rather than from less—at least on those problems for which over-all planning seems appropriate. There has been some criticism, almost certainly justified, that planning, and analysis is sometimes confused with an attempt to achieve an impossible degree of coordination and detailed prediction, resulting in a stifling of ideas and an undue complexity in projects, but the need for long-range analysis of the proper sort is not disputed.

Aside from the three services, about the only other place which carries on such analysis is the Office of Secretary of Defense. However, most of those in OSD who are actually spending much time on long-range problems are located in such agencies as Weapons Systems Evaluation Group, Research and Engineering, Advanced Research Projects Agency, and so on. Because of their location, their attention is often restricted to relatively parochial subjects and almost always directed to the purely "hardware" aspects of the future; they do not engage in truly "national" studies. Actually, the three services do much more long-range thinking than OSD. Each of the services has "loyal" operations analysis groups, such as the Headquarters Operations Analysis Group in the Air Force and the Operations Evaluation Group in the Navy. In addition, the Army and the Air Force also have large, competent, and influential scientific advisory boards that have direct access to the corresponding chief of staff. These boards have permanent secretariats and civilian and military directors. They are composed of both "hard" and "soft" scientists from outside the government who spend a good deal of time in evaluating current and future trends and in suggesting new ideas. All of these are in addition to numerous committees and staffs, both military and civilian, that try to plan ahead.

In spite of the elaborate in-house capabilities, the Army and Air Force still contract out with private agencies to do the special kind of long-range planning and the analyses that we have been discussing. The Army's contracts are with the Operations Research Office (Johns Hopkins), Stanford Research Institute, and others. The Air Force contracts are with The RAND Corporation, Anser, Institute of Air Weapons Research, Mitre Corporation, and others.

The RAND Corporation, with which I have been for some years, is the largest and possibly the most prestigious of these organizations. It has over 900 employees, approximately two-thirds of whom have technical backgrounds. Its Air Force budget runs to some $13,000,000 annually. In spite of its size and expense the RAND Corporation has no formal staff responsibilities. Only a small percentage of the studies undertaken at the organization are created "to order" and must meet deadlines imposed from outside. In essence, RAND researchers have access to every level and every part of the Air Force, yet nobody has to act on their advice and they do not (usually) have to research exactly what outsiders think they want at the moment. RAND's Military Advisory Group is formally charged with the duty of advising the Air Staff on how best to make use of the resources of talent in the corporation.

It was a great shock to me to discover that there is very little comparable activity on the civilian side of the federal government (or in the military or civilian side of allied and neutral governments). In fact, it might be fair to say that there is no full-time, independent planning or analysis of the larger problems. There are frequent committees, which sometimes perform a valuable service, but their charter only runs for a few months. They generally serve only as a filter and clearinghouse for already existing ideas; rarely if ever do they add to our intellectual capital. Equally important, the committees just write their reports and then disband; therefore, in the important sense of not being responsible for defending their recommendations in detail or advising on implementation, they can justly be charged with being "irresponsible" or at least "unresponsible." In any case, they are under no pressure to supply adequate documentation or to differentiate between judgment and analysis. As a result, important issues are sometimes decided or analyzed on an almost "frivolous" basis.

The permanent staffs, almost without exception, have their time taken up by the day-to-day jobs of administration, coordination, and liaison, and by the annual budget and other crises. This over-concern with immediate problems is true of the current National Security Council organization. In any case, the more complicated problems cannot be handled either by individuals or by part-time intragovernmental committees, even if they were to have the time and talent. Every study with which I am familiar that has resulted in new views or the production of orienting "philosophy" has taken more than two years to complete and has required a team of disciplined and interested technical and nontechnical people. In fact, I have found that operations analysis organizations with hundreds of members, many of them of almost extraordinary competence, are just able, working full-time, to keep abreast of current military developments; only rarely do they successfully initiate detailed long-range planning. In these relatively few successful studies it was also necessary to have, in addition to the team members, access to competing expert consultants who took an interest in the project and were not bound by special loyalties. It should be clear that even the talented individual in or out of government will have difficulty in doing an equivalent project on his own.

I am not trying to say that the above approach automatically produces acceptable work; often it does not, and I have written elsewhere on some of the reasons why it does not. I am saying that there does not seem to be any other environment than that supplied by the relatively large independent planning organization in which it is possible even to hope to treat certain complicated problems with any completeness—problems that must be treated if we are to try to anticipate events and supply our decision makers with the basic knowledge they have to have.

It seems to me of the highest importance that we create a National Security Research Organization whose major purpose will be to house large study projects. Such an organization could do many things, any one of which might have a large enough impact to easily justify its existence, but its *raison d'être* should be the large study.

Let us now consider some of the other functions of such an organization. First, it could house independent scholars, technicians, and experts who are working by themselves on either narrow problems or the most global aspects of world affairs. It could only help both the independent work and the in-house projects to have systematic interaction, advice, and criticism. Second, the NSRO could do a certain amount of what I would call loyal analysis for the government—that is, analysis to the order of some governmental agency.

Such agency work would increase the prestige of the organization because this agency would be more likely to appreciate the skills and techniques of the organization and would also tend to identify itself with the organization. This, in turn, would make more palatable the organization's independence—even to those officials who are dubious about long-range and large-scope studies that might cut across bureaucratic lines. It should be clear, however, that doing loyal studies or analyses to order must always be kept a secondary function, even if this can only be done by occasionally antagonizing senior government officials and departments whose pet projects have been turned down. This is necessary to protect not only the intellectual independence of the organization, but its resources as well.

In practice it is difficult to prevent demands on the time and resources of such an organization from becoming inordinate—in fact, it is clear that the better the organization is, the more demands will be made and the more difficult it will be to protect the independent scholarship and free study that are important parts of its activities.

The NSRO could also act as a high-level training center for selected people in and out of the government through formal lectures, short or long courses, or, better, by having people actually spend a year or two with the organization either as working members, or with some liaison assignments relevant to their previous work. If this were done, the organization could diffuse a larger and more expert point of view toward crucial questions in all parts of the government and academic worlds. It might even be desirable to have "trainees" from the "outside" world—that is, the political, business, and professional worlds.

In addition, NSRO might spawn new organizations to handle specialized tasks of various sorts. The most natural way that this would occur would be when a project became permanent and large. It would then be transferred to another organization or a new organization would be set up; probably with some transfer of personnel. The original organization, of course, would not normally undertake such large permanent obligations, particularly if they involved operating responsibilities. Otherwise, we would have the familiar problem of the tail wagging the dog.

NSRO could act in lieu of or as a supplement to an in-house staff for any department of the government—but always on a restricted and temporary basis. Doing this would create two familiar problems. First, the personnel involved would tend to lose their independence and would not be able to serve the department in the way we originally conceived. Second, if the organization had easy access to decision makers, it might be forced to give up some of its informality and independence. For NSRO to do its work, its staff would have to be allowed the freedom to make mistakes and blunders. But no responsible organization could allow that much freedom to its employees if they were regularly influencing major decisions. It would have to monitor, regulate, and referee the work much more closely, which in turn would stifle the mechanisms on which we would be depending for the major product.

No one should be required to coordinate with the long-range planning organization, although their comments on a restricted number of staff papers may be requested. In particular, the organization should not be required to give opinions on all important issues. It is absolutely necessary for the staff of this agency to be able individually and collectively to suspend judgment or even to withdraw into academic isolation on issues on which it does not feel competent.

The staff itself must be the final judge of what it considers to be subject to research. While it should generally set itself the widest practical goals, the qualification "practical" is an important one. For example, the organization might well try to study the impact on consumers, taxpayers, and the general price level of trying to get a six percent annual increase in GNP, but it could scarcely come up with a conclusion that the sacrifices and risks are or are not worthwhile. It can only describe them. To give another example, it can try to decide whether giving our overseas allies IRBMs will really give them an independent nuclear deterrent, but the problem of whether it would be *desirable* to give them an independent nuclear deterrent may not be as researchable, though the staff could clearly make relevant comments on this issue.

To summarize, such an organization has many needs that are hard to supply—financial stability, flexible hiring policies, and incredibly elastic working conditions; access to all kinds of proprietary and secret information; independence of individual projects to the point where it is almost the rule that many project leaders will make fools of themselves; protection against crash programs and too many urgent requests for help; and so on. There are also some things it does *not* need—immediate and sympathetic access to the highest levels of policy-making, for example.

While it is often desirable to have the researchers present their ideas directly, it is usually helpful rather than harmful to let them do a little fighting to get them presented. Regular governmental staffs should have all the opportunity they need for review and criticism of studies before they go to the top levels. In addition, to the extent that they wish, these staffs should be allowed and encouraged to incorporate ideas in their own programs on the staff and working level rather than have the suggestions come down from on high. This sometimes leads to morale problems with those of the original researchers who come from an academic tradition in which each man owns and presents his own ideas, but a sympathetic and knowledgeable management should have no trouble in handling these problems.

Some desirable characteristics that NSRO should have (some of which have already been mentioned) include:

1. It should not be monolithic. All reports, except for formal organizational recommendations, should be signed by the researchers themselves. There should be review within the organization, but if an author insists on being in error, he should have the

privilege. Others should have the corresponding privilege of objecting or of amplifying by including signed notes, marginalia, and appendices in any controversial reports.

2. It should be allowed to fund its obligations as it goes along, so that it can, for example, make what amounts to tenure appointments. If possible, funds appropriated for special studies should be given on a "No year" basis.

3. In order to allow it to establish close working relations with government and with private organizations, it should be allowed to send and receive liaison people, transfer money, give and take dollar-a-year contracts, certify a "need-to-know" for its employees, consultants, and liaison personnel, and so on.

4. It should be allowed to subcontract work to private and public agencies for research, development, and analysis. So long as the contract is small, say less than $100,000, no question of duplication of an existing agency's function should be allowed to arise.

5. It should have some mechanism for setting up independent organizations to take over desirable projects, especially those which start small but later become too large to keep conveniently within the organizational setup. Giving birth to new organizations should be one of its major functions.

6. It should be allowed to receive proprietary and sensitive information which it will not divulge to anyone without the written permission of the supplier of the information.

7. NSRO should be a quasi-independent organization with a Congressional charter, an endowment sufficient to enable it to live partly off the income, and the right to request annual or special appropriations. Its director and most of its trustees or policy-making officials should not be members of government; however, the Executive Branch should be represented on its board of trustees. It should be affiliated with and responsive to the Executive Office of the President and should be a research arm of the National Policy Planning Staff already described. While the bulk of its work should be self-generated, some of its projects would come from the Executive Office in the form of suggestions or assignments from the President, the National Security Council, the National Policy Planning Staff, or other Executive Office elements concerned with national policy.

8. The sphere of interest of NSRO would be primarily in national security affairs. However, this concept should include the study of domestic programs and policies having impact on national security. Its sphere of interest should include the social as well as the physical sciences; indeed, problems in the political-military-economic field are as important as, and perhaps knottier than, those in the technological and scientific areas.

The following are suggested as illustrative of the kinds of areas that might be examined:

    a. All aspects of arms control.

    b. Policy implications of the arms race and technological progress.

    c. Long-range policy with respect to the communist bloc.

    d. A viable strategy for NATO in the nuclear age.

    e. Aid to underdeveloped nations.

    f. Cultural penetration as an instrument of U.S. foreign policy.

    g. The use of agricultural surpluses in foreign-aid programs.

    h. Prospects and techniques for an effective air defense.

    i. Alternative mixes of offensive weapons systems.

    j. Problems of taxation, inflation, and economic growth and stability.

9. As a supporting element of the Executive Office, NSRO ought to receive the assistance of all other government agencies in obtaining the necessary data, personnel, and access to information. In some instances, particularly in the beginning, Presidential authority may be needed for this purpose; however, as the organization proves itself it may be anticipated that access and assistance will be readily available on the working level. Liaison offices or senior points of contact in the major agencies will facilitate these efforts.

10. The interchanges of information with and the use of personnel from private colleges, institutions, and study groups at home and abroad should be a matter of routine. Only by such interchanges can NSRO keep abreast of what is being done outside the government and tap the talents and the energies of individuals serving in private capacities, without disrupting the work of the institutions to which they belong. It might be well to establish a

permanent contractual arrangement with selected universities and institutions so that they can have a voice in the direction of effort and could coordinate the use of their resources in support of NSRO. Whatever method is used, it can only help NSRO to carry out its assigned responsibilities if it serves as a link between governmental and nongovernmental activities.

An important element of this link would be a liberal policy for the open publication of material. This can also serve as a means of disseminating information and of arousing public interest and concern with the problems facing government. While many of the studies that NSRO undertakes (especially those requested by the Office of the President) will be of a classified nature, every effort should be made to publish as much of the material as possible, subject only to normal security clearances and to a liberal interpretation of the client relationship that NSRO will have with the Office of the President. In particular, material which dissents from approved programs and policies should not be restricted routinely on that basis alone.

In order to stimulate thinking about the organization, I would like to close this chapter with some specific organizational suggestions, presenting items without much discussion. They are offered to give the reader an idea of what the organizational structure might be.

A. Board of Trustees (BOT)
1. Composition: six from academic or professional life, six from "public affairs," three from industry, three from governmental or political life, three from its organizational management.
2. Self-perpetuating, but the President or Congress might have veto rights.
3. Should have enough salary to justify part-time participation in the corporation's affairs.
4. Full semiannual meetings and more frequent meetings of subcommittees.
5. Mediates between NSRO and EAG (Executive Advisory Group, described later).
6. Mediates between Management Committee and NABS's Director.

      7. Reviews programs.

      8. Makes basic decisions.

      9. Handles all the normal functions of a board of trustees.

B. Executive Advisory Group

      1. May be required by statute or just by contract.

      2. Should have about twenty-five full members, about fifty auditors.

      3. Allocation of full members: headed by President's Assistant for National Security Affairs, two from OCDM, two from DOD, three from the services (one from each), two from the State Department, eight from other members of the cabinet, one from FRB, one from AEC, one from NASA, one from BOB, one from NAS, one from CIA, one from CEA, one from Vice-President's office.

      4. Each full member is allowed to bring one auditor to meetings. In addition, auditors should be invited from such other agencies as seem appropriate.

      5. Should have full-time secretariat whose head (and maybe sole member) is on NSC Planning Board and is chosen by the President's Assistant for National Security.

      6. Should have the right to suggest specific studies. In case of controversy, the trustees should mediate.

      7. Major functions:

        a. Advises government on how to use NSRO;

        b. Hears formal briefings from NSRO about once or twice a year;

        c. Provides two-way channel for information and flow of ideas;

        d. Formally advises trustees of their evaluation of how NSRO is functioning;

        e. Advises on level of NSRO budget and any basic changes in function;

        f. Mediates between Legislative Advisory Group and the Executive Advisory Group or NSRO;

        g. Determines which of the briefings the Legislative Advisory Group is to hear;

        h. Advises other executive agencies to hear briefings and sometimes asks these other agencies to take a formal position on these briefings.

C. Legislative Advisory Group
   1. May be statutory or just "courtesy."
   2. Full members are appointed by Majority and Minority Leaders of Congress.
   3. Auditor members should include Congressional staff.
   4. Has no normative or regulatory functions.
   5. Has full-time secretariat, hired by NSRO or some part of Executive Office. This should reduce the problem of unauthorized leaks to members of Congress or their staffs.
   6. The secretariat and Legislative Advisory Group briefings should provide the major channel through which information is fed to Congress. Unlike the Executive agencies, Congressional staffs should not have direct working relations with NSRO, although authorized information-gathering would be encouraged.
   7. Specific requests for studies or sensitive information by members of Congress should be discouraged, although not forbidden. Possibly these should be filtered through the Executive Advisory Group. There should be at least informal liaison with the Legislative Reference Service of the Library of Congress.
D. Internal Organization of NSRO
   1. Possibly six semi-independent functional divisions:
      a. Technology;
      b. Social Science (including foreign policy, economics, geography, and history);
      c. Physical Science (including mathematics);
      d. Strategic Analysis (coordinates research in strategy and tries to furnish leadership for certain kinds of projects);
      e. Operations (studies costs, operations, legal questions, administrative efficiency, etc.);
      f. Services (security, guards, publications, personnel, etc.).
   2. The heads of the divisions shall form a management committee to advise the Director on fundamental policies. In case of disagreement, the Director can choose to have his own views prevail, but the trustees shall then be informed of the dispute and its disposition.
   3. While each division will be allowed (within its budgetary limits) to hire consultants and employees with skills that

would naturally lie in another division, the excessive use of this privilege should be discouraged.

4. Projects should normally be organized across divisional lines. Project leaders can come from any of the divisions.

The reason for suggesting three such groups as the Board of Trustees, the Executive Advisory Group, and the Legislative Advisory Group is that while the NSRO will be formally a creature of the Executive, one would like it to have a semi-independent existence and exert part of its influence by educating senior people in and out of government. I conjecture that the formal structure just suggested could go a great distance in facilitating this activity. We are preparing for large, important, influential, and responsible captive and critical audiences for our findings.

When the NSRO builds up its competency and prestige it could do other things along this line. It might be quite reasonable for the trustees and legislative advisers, in particular, to play a rather special role in trying to raise the general intellectual level of discussion on national security affairs. In addition, the NSRO might issue signed reports in the same way the National Academy of Sciences, the National Planning Association, or the committee for Economic Development do. Some of these reports to the general public would really be the result of an informed intuition rather than an analysis. While not directly related to studies, such reports could be very useful. These should be signed by members of the Board of Trustees as semipersonal documents. Such reports should, of course, be sharply differentiated from the direct output of the analytical side of the organization.

The eventual hope is to have decision makers so competent and so well informed (a sort of intellectual pressure group for long-range thinking) that we have some of the benefits of an "aristocracy" in treating long-range programs without the well-known disadvantages of aristocracy.

There are many reasons for having independent functional divisions rather than organizing on a project basis. Experience has shown that it is almost impossible to hire really first-rate technical and scientific people except into a division which is a natural professional home. Few good mathematicians, for example, would be willing to tie themselves to a permanent non-mathematical project, but quite a number would join a Math division which looks and acts a great deal like an academic mathematics department, and then work part- or full-time on a number of projects, as their interests and the work load dictate.

I would also like to mention the extreme importance of being able to organize new projects easily and being able to release to a pool people no longer needed. A functional organization is very suitable for this purpose.

The reason we are having a special strategic analysis division in which we could put many of the senior project leaders has to do partly with the extreme desirability of having such people working closely together (in the sense of interaction and information rather than coordination) and partly for preventing a stratification and a hardening in the informal organizational structure by breaking up some of the lines from project leaders to team. Experience has shown that first-rate project leaders tend to be very competitive as individuals. If left in their separate divisions there is a tendency for them to try to hoard the resources most easily available to them, and not to make available to project leaders in other divisions the resources that they may need. The competition also tends to lead to a lack of communication and cooperation between project leaders in different divisions. I believe that putting the senior people in a single division and having them report to a single head should help overcome all these possible drawbacks. Lastly, the breaking up of some of the authority lines which were established when these project leaders were in divisions is important to give young people a chance to grow.

V

Education

We can envision the time of universal individualized education, when every person will be educated and no two will be educated alike, when teachers deeply committed to the art of teaching and thoroughly versed in the science of learning will have at their disposal a full panoply of learning materials to which they will direct each individual student in accordance with his needs, abilities, and interests. There will be no lockstep and no common schedule. Each student will proceed at his own pace through a curriculum uniquely adjusted to his needs.
—NORMAN D. KURLAND, *at a conference* (1968)

ON EDUCATION

by DON FABUN

Says Francis Keppel, once U.S. Commissioner of Education and now chairman of General Learning Corp., in his book, *The Necessary Revolution in American Education*, "The first revolution in American education was a revolution in *quantity*. Everyone was to be provided the chance for an education of some sort. That revolution is almost won in the schools and is on its way in higher education. The second revolution is *equality* of opportunity. That revolution is under way. The next turn of the wheel must be a revolution in *quality*." And it is to the question of quality that we will now turn, for if education fails to prepare people for the kind of world in which they will be living as adults, it will have failed of its purpose, no matter how many millions of people happen to get through school.

We are, in the main, a quantitative society, and questions of quality not only bother us, but frequently are not asked, or, if asked, not answered. When it comes to the question of quality in education, one of the ways of answering it is to ask, "What is the purpose of education?"

In America, the first aim of education was to prepare children to read the Scripture and its intent was religious. Later on the purpose was enable people to read and write, and thus participate in a democratic process which required an understanding of the issues and candidates involved. Still later, the purpose increasingly became to prepare young people for jobs in an industrialized society. At no time was the aim of education to prepare students to become individuals or complete human beings. This aspect of education was left to the home, church, mass media, and the city streets. To a certain large extent, it still remains there. Yet in a

Reprinted from *Kaiser Aluminum News,* © 1967, Kaiser Aluminum & Chemical Corporation. By permission of the author.

society that can easily be foreseen, one in which cybernation and mechanization will minimize the human factor in industrial production, the purpose of education must once again change. It must begin to educate people to live full and meaningful lives in which "jobs" are at best only incidental; or at least for jobs that are oriented toward human service rather than physical productivity.

Throughout the changes in American education, certain constants have remained and only quite recently have they begun to change. These constants are pretty much the same regardless of the size and grade of the institution. The most pervasive (and unexamined) is the teacher-pupil relationship. In this an older person imparts to a younger person (or a less "educated" person) the cultural wisdom or the skills which the teacher has learned. This is the pattern of education in even the most primitive societies, and it presupposes a constancy of environment in which the cultural inheritance that is passed on is still pertinent. There are some serious questions whether most of the cultural inheritance of America's past is any longer relevant to the future in which the child will live as an adult.

What is created is an authoritarian figure in the teacher and a subordinate figure in the student. This role-playing usually carries over into adult life, where fear of the authoritarian figure—whether politician, "boss," or "expert"—often expresses itself as the antithesis of "consent of the governed."

"Education has not yet caught up with the fact that the educational pattern of the past, in which it was assumed that the old know and the young must learn, is no longer valid," says Robert Theobald. "We are teaching young people to respect authority at a time when authority is no longer possible, and when we ought to be struggling together to understand the world in which we live. We still say to them, *listen and learn,* rather than *strive with us.*" And, certainly, it is possible to contemplate an educational system in which teachers and students are engaged in a common enterprise in which they participate with equal interest and equal respect for each other.

Another constant of the educational system is what has been called its "regurgitative" aspect. Here the student is fed "facts" and, on request, is supposed to repeat them back. What this has to do with learning is a little difficult to see, particularly in an age where the facts are easily available in books or on film and tape. Actually, the "rote" method goes back to the days when stored sources of information were few and far between. One can imagine a system of education that teaches students the techniques for fact-finding, without cluttering up their minds with facts that can be found in any branch library.

Other outmoded accouterments of the educational system are classes—in the sense that children of a certain age level are grouped together (as if everyone of the same age learned at nearly the same rate)—and the grading system, in which some quantitative measure is applied to the individual student's performance and compared to similar quantitative judgments concerning other students.

There is nothing in either learning theory or actual experience that supports the view that students of the same age should be herded together. Learning rates differ from student to student of the same age, and with the same student, from subject to subject. The ungraded, non-class school is already becoming more common in the American educational scene. In such schools, the student moves along "tracks" determined by his own learning ability and interest; spending perhaps more time in third-grade arithmetic (because he is "not good at figures") and participating in a tenth grade English composition class (because he has a flair for writing).

As far as the quantitative assignment of grades is concerned, there is some serious question whether they are necessary at all. As the grade system has traditionally been used in the past, each student is pitted against the other. Yet in the "real" world in which he will live as an adult, his most important ability will be his willingness and skill in working cooperatively with others. This is particularly true in the business world, which is predominantly a cooperative enterprise and not a competitive one. No automobile ever got designed, engineered, produced, and distributed without the cooperation of literally thousands of people. Competition occurs only in the ultimate market place.

One can conceive of an educational system in which each member of the class endeavors to help the others in a common enterprise, which is the learning process and development of attitudes toward learning. In such classes the entire group would be graded on the performance of the weakest members, and if the class desires to achieve "good grades" then it becomes incumbent on the able and knowledgeable to bring the performance of the slowest member up to their level.

Finally, in discussing age-old methods of operating that turn out an individual who enters adult life with ingrained aggressiveness toward his fellow man (an attitude which fits badly into the teamwork concept of modern business operations), there is the larger problem of the fragmentation of knowledge. This comes about through at least three major mechanisms, all of them anachronistic. The first is the fragmentation of time; the second the fragmentation of space; and the third is the fragmentation of "disciplines." The three forces act together to produce a fragmented man who, for the rest of life, will find it difficult to relate to the flow and process of living, and who tends to become a frozen layer cake of unresolved conflicts between the various disciplines he has learned and failed to learn. In later years, these people dominate the power structure of business, industry and government: still specialists, still fragmented, still using but a fraction of their individual ability. Such a system turns out "specialists" who have great competence in some special field, such as the law, accounting, business management, personnel administration, etc., but who must be classified as functional illiterates in most other fields. Such a system seldom turns out "generalists" whose thinking covers a broad spectrum of human activity. And it is precisely the generalist who is most needed to run today's increasingly complex and interwoven business structure.

The fragmentation of school time has many aspects, but can rather easily be grouped into three major categories, all of them anachronisms in late twentieth-century America. The first of these is the year at which formal education begins. Typically in this country it is the age of five or six, and this develops not from the learning capacity of children, but from the days when schools were few and far apart, transportation was inadequate, and the child was kept home until he was big enough to walk to the schoolhouse. Nevertheless, there are adequate demonstration and research projects that prove that the child of two or three is quite ready for instruction. The tragedy of the late start is that by the time the student enters school, he has used up nearly all of the first seven years, believed to be the formative years of his life.

Charles E. Silberman in *Fortune* (April 1961) reports that "Professor O. K. Moore of Yale has shown that even two- and three-year-olds of average intelligence can learn to read, write and type. Public schools have been wasting valuable years by postponing the teaching of many important subjects on the grounds that they are too difficult."

Francis Keppel says, "In some schools two- and three-year-olds were being taught to read and write, first graders were being asked to deal with the fundamentals of economics and algebra; second and third graders were encouraged to discover set theory in mathematics; junior-high-school students explored anthropological concepts and high-school students studied physics and literature in courses formerly taught only in college." Sloan Wayland reports that normal children can make up the first six or seven years with a few months of good teaching. (Reported by Paul Goodman in *The School Dropout*, National Education Association, 1964.)

In short, the learning process could begin much earlier in life for most normal students, bringing them to the college level at the age of twelve to fourteen, with considerable savings in educational expenditure, and giving the student himself a longer period for post-graduate study in his field of specialization before he reaches the difficult age of establishing a family and a home, or committing himself to a particular kind of job. This, in turn, would provide business, industry and government with a better educated prospective employee at an age where on-the-job training programs would be more effective.

Two other anachronisms that haunt today's educational process also relate to our agrarian past. The typical school day may run from 8:30 to 3:30. This is to allow Johnny to do the morning chores before leaving for school, and to get back home in the afternoon in time to bring in the firewood, slop the pigs, round up the cows, and bring in water for the early evening supper (since there was no electric light), before dark. Johnny these days performs none of these chores in the typical urban home; but he does have a long time to "kill" between school and dinnertime. A longer school day would appear to hasten the educational process and help solve some problems of juvenile delinquency.

The other anachronism concerns the school year. Typically students begin their school year in September and conclude it in June, with a three-month hiatus, originally designed so that Johnny could help on the farm during the important part of the growing season. This consideration has little relevance to the urban child, who finds, instead, three months with not much to do.

An educational system that began earlier in life, during the "fast learning" years, that used longer days in school attendance, and operated the year round (on a trimester or four-quarter system) would appear to have the promise of occupying more of the child's time with useful activity and bringing him to the graduate-school level much earlier in his life where the high degree of specialization and technological proficiency required in today's world would have ample time to develop.

One other aspect of the use of time, as it relates to "fragmentation," is the breaking down of the school day into hours devoted to separate subjects. There is a belief, with little or no support from learning theory, that a child learns faster when exposed to small increments over a period of time, rather than intensive training in a single subject over a sustained period. Why, if there are to be five subjects, is not each taught intensively one subject each school day; or for one week at a crack?

Nor is there any reason why a subject should take standard sixty-minute periods. Robert E. Jenkins, superintendent of schools for San Francisco, has suggested (San Francisco *Chronicle*, November 18, 1966) that in the future "class lengths through the day may vary from 20 minutes to perhaps 60. Not all lessons or subject areas require the same amount of time for all students. Flexible scheduling and short time modules (of 20 minutes) are opening new areas for improving instruction."

Closely allied with the use of time in the fragmentation of the student (and therefore of the adult he will become) is the use of space. Little can be said here about school design and architecture, except that for the most part it is an anachronism that stems from memories of the little red schoolhouse and the concept that education somehow must take place in a structured environment in which a teacher imparts "knowledge" to a class of students. Most school architecture, then, is based on putting together a group of little red schoolhouses.

"The school composed chiefly of classrooms is obsolete," declares Francis S. Chase of the University of Chicago. "In schools of the future, upwards of one half of the student's time may be spent in the library, in science laboratories, or in other workrooms where he can search for knowledge, analyze data, reflect upon the ideas which he is encountering, and put his conclusions in writing." A system of little boxes does not provide this kind of work area; it does help to preserve the isolation of one field of instruction from another, and to reinforce the fragmentation effect of the use of the student's time. This compartmentalization of knowledge, implemented by an anachronistic school architecture, usually gives off as its end product fragmented specialists who may know accounting or medicine very well, but very little about anything else.

One wonders what the effect would be of a single large structure (such as the successful Granada elementary school in California) in which there are no partitions and students (as well as teachers) move freely from one learning group to another, according to their individual interest or need. Such structures, properly designed, can also serve as recreation halls, community centers, auditoriums and cafeterias, thus eliminating the monolithic single-purpose structures that are such a large part of the total educational facilities investment.

With the tremendous investment that American business has, both indirectly and directly, in the financing of the education system and with its total dependence on the quality of persons who will ultimately become its management, its employees, and its customers, it would seem that a closer interest in how school time and school facilities are used would be in order. Business and industry also have an important stake in the *quality* of that education, and for that reason must take a deeper interest in the many transformations that, starting in the late of 1950's, are beginning to take place in the educational system.

DIVERSITY IN EDUCATION

by JOHN R. PLATT

THE AREA where there is perhaps the greatest need of all for more diversity today is the area of education. Students nowadays can hardly realize how much the alternatives available to them have been closed up by the zealous professionalism of the professors in the last 30 years. In the 1930s the colleges knew they had been liberalized by John Dewey and they offered what is now sneered at as a "cafeteria system" of education. Yet what an enriched program it permitted us! When I was an undergraduate physics major at Northwestern University I not only took physics and math courses but I had time for electives that included two years of French and three years of German (Goethe and Schiller), plus astronomy, economics, philosophy, public speaking, music, and a seminar on the origins of war.

Our present survey courses are more thorough and systematic but not so well tailored to each individual's curiosity and enthusiasm. Many colleges have pushed electives almost out of the curriculum, in favor of so-called "honors programs." All too often these should be called "narrows programs," for what they make is one-dimensional men.

It particularly worries me that physics and chemistry majors and other science majors have now lost most of their free electives. Scientists are now rising to executive positions in business and industry and are becoming advisers on major international and military matters. About one-third of all physicists eventually become administrators. I do not want—and I do not think any sane person wants—a world in which the major decisions on technology and military and international affairs are made by

Reprinted from *Science*, Vol. 154, pp. 1132–1133, 2 December 1966. Copyright 1966 by the American Association for the Advancement of Science. By permission of the publisher and the author.

one-dimensional men, men who have never had time to explore art or music or history or philosophy or literature or the nontechcal achievements of mankind!

The only thing that saves us is the fact that the good students learn many things outside the curriculum. I think that in many cases the reputation of the hard-driving schools, both the high schools and the colleges, is not due to the courses or the staff at all, but is due to the quality of the students they are able to get. If you have hotshots, it makes little difference what you teach them—or whether you teach them at all; they will find out from each other (as the whole human race did!) how to be great contributors to society. The importance of this initial student selection factor has never been sorted out in assessing our schools. Many a school has good graduates not because its education is good but because its students were good when they came in and have not been much damaged.

Even so, the hotshot dimension is not the only one to be emphasized. Why should we assume or insist that our students have only one important coordinate of variation? This is the fallacy of exams and IQ tests. Yes, I want those fast-growing pines, but I also want rose bushes in my classes, and persevering oaks. It is good that Jacob Getzels and Philip Jackson and others have emphasized recently that there is a dimension of "creativity" in students that has little relation to IQ. How many other such dimensions of achievement are still to be explored?

We do not even allow for the physiological variations in students. Students, like professors, are not all wakeful or sleepy at the same time. We often start by trying to teach them things when they—and we—are half-asleep; and then we try to get them to go to sleep when they are wide awake. Would it be impossible to have classes at one time of day for the skylarks and at another time for nightingales? Even professors might like it. Some of the world's greatest leaders napped in the daytime and worked around the clock. Classes in the evening might lead to the best discussions of all if you could sleep in the morning. I have never understood why these possibilities are not seriously examined by educators, who are supposed to know something about the psychology and physiology of learning.

While we are speaking of the right to physiological diversity, let us not forget the right of some of the students to be women. It is easy to show that prejudices and handicaps to women's education still abound. Fathers send sons to college, rather than daughters; and not only fathers but deans will cut off a college girl's financial support if she gets married, where they would not cut off a boy's. I have known professors in several departments who refused to take girls as graduate students on the grounds that they would probably get married and not use the education. The "nepotism rules" of many schools result in failure to hire good women teachers if they have the misfortune to be married to good men teachers, so the image of the woman intellectual that the student sees is almost always that of a woman who has renounced marriage. One great university lost a great woman scientist in this way, through refusing to pay her a salary separate from her husband's—until she became famous.

What is worse, however, is the fact that the colleges and counselors do nothing to combat the double standard of the college men, who may learn far-out things in biology or anthropology but are never shaken out of their conventional station-wagon images of what marriage should be. They go on assuming that the college wife, or the graduate-student wife, is the one who shops and cooks and cleans, even if she is carrying courses and trying to do equal work. The result of this conventional image—which the girls have often picked up as well as the men—is that American women are concentrating on conventional and subordinate jobs and that, compared to women of other countries, they are making fewer and fewer contributions to our national life, either as educators or editors or scientists or doctors or lawyers or judges or legislators or political leaders. We are only getting half-power out of our educated and intellectual women, and it impoverishes us all.

To come back to the narrowing pressures on student life in general, I think it is not at all clear that the intellectual and economic pressures on students today are either good education or good economics. Students are probably the most overworked and underpaid class in our society. Their training has now been shown by many studies to be the most important element in the economic development and prosperity of a country, and yet they are not paid as well as their brothers who became plumbers' apprentices. The 18-year-old brother or sister who works in a factory or a store gets off at five o'clock and has enough income to have an apartment and a car and books and records and recreation and a paid vacation. He can have guests in and can come in or go out at any hour. But the student is treated, not like his brothers or parents or teachers, but like a monk with a vow of poverty, austerity, and overwork—a vow which is not even his own vow but has been taken for him. He often works until midnight or later at subjects his brothers might never master, and he is supposed to get money from his family, or borrow it, or be grateful for a fellowship that still leaves him below the poverty level. He is frequently locked in at night and forbidden to have a car or an apartment, and has little money for his own books or for good meals or concerts. He is given cafeteria fare in cinder-block buildings and never learns to live like a human being. It is an affluent-society parody of medieval monasticism, with the universities—the primary sources of new economic development today—treated as priestly beggars, and with the professors themselves, who have grown up in the system, approving this treatment of the students and feeling, always, that they have too much money and do not work hard enough.

It is an odd four-year gap in our economic scheme. Students are overworked and underpaid undoubtedly because they are the only group in our society who are too old for child-labor laws to protect them and too young to have the support of a union or of professional-market competition—as their parents and their professors have—to help them get more civilized hours and treatment.

And, oh, how long are those hours that we are forcing on ambitious students in good high schools and colleges today! You professors who have measured the rates of learning, have you measured the optimum number of hours for intellectual work? Do they agree with the standard homework assignment? It is estimated that a medical student is expected to learn 30,000 bits of information in his first year, or 100 bits per day, if he obeys every demand of the instructors. Is it actually possible to learn at this rate, or does this not simply overload the brain and block any real organization of the material? No wonder the dropout and failure rates are high. No wonder the suicide rate is high.

Men do not become wise and full by studying 14 hours a day, or 10 hours a day, or possibly even eight hours a day. This is not education for the good life or the good society. There is a limit to human capacity to pack in new knowledge just as there is a limit to the capacity of a stuffed goose. The limit may be no more than a few hours before we need a change of pace for the rest of the day—a period of exercise or recreation or idleness, eating and chatting—if we are really going to assimilate new information and fit it together.

The trouble is that the faculty itself still thinks this is the only way of education. The student is not taught how to be broad and human because the faculty frequently does not know how to be broad and human. *Nemo dat quod non habet*—No one can give what he does not have. The student is overloaded with information because the professor is overloaded with information, with a piled-up desk and a bulging briefcase. He does not know how to handle it himself, so he passes it on. And many a professor equates education with judgments and grades. I have heard of one man, a kind man in his personal life, who gave out several Fs in a class of 25 undergraduate majors because some students either were not prepared for his three-hour course or were unwilling to spend 20 hours a week on it, and because he had not the perception or the humanity to tell them earlier that they should not be in the course. This little piece of righteousness will cost these unfortunates hundreds of thousands of dollars in lost fellowships and graduate education and potential job opportunities over their lifetimes. In any other line of work, a man who did such a thing could be sued. In a university, he tells his colleagues it shows how poor the students are today, and they cluck sympathetically. Sometimes such men mellow as they mature, but all too often these black-and-white academics only get more and more self-righteous all the way to retirement.

The student comes for teaching and what he gets is grades. We are hypnotized by grades. They seem so exact and discussable. I have seen departments where one-quarter of the teachers' time and energy was spent in making up exams and grading them. If any administration doubts this, let it measure the ratio. This amount of time spent with individual students could have pulled many of them over the borderline; but we prefer to retreat to written questions. It gives us renewed proof that our students are one-dimensional. What Montessori said should be written on every bluebook in letters of fire: "The business of a teacher is to teach, not to judge." The business of a professor is to give, not grades, but intellectual contagion.

Do not misunderstand my criticisms here. I think the academic life can be the most varied and imaginative and interesting life in the world, and I love it. But I am talking about its distortions and about how they narrow it from what it might become. Its great men are so very great and its little men are so little. And it pains me when I see one of those academic men who has deliberately narrowed himself to an intellectual pinpoint and has cut off all that life might be. Emerson must have been thinking of such men when he said: "The state of society is one in which the members have suffered amputation from the trunk, and strut about like so many walking monsters—a good finger, a neck, a stomach, an elbow, but never a man."

The academic world is perhaps no worse in this respect than the world of government or the world of business, but it is sad all the same. The teacher is the one man who most needs to know what it is to be a complete man with wholeness and diversity and humor. When his vision is distorted, the vision of a whole generation may be warped.

I think it is time to say loudly and clearly that the interval of higher education should be an interval of learning to live like cultured human beings instead of like monks and academics. Instead of overload and punishment let us have excitement and leadership. Along with excellence let us enjoy diversity. Let us try to find ways in which students can be given the money and leisure they ought to have as valuable apprentices in an affluent society. Let us bring up a generation of young adults full of the delight of living, interested in many things, and knowing not only how to be intellectual but how to be full and creative men.

I think that this goal I have suggested, of trying to make the college years more humane, more cultured, and more diverse, is just a part of a new educational revolution that will totally change the structure of our schools in the next twenty years. This revolution may be even more thoroughgoing than the revolution that was made by John Dewey and the other reformers seventy years ago, when they swept out the obsolete and stuffy classical education of the nineteenth century and redefined the goals of education as education for society and education for living.

Today our education has indeed become an excellent education for our society, so far as its professional content is concerned, but it is still obsolete and clumsy in its teaching methods. Since World War II, a revolution has occurred in information and communication and in our knowledge of the biology and psychology of the brain and the psychology of learning. It is beginning to be urgent for us to adapt our educational system to take account of these advances. Mass education up until now has been hard and punitive, with more of the stick than of the carrot. It has been hardest and most punitive in the colleges, where many departments and schools are actually proud to have standards so strict that they flunk one-third of their freshmen.

But it is now possible to move away from this traditional pattern. It has become clear that the psychology of positive reinforcement, of encouraged curiosity and reward, works much better than the psychology of negative reinforcement, as great teachers have always known. It is time to try out on a large scale the new discoveries and methods of this new educational psychology, discoveries such as the remarkable effect of early enrichment at ages one to four, and methods such as use of the new phonetic alphabets and the programmed learning and teaching machines and programmed texts that promise to make spelling and geography and physics and anatomy and many other subjects easier and more quickly mastered.

The new ideas have already made a revolution across the nation in the teaching of high-school science courses, and efforts are well under way to create science programs with the same exciting immediacy all the way down to the kindergarten level. In fact it now appears that the whole difficulty with many subjects is that we have been teaching them too late. A seven-year-old can learn reading and writing more easily than an eighteen-year-old can, and we are now finding that he may also learn about sets and binary arithmetic and rates-of-change and the difference between mass and weight more easily than many college sophomores.

The difficulty today is that these remarkable new methods have not yet been drawn together into a unified educational approach. We have a better engine, a better transmission, and a better steering mechanism, but they have not yet been fitted together to make a complete car. It seems very likely that, when they are all put together, these new developments in education will reinforce each other and will make possible further gains that would not come from any one alone. Pre-school reading and writing would make room for beginning science in the early grades. Binary arithmetic in the second grade may make a child ready and eager for number theory and computer programming in the sixth. Rates-of-change at age seven would permit introduction to economics at thirteen.

What is evidently needed now is to get out of the rut of our standard educational structure and to set up complete new kinds of pilot schools to try out this new personal and concrete and manipulative education in an integrated program all the way from age one to age twenty-one and beyond. We need to try schools of several different kinds, in different types of communities, in slum areas and rich suburbs, in company towns and scientific laboratory communities, to find out which kind of program under different circumstances produces the most alert and creative citizens. If we can find some educational leaders who will take the initiative in establishing private schools of this sort, or who can persuade some forward-looking school boards to try them out, this may be the most exciting educational adventure of the next decade.

I think that, if we put together all the speed-ups and simplifications that these new methods make possible, the children in such schools would no longer be overworked. The subjects we now teach them might be mastered in a much shorter school day, perhaps no more than three or four hours. There would be less boredom and resistance in school and more time for creative leisure outside. Some parents may shudder at this, because they do not want the children home half the day. But, with the new trends of productivity and automation in our adult life, perhaps creative leisure is one of the things we need to teach children earliest. And, if we let the adult's leisure enrich the children's leisure, homework might even become home play. The interaction between the generations might make for better relations than we have had for years. In fact the children, with their shorter hours, going home from school may soon meet the adults, with their new leisure, going back, hoping to learn in a more voluntary and serious way the subjects they missed in all their years of report-card education.

All this would change our stereotyped pattern of education in a remarkable way. The intense program of work now imposed across a few years in the late teens—where we have to study all day and all night because the earlier grades have taught us so little—might be replaced by an easier longitudinal pattern that would start with easy and fast learning methods at age one or two and would then go on all our lives for two or three or four hours a day. The children and the college students and the leisured adults might acquire a new attitude toward education. Formal teaching might blend inseparably into more individual and creative leisure-time activities, such as building boats together or learning music or ballet or skiing—or studying embryos and catching striped bass before dawn. Education would be by contagion and long discussion, and the generations might learn to talk to each other again.

A lifetime ago we made the transformation to education for living. It is time now to make the transformation to education for wholeness, for delight, and for diversity.

FREEDOM AND LEARNING: THE NEED FOR CHOICE

by PAUL GOODMAN

THE BELIEF that a highly industrialized society requires twelve to twenty years of prior processing of the young is an illusion or a hoax. The evidence is strong that there is no correlation between school performance and life achievement in any of the professions, whether medicine, law, engineering, journalism, or business. Moreover, recent research shows that for more modest clerical, technological, or semiskilled factory jobs there is no advantage in years of schooling or the possession of diplomas. We were not exactly savages in 1900 when only 6 percent of adolescents graduated from high school. Whatever the deliberate intention, schooling today serves mainly for policing and for taking up the slack in youth unemployment. It is not surprising that the young are finally rebelling against it, especially since they cannot identify with the goals of so much social engineering—for instance, that 86 percent of the federal budget for research and development is for military purposes.

We can, I believe, educate the young entirely in terms of their free choice, with no processing whatever. Nothing can be efficiently learned, or, indeed, learned at all—other than through parroting or brute training, when acquired knowledge is promptly forgotten after the examination—unless it meets need, desire, curiosity, or fantasy. Unless there is a reaching from within, the learning cannot become "second nature," as Aristotle called true learning. It seems stupid to decide a priori what the young ought to know and then to try to motivate them, instead of letting the initiative come from them and putting information and relevant equipment at their service. It is false to assert that this kind of

Reprinted from *Saturday Review,* May 18, 1968, copyright © 1968 by Saturday Review, Inc. By permission of the publisher.

freedom will not serve society's needs—at least those needs that should humanly be served; freedom is the only way toward authentic citizenship and real, rather than verbal, philosophy. Free choice is not random but responsive to real situations; both youth and adults live in a nature of things, a polity, an ongoing society, and it is these, in fact, that attract interest and channel need. If the young, as they mature, can follow their bent and choose their topics, times, and teachers, and if teachers teach what they themselves consider important—which is all they can skillfully teach anyway—the needs of society will be adequately met; there will be more lively, independent, and inventive people; and in the fairly short run there will be a more sensible and efficient society.

It is not necessary to argue for free choice as a metaphysical proposition; it is what is indicated by present conditions. Increasingly, the best young people resolutely resist authority, and we will let them have a say or lose them. And more important, since the conditions of modern social and technological organization are so pervasively and rigidly conforming, it is necessary, in order to maintain human initiative, to put our emphasis on protecting the young from top-down direction. The monkish and academic methods which were civilizing for wild shepherds create robots in a period of high technology. The public schools which did a good job of socializing immigrants in an open society now regiment individuals and rigidify class stratification.

Up to age twelve, there is no point to formal subjects or a prearranged curriculum. With guidance, whatever a child experiences is educational. Dewey's idea is a good one: It makes no difference *what* is learned at this age, so long as the child goes on wanting to learn something further. Teachers for this age are those who like children, pay attention to them, answer their questions, enjoy taking them around the city and helping them explore, imitate, try out, and who sing songs with them and teach them games. Any benevolent grownup—literate or illiterate—has plenty to teach an eight-year-old; the only profitable training for teachers is a group therapy and, perhaps, a course in child development.

We see that infants learn to speak in their own way in an environment where there is speaking and where they are addressed and take part. If we tried to teach children to speak according to our own theories and methods and schedules, as we try to teach reading, there would be as many stammerers as there are bad readers. Besides, it has been shown that whatever is useful in the present eight-year elementary curriculum can be learned in four months by a normal child of twelve. If let alone, in fact, he will have learned most of it by himself.

Since we have communities where people do not attend to the children as a matter of course, and since children must be rescued from their homes, for most of these children there should be some kind of school. In a proposal for mini-schools in New York City, I suggested an elementary group of twenty-eight children with four grownups: a licensed teacher, a housewife who can cook, a college senior, and a teen-age school dropout. Such a group can meet in any store front, church basement, settlement house, or housing project; more important, it can often go about the city, as is possible when the student-teacher ratio is seven to one. Experience at the First Street School in New York has shown that the cost for such a little school is less than for the public school with a student-teacher ratio of thirty to one. (In the public system, most of the money goes for administration and for specialists to remedy the lack of contact in the classroom.) As A. S. Neill has shown, attendance need not be compulsory. The school should be located near home so the children can escape from it to home, and from home to it. The school should be supported by public money but administered entirely by its own children, teachers, and parents.

In the adolescent and college years, the present mania is to keep students at their lessons for another four to ten years as the only way of their growing up in the world. The correct policy would be to open as many diverse paths as possible, with plenty of opportunity to backtrack and change. It is said by James Conant that about 15 percent learn well by books and study in an academic setting, and these can opt for high school. Most, including most of the bright students, do better either on their own or as apprentices in activities that are for keeps, rather than through lessons. If their previous eight years had been spent in exploring their own bents and interests, rather than being continually interrupted to do others' assignments on others' schedules, most adolescents would have a clearer notion of what they are after, and many would have found their vocations.

For the 15 percent of adolescents who learn well in schools and are interested in subjects that are essentially academic, the present catch-all high schools are wasteful. We would do better to return to the small preparatory academy, with perhaps sixty students and three teachers—one in physical sciences, one in social sciences, one in humanities—to prepare for college board examinations. An academy could be located in, and administered by, a university and staffed by graduate students who like to teach and in this way might earn stipends while they write their theses. In such a setting, without dilution by nonacademic subjects and a mass of uninterested fellow students, an academic adolescent can, by spending three hours a day in the classroom, easily be prepared in three or four years for college.

Forcing the nonacademic to attend school breaks the spirit of most and foments alienation in the best. Kept in tutelage, young people, who are necessarily economically dependent, cannot pursue the sexual, adventurous, and political activities congenial to them. Since lively youngsters insist on these anyway, the effect of what we do is to create a gap between them and the oppressive adult world, with a youth subculture and an arrested development.

School methods are simply not competent to teach all the arts, sciences, professions, and skills the school establishment pretends to teach. For some professions—e.g., social work, architecture, pedagogy—trying to earn academic credits is probably harmful because it is an irrelevant and discouraging obstacle course. Most technological know-how has to be learned in actual practice in offices and factories, and this often involves unlearning what has been laboriously crammed for exams. The technical competence required by skilled and semiskilled workmen and average technicians can be acquired in three weeks to a year on the job, with no previous schooling. The importance of even "functional literacy" is much exaggerated; it is the attitude, and not the reading ability, that counts. Those who are creative in the arts and sciences almost invariably go their own course and are usually hampered by schools. Modern languages are best learned by travel. It is pointless to teach social sciences, literary criticism, and philosophy to youngsters who have had no responsible experience in life and society.

Most of the money now spent for high schools and colleges should be devoted to the support of apprenticeships; travel; subsidized browsing in libraries and self-directed study and research; programs such as VISTA, the Peace Corps, Students for a Democratic Society, or the Student Nonviolent Coordinating Committee; rural reconstruction; and work camps for projects in conservation and urban renewal. It is a vast sum of money—but it costs almost $1,500 a year to keep a youth in a blackboard jungle in New York; the schools have become one of our major industries. Consider one kind of opportunity. Since it is important for the very existence of the republic to countervail the now overwhelming national corporate style of information, entertainment, and research, we need scores of thousands of small independent television stations, community radio stations, local newspapers that are more than gossip notes and ads, community theaters, high-brow or dissenting magazines, small design offices for neighborhood renewal that is not bureaucratized, small laboratories for science and invention that are not centrally directed. Such enterprises could present admirable opportunities for bright but unacademic young people to serve as apprentices.

Ideally, the *polis* itself is the educational environment; a good community consists of worthwhile, attractive, and fulfilling callings and things to do, to grow up into. The policy I am proposing tends in this direction rather than away from it. By multiplying options, it should be possible to find an interesting course for each individual youth, as we now do for only some of the emotionally disturbed and the troublemakers. Voluntary adolescent choices are often random and foolish and usually transitory; but they are the likeliest ways of growing up reasonably. What is most essential is for the youth to see that he is taken seriously as a person, rather than fitted into an institutional system. I don't know if this tailor-made approach would be harder or easier to administer than standardization that in fact fits nobody and results in an increasing number of recalcitrants. On the other hand, as the Civilian Conservation Corps showed in the Thirties, the products of willing youth labor can be valuable even economically, whereas accumulating Regents blue books is worth nothing except to the school itself.

(By and large, it is not in the adolescent years but in later years that, in all walks of life, there is need for academic withdrawal, periods of study and reflection, synoptic review of the texts. The Greeks understood this and regarded most of our present college curricula as appropriate for only those over the age of thirty or thirty-five. To some extent, the churches used to provide a studious environment. We do these things miserably in hurried conferences.)

We have similar problems in the universities. We cram the young with what they do not want at the time and what most of them will never use; but by requiring graded diplomas we make it hard for older people to get what they want and can use. Now, paradoxically, when so many are going to school, the training of authentic learned professionals is proving to be a failure, with dire effects on our ecology, urbanism, polity, communications, and even the direction of science. Doing others' lessons under compulsion for twenty years does not tend to produce professionals who are autonomous, principled, and ethically responsible to client and community. Broken by processing, professionals degenerate to mere professional-personnel. Professional peer groups have become economic lobbies. The licensing and maintenance of standards have been increasingly relinquished to the state, which has no competence.

In licensing professionals, we have to look more realistically at functions, drop mandarin requirements of academic diplomas that are irrelevant, and rid ourselves of the ridiculous fad of awarding diplomas for every skill and trade whatever. In most professions and arts there are important abstract parts that can best be learned academically. The natural procedure is for those actually engaged in a professional activity to go to school to learn what they now know they need; re-entry into the academic track, therefore, should be made easy for those with a strong motive.

Universities are primarily schools of learned professions, and the faculty should be composed primarily not of academics but of working professionals who feel duty-bound and attracted to pass on their tradition to apprentices of a new generation. Being combined in a community of scholars, such professionals teach a noble apprenticeship, humane and with vision toward a more ideal future. It is humane because the disciplines communicate with one another; it is ideal because the young are free and questioning. A good professional school can be tiny. In *The Community of Scholars* I suggest that 150 students and ten professionals—the size of the usual medieval university—are enough. At current faculty salaries, the cost per student would be a fourth of that of our huge administrative machines. And, of course, on such a small scale, contact between faculty and students is sought for and easy.

Today, because of the proved incompetence of our adult institutions and the hypocrisy of most professionals, university students have a right to a large say in what goes on. (But this, too, is medieval.) Professors will, of course, teach what they please. My advice to students is that given by Prince Kropotkin, in "A Letter to the Young": "Ask what kind of world do you want to live in? What are you good at and want to work at to build that world? What do you need to know? Demand that your teachers teach you that." Serious teachers would be delighted by this approach.

The idea of the liberal arts college is a beautiful one: to teach the common culture and refine character and citizenship. But it does not happen; the evidence is that the college curriculum has little effect on underlying attitudes, and most cultivated folk do not become so by this route. School friendships and the community of youth do have lasting effects, but these do not require ivied clubhouses. Young men learn more about the theory and practice of government by resisting the draft than they ever learned in Political Science 412.

Much of the present university expansion, needless to say, consists in federal- and corporation-contracted research and other research and has nothing to do with teaching. Surely such expansion can be better carried on in the government's and corporations' own institutes, which would be unencumbered by the young, except those who are hired or attach themselves as apprentices.

Every part of education can be open to need, desire, choice, and trying out. Nothing needs to be compelled or extrinsically motivated by prizes and threats. I do not know if the procedure here outlined would cost more than our present system—though it is hard to conceive of a need for more money than the school establishment now spends. What would be saved is the pitiful waste of youthful years—caged, daydreaming, sabotaging, and cheating —and the degrading and insulting misuse of teachers.

It has been estimated by James Coleman that the average youth in high school is really "there" about ten minutes a day. Since the growing-up of the young into society to be useful to themselves and others, and to do God's work, is one of the three or four most important functions of any society, no doubt we ought to spend even more on the education of the young than we do; but I would not give a penny to the present administrators, and I would largely dismantle the present school machinery.

CONCLUSIONS AND RECOMMENDATIONS

---

by CALEB GATTEGNO

I

Because the education that is necessary for our time will be the creation of the witnesses who will free the coming generation from the task of absorbing what it is not yet (but otherwise would become) committed to and which it need no longer bow to, education thus becomes the social and technical action that will permit the new man to emerge—to emerge conscious of what he can objectify in his life, recognizing in himself incomparably greater powers in his mind and finding more to explore in the universes that he unfolds by the process of living in them intensely and thoroughly.

Reprinted in excerpt from *Towards a Visual Culture: Educating through Television* by Caleb Gattegno. Copyright © 1969 by Caleb Gattegno. Published by Outerbridge & Dienstfrey, New York, New York. By permission of the publisher.

What will give him this consciousness and make him into a man of the new culture is his awareness that understanding reality simultaneously involves the perception of the self in time and of what the mind is capable of noticing in the universe of which it is a part. No abrupt separation exists between an individual and the world around him ; each gives reality to the other. Recognizing this, the new man would then know that every thought can be revised, that every impression is a stage in one's awareness, susceptible of change and of delivering up a new meaning.

The man of the new culture will know that the fabric of things is made of relationships that are never exhausted and when apprehended always betray the observer, as well as the observed, as being at a particular stage and moment.

The man of the new culture is ready to revise any and every one of his thoughts, ideas, attitudes, ideals, because he knows that his knowledge depends on his knowing and that this in turn depends on where he has taken himself on the road of perception. Because relativity is a universal attribute he has perceived in himself, in his knowing, and in what stands for his universe, he approaches every moment of life as one that is what it is, though he cannot say quite what.

To perceive a reality that changes in time is to perceive the real reality, not an unreliable set of illusions. The illusion is to believe in (and to believe one sees) an unchangeable or unchanging reality, for there is not a single example of such stability within or without.

The television set, once lit with its images, is a reminder of what we actually live in, a world in flux, an indefinitely renewable universe capable, once we become one with an image by surrendering ourselves to it, of generating a constant renewal of consciousness by acting on the sensitive springs within the viewer.

We now have the facility of knowing our self as time and to live its transformation into experience. Mastering the economy of the transformation of time into experience is one of the main jobs for the man of the new culture.

Looking at how we can educate through television, we find that we must see to it that as many people as possible recognize television for what it is. This is task number one.

When those who understand that television is a preeminent

channel towards the visual culture are strong enough to be heard, they will display in their being the characteristics that will make them attractive, inspiring, and capable of generating change among others. Task number two is hence the formation of an elite of the new culture in the sense that some of those who know television for what it is find in themselves the means of expression that are conceived by others as a power worth possessing.

Task number three consists of the demonstration

that those who are not yet committed to the values of the present cultures will not need much in order to become people of the new culture,

that as people of the new culture they will function so much more easily in a much richer universe than their fathers did,

that they will achieve returns for their thoughts and actions that are rarely realized at present.

From all this it will appear to all that the new culture is preferable to the previous ones.

The men of the new culture will remain uncommitted because the new culture, unlike previous ones, does not demand identification with one vision, one form, one static reality.

As to the people who, in the process of receiving their education, have been made to give up the consciousness of their own role in grasping reality, it may be task number four to re-educate them.

II

Since adults are defined here as the people who are responsible for the changes in society, it will be their responsibility to give themselves the programs they need to make sense of where they are going and what they are doing with themselves, with others, and for others.

Still, because the members of these three groups have finished or are finishing their formal education, most of them will have acquired ways of thinking that mainly are reflections of the cultures of the past. They might not be able to discover easily what a visual culture could be and could do for them. On a number of occasions, they are likely to be caught between a world functioning in ways to which they have not been introduced and one functioning in the ways they were forced to acquire when they were not those who decided what to do with people.

The following proposal is but one of those that could be made to serve all three of these groups, whose members, in so far as their modes of thought are concerned, are in serious need of re-education.

What we usually do when we think via the medium of memorized words, which form so much of our verbal education, is to generate a static universe. Many of the transformations that underlie the acquisition of languages are beaten out of our consciousness, and we are made to believe primarily in the existence of individual objects without much link between them, our perceptions culminating in an atomized universe whose meaning remains beyond our reach. Our critical powers are not developed in the direction of questioning evidence, of looking for whatever is needed to make sense of anything. We are made dependent on those among ourselves who are thinkers, and we look to them for solutions.

To bring a change in this situation we must re-educate adults so as to make them trust their perception more than they trust other people's words, and help them to acquire a dynamic imagery that permits them to scan a world of possibilities contained in situations that involve variables; and enable them to learn, by working on new problems that have not been part of their education, that they are capable of developing mental tools no matter what their age—and then have them test these tools on meaningful challenges that are indicative of how the future will work.

One thing is becoming increasingly clear every day and this is that we have to develop a dialogue of informed people rather than put someone who knows in front of a person who does not know and let the one tell the other what he knows whether or not the second has any criteria to ascertain the truth of what he hears from the first.

Whenever we place two people in front of a situation they can look at, it is almost impossible to say who will see more and what significant things will be seen by which of them. Most of us are equal when it is a matter of looking and seeing, regardless of the fact that we might choose to stress some features of the situation rather than others.

Adults who functioned early in their childhood as "visuals" have been distorted by a verbal education and no longer know what it is to be a "visual." *Television, as they see it, is an extension of the radio. But it is not.* Television forces us to receive an infinite number of items at once all the time we are viewing. We only need to remove the verbal side of the programs to force viewers to use their gifts of vision. We must seek to develop a complete visual code that feeds information without words and forces viewers to drop the habit of verbalization they currently need in order to feel that they understand a message.

Adults in the space age, the nuclear age, the computer age, are still functioning as their ancestors did in the Middle Ages. Verbalization is really valid only for the areas where words can trigger images that become the carriers of meaning. People who feel the necessity to verbalize can be confounded if they are requested to express what verbally is inexpressible, or even extremely complicated.

Facing the world of tomorrow, with the new demands it will make, requires that we use our mental tools for what these tools do best. There is a place for words, but not every place. There is a place for quick thinking, a place for thinking of wholes, and a place for awareness of the appropriate mental tools needed by situations.

Television can contribute to giving adults once more the use of their imagery, of a quick and complex way of thinking. To achieve this we need a kind of film in which the components are so selected that they force ideas to emerge without the accompaniment of words and in such a way that, on the part of the viewers, no words have the time to form themselves.

Because we can get an impact through our eyes that does not need to be remembered and remains in us by the energy it adds to the mind in the form of an image that can be recalled at once and in terms of mental energy, we can now through television submit people to the impact of colors, shapes, and intensities of our choosing and be sure that these selections have affected them. This means that, for any future learning, we can count on this wealth being in their minds, and we can act upon its presence by means that at a very small cost in energy generate infinite

classes of equivalences, whose operation is a basic mode of thought. In the process, the mind will enrich itself with
—the infinities that it perceives in the transformations
—the capacity to transform any image into another.
When this mode of thought becomes second nature, the viewers can act upon their own thinking, looking for transformations compatible with attributes of classes that they find in their mind.

Today we know enough about how to achieve this to generate a large number of programs that will give every adult what ignorance and preconceptions have prevented him from acquiring during his education, a power to think quickly and correctly in a complex way on complex things.

A VISION OF TECHNOLOGY AND EDUCATION

by ANTHONY G. OETTINGER

B<small>Y LACKING</small> an understanding of the dynamics of interactions between technological and social change, most views concerning their relationship tend to be polarized and naïve. To those "outside," major technological programs such as the lunar landing program appear to be the product of lobbying by powerful special interest groups, advocating big spending by the government and social change at any cost, without seriously considering the consequences of such spending or change. Viewed from the "inside," social reaction to potential technological advance may seem shortsighted if not downright Luddite. For example, the reaction to potential large-scale introduction of atomic power led to efficiency increases and cost reductions by the

Reprinted from *Communications of the ACM* (IX/7, July 1966), copyright © 1966 by Association for Computing Machinery. By permission of the author.

conventional power industry, and this development has effectively delayed the introduction of nuclear power into the mainstream of peacetime affairs.

In approaching the problem of the interaction of educational technology with society, I shall first present a vision of technological possibility deliberately unclouded by economic or temporal realism. I shall then explore both some effects this vision, if realized, might have on the fabric of society and also some of the factors likely to inhibit its realization. The questions raised will be at best superficial problems whose interactions with one another are ignored. It is very unlikely that so simple-minded a view will describe a future reality, but no more seems possible at this time.

In the first tableau of our vision, we see that it is technically feasible for sound, pictures, and even objects stored at appropriate centers to be available with the greatest of ease and negligible cost at innumerable local points of access, first perhaps in schools, libraries, or factories and only a little later, in our visionary perspective, in every home. The price of getting there is one of the things that should give us pause, but potential means, safely short of involving extrasensory perception, are now at our command. Once this much is granted, an entirely new look at the means for education is possible.

It does not matter for our purpose whether or not we assume that computer technology will replace the libraries we now know. Reasons of cost and reliability might lead us to prefer storing information in microscopic film or solid-state devices and transmitting it by electronic means rather than propelling conventional books hither and yon through a national network of huge pneumatic tubes, but this choice need not concern us here. Careful design might well require certain frequently used materials to be available in local depositories, but the basic assumption is simply that anything available in any library can be made available to anyone anywhere within what he thinks is a reasonable time.

In the next tableau we see individual consoles linked to the common information pool serving as the basic tool for virtually all formal education. The key idea is that, by pushing buttons or otherwise signaling from an appropriate terminal, a student has visual access to:

1. The catalogs of great libraries, hence access to everything in their collections.
2. The catalogs of new videotape or film libraries which will include recorded lessons on specialized topics (possibly in the manner of an illustrated encyclopedia) and also source materials such as records of significant contemporary events, outstanding dramatic productions, clinical demonstrations (perhaps of a difficult operation particularly well performed in a leading hospital), and so on.
3. Teaching programs of the kind already in widespread experimental use.
4. Tools to aid symbol-manipulation and concept-formation, such as numerical and algebraic manipulators, dictionaries, thesauri, editing programs, etc.

The teaching programs provide routine directions through the maze of materials. However, many of the documents in the consulting collections may themselves contain references to other entries. The library system is thus visualized as a kind of Gargantuan version of Vannevar Bush's Memex.

The local teacher gives guidance, perhaps after having mastered the materials himself as part of a machine-aided program of continuing education. Indeed, guidance is all important since the individual has greater responsibility for his own education than he has had in the past; the teacher's role thus becomes far more humanistic and far less mechanical than it is now.

The manipulative tools are very important both for education and for research. At present, visual display systems are useful in helping men understand the results of experiments or calculations; they may be used by students of introductory differential equations to generate direction fields and thus to gain immediate insight into the global character of the solutions to these equations; they may be used by research scientists, perhaps to make visible various proposed structures for complex organic molecules and to view these from arbitrary orientations and across arbitrary sections. Such tools enable the easy confrontation of model and reality, as in the visual superposition of calculated streamlines on those in a real fluid flowing around a real obstacle in a real tank. To those who have observed them, such confrontations have dramatic immediacy and perspicuity. This is a means for expanding man's consciousness and giving him a new way of grasping ideas that is especially valuable where scientists must use intuition and complex calculations to study phenomena increasingly remote from their unaided senses.

The system also provides expert help for those at both ends of the ability scale. Special materials are available for the very advanced or the particularly slow. Outstanding people or trained remedial specialists are provided for consultation via a directory of consultants incorporated in the system. Students who are now at the low end of the scale but who do have intellectual potential could be reached by the new techniques, because they respond well to individualized education, especially when personal contact with a teacher keeps learning from being a fearful experience. As the teacher is released from routine chores for guidance activities, he can provide much more individual attention than now. For some, although obviously not for all, the unassisted machine may carry the impersonality of the confessional or the couch to a logical and beneficial extreme. Finally, the use of reinforcements designed especially to appeal to the culturally deprived might also reach intractable students in this category.

In certain areas, notably in mathematics and its applications, the student may use computers not only as tools for tackling and solving more exciting and deeper problems than can now be handled, but also as a means for remembering techniques that he has developed. The computer puts these powers at the student's fingertips throughout his school career and beyond, on the assumption that the system itself remains available to him wherever he goes. Universal access obviously requires a national or worldwide system of standardized consoles and the cheap communication channels we have already postulated.

Such an approach fundamentally changes the entire teaching process. Whatever teaching by rote is necessary can be handled by the programmed teaching devices incorporated in the system; but beyond this, people can learn to use library resources of all types and can master the manipulative tools put at their disposal.

The system helps them remember both the tracks they and others pursued in browsing and the problem-solving techniques they developed for their own individual purposes. The system could thus be regarded as the crude beginnings of a cultural or social memory, comparable in complexity and accessibility to that of the individual human being. In a sense, such a collective mind already exists in libraries and in the complex and growing organism we call scientific literature, but we have much more limited powers of recall and articulation than are envisioned here.

One immediate interesting consequence of these visions is that they leave no obvious intellectual need for the separation of children in grades or other forms of lockstep. The child can progress through the system as rapidly as he is able or wishes to. Another interesting feature of the system is that it relieves the school of what is the bulk of its concern today, namely the abstract and the verbal. The school as such may concentrate instead on the concrete, the social, and the human. In principle, everything that has been described here could be done as well in the home as in the school. Such learning would be an individual activity; the long use in Europe of individual tutoring as the primary means of education shows that group activity is not always a prerequisite for learning. The school would, however, continue to provide what Buckminster Fuller has called its baby-sitting function, as well as a situation for the meeting, the rubbing, and the blending of individuals who must later take places as partners in society.

As the school thus comes to resemble society, the transition from school to job would be far less traumatic; the continuum of learning would be more obvious; and the tools and techniques of acquiring knowledge could be switched to higher education or to professional activities without severe discontinuities. The materials used may change but the human methods need not. In a job interview, the student might describe the materials he has mastered and, perhaps, demonstrate directly that he can use the techniques on problems relevant to the job.

Some might insist on grading in the form of a profile of the levels of achievement (or of familiarity in various directions available) in the system. Such a profile need not pretend to quantify proficiency but, by pointing to those areas in the common information pool which a student has reached, simply make plain where his strengths and weaknesses lie. While the greater snob value attached to certain profiles might affect a student's choice of subject, the system, nevertheless, leaves a greater scope for individual freedom and greater opportunity for the student to match himself to the outer world rather than to the mores of a school than is possible today. This flexibility can be a relief since, for many people today, things are never again quite so grim as in school.

The school, free to concentrate on guidance and counseling, may also emphasize such concrete matters as laboratory exercises in the sciences or student productions of plays, poetry readings, and discussions of books in the humanities. Picture the student who has seen video lectures on certain physical principles presenting himself to the laboratory instructor and claiming that he is ready to perform a certain experiment. This is one of the points at which the teacher can check the student's progress since, if the student fumbles miserably in the laboratory, he can be sent back for further study at the machine. Furthermore, the student's progress and the outcome of his experiment might well determine the path of his future inquiries into the machine pool of knowledge.

The emphasis on the concrete within the school has two desirable social effects. First, it tends to reduce upper-class alienation of the type that repels the children of the well-educated and the well-to-do from science and technology. Second, the undesirable barrier between the academic school and the vocational school can disappear. While the better-off students would be faced with the concrete in the laboratory, those hitherto relegated to vocational schools might, through initial exposure to concrete mechanisms, devices, demonstrations, and so on, be then stimulated to attempt a deeper abstract understanding of such phenomena by exposure to appropriately leveled sources in the machine bank of information.

A student who has used a wrench to loosen a rusty bolt or to tighten one would, either on his own or with the guidance of his sympathetic teacher, quickly notice that the longer the handle on the wrench the easier it is to turn the bolt. The step from this experience to motivation for looking at a videotape of an elementary lecture on simple machines is a small one, but rarely taken in the present day vocational school where the teacher, although sympathetic, is usually unable to supply the lecture himself. The student so stimulated might then, if he has the innate intellectual equipment, be able to catch up to others on his own time and in privacy.

The difference between being in and out of school is reduced since industrial plants have access to the same information and education system. Hence, where a man has achieved his level profile becomes less relevant than what the level is. An easy flow back and forth between school and work is conceivable for people of all ages.

Little need be said of feasibility and economics. While everything described in the preceding section can be done in principle, doing it is a matter of enormous funds and effort. If the vision is to come true at all, most likely it will come about through an evolutionary process and, in the course of evolution, deviate radically from its present detail. Many specific criticisms can obviously be leveled at the vision. The following is merely a sample.

What, for example, guarantees that such a system could work in practice as well as in principle? The information available at the terminals will be prepared by people, and it is questionable whether the available people will have enough ideas and enough command of the technology to do a job good enough to interest the students.

Where, indeed, do the teachers come from? What degree of contact can remain between really good, sensitive teachers and the students when the machines frequently know more than the teacher? How can student-teacher contact be encouraged? How, in the long run, can teacher training provide guidance in the creative arts and laboratory work? And what about the transitional problem of reeducating teachers of the current school?

The teacher in the wrench example of the preceding section would have to be able to move freely between the abstract and the concrete, a knack which all too few possess. Hence, in spite of the high degree of automation of the envisaged system, there might not be enough talent to start it. The vision implicitly assumes that teachers will be able to guide students from all walks of life and levels of competence. If this ideal is unattainable, it would quickly seem more efficient to group students by ability around appropriate advisers. Thus, grading and lockstep would be reinvented.

The new system might overcome the current great advantage of factors of birth in determining which students receive higher education but it might also leave the student without intellectual potential far behind. The natural elitism of the intelligent and educated might therefore be sharpened. Considering the present parental agitation against grouping by ability, the very possibility of implementing an ability-oriented system within the American social structure must be seriously questioned. Elected school boards are not likely to take kindly to some of the implications of the vision, and its implementation might require either a tremendous change in public attitudes or an authoritarian educational system. The problems of fluoridating water would pale in comparison.

It is conceivable that terminals in the home would lead to serious problems of addiction and competition. With home and school indistinguishable, the tendency to stay glued to the console might be irresistible for those with a competitive bent, and this would have a marked effect on the quality of their lives. A system based on remote information storage might make control over subject matter far easier than it is in our present society. One need only picture the use a Hitler or a Stalin could have made of a national educational information pool to understand the seriousness of this problem. Using regional rather than national information centers, or foreign as well as domestic sources, might reduce this uniformity. On the other hand, some of the homogeneity now evident in the lower schools would disintegrate before a system which can give access to a much wider range of literature than a bigoted local school board would allow today.

In general, new technology tends to produce greater interdependence and uniformity. The vision includes discussion and questioning in the school and diversity in the system, but the impersonal use of canned materials on a large scale might produce in students the illusion of infallibility, since the printed, recorded, or filmed word or action often seems to wield greater authority than does the fumbling middle-aged type at the blackboard or in the kitchen. Teaching all children the same history might be all too easy and gaining control over the mind of a nation all too possible unless this possibility is most carefully studied and intellectual freedom most jealously guarded.

Finally, to hint for once at a second-order effect, it seems likely that any partial step toward the vision would be based on an evaluation of the educational system and of the economics of computers, communications, and so on, as they are now. It should be clear that the prospect of a system which might radically alter patterns of book distribution and hence the stability of the book trade would lead to reactions that might alter the assumption on which original plans are based so significantly that their rational implementation would be blocked.

Unfortunately, there is too little knowledge or sense of alternatives now available to help us answer these questions.

VI

Planning

Let's not wait for those cripples in the administration to hand out money or land, and let's not wait for them to grant us the future that they owe us. They won't. They can't. Let's start thinking in terms of permanence now and build our own damn future.

—JEFF NUTTALL,
Bomb Culture (1968)

THE BELLAGIO DECLARATION ON PLANNING

W e, the participants of the Organization for Economic Co-Operation and Development Working Symposium on Long-Range Forecasting and Planning, having discussed in Bellagio, Italy, the importance which the subject may have at the present stage of social crisis, feel compelled to put forward our views on the planning potentials as a method of approach to solving many contemporary problems.

Social institutions face growing difficulties as a result of an ever-increasing complexity which arises directly and indirectly from the development and assimilation of technology. Many of the most serious conflicts facing mankind result from the inter-action of social, economic, technological, political, and psychological forces and can no longer be solved by fractional approaches from individual disciplines. The time is past when economic growth can be promoted without consideration of social consequences and when technology can be allowed to develop without consideration of the social prerequisites of change or the social consequences of such change. Diagnosis is often faulty and remedies proposed often merely suppress symptoms rather than attack the basic cause.

The quality of individual life and that of the community is changing rapidly and in many senses deteriorating; foreseeable technological developments will have a still greater influence, presenting both opportunities for a richer life and attendant dangers.

In the corporate environment, the individual enterprise tends to become larger and more complex. Multinational industrial activities are developing which can be expected to influence in-

Reprinted from *Futures* (I/3, March 1969). By permission of the publisher.

creasingly political relationships between the nations. This necessitates international planning.

Complexity and the large scale of problems are forcing decisions to be made at levels where individual participation of those affected is increasingly remote, producing a crisis in political and social development which threatens our whole future. It is in relation to this crisis that we feel the planning function and related arts such as forecasting assume new significance.

Having discussed the present state of the art of planning and the diversity of its new approaches, we believe that its possibilities including the appreciation of human values transcend mere technocratic objectives. Scientific attack on these problems of complexity and interdependences is a matter of the utmost urgency, and whilst we have what we consider to be a healthy divergence of views regarding the pertinence and scope of individual method and approaches, we are nevertheless convinced that a corpus of knowledge already exists capable of immediate exploitation, and that there is expectation of further and fruitful development.

The need for planning is not generally recognized. Further, the pursuance of orthodox planning is quite insufficient, in that it seldom does more than touch a system through changes of the variables. Planning must be concerned with the structural design of the system itself and involved in the formation of policy. Mere modification of policies already proved to be inadequate will not result in what is right. Science in planning today is too often used to make situations which are inherently bad more efficiently bad.

The need is to plan systems as a whole, to understand the totality of factors involved, and to intervene in the structural design to achieve more integrated operation. All large, complex systems are capable of some degree of self-adaptation. But in the face of immense technological, political, social, and economic stresses, they will have to develop new structures. This can easily lead to grave social disturbances if the adaptation is not deliberately planned, but merely allowed to happen.

Recognition of such facts leads us to specify a number of operational conditions which must be satisfied if planning is to evolve its coherent, creative, and useful features. In particular:

- The scope of planning must be expanded to encompass the formulation of alternative policies and the examination, analysis, and explicit stipulation of the underlying values and norms.
- Planning must cope with new situations and devise new institutions. New possibilities of quantitative analysis and simulation of complex dynamic systems using the computer greatly extend our capabilities in this direction.
- Social and institutional experiments, carefully designed and evaluated, should be promoted to develop a better basis for planning and its implementation.
- Planning must be understood in relation to the consequences, and in particular the consequences to the individual, of decisions and actions within social systems. It should therefore be performed at the lowest effective level to make possible a maximum of participation in the planning itself and in its implementation.
- Planning must nevertheless be undertaken simultaneously at different levels and must be integrated across these levels.

These views and recommendations are expressed in response to trends that are irreversible and world-wide in their consequence. We believe therefore that they are urgent and relevant irrespective of political, social, and economic ideologies.

The difficulties if ignored will not disappear. We take it upon ourselves therefore to issue this collective warning that social and technological developments already clearly foreseen can exacerbate matters beyond any hope of peaceful relief. In doing so we express the belief that a basis of remedy already exists to help man to define and create his own future.

A PROPOSAL

by L. MOHOLY-NAGY

Hᴇ ᴡʜᴏ ʜᴀs the youth has the future." Prepara-
tions are made in all quarters to "have" the youth, often casting
the adult generation aside. However, for a better world yielding
more from its resources for the struggling millions, one should
also make a blueprint for a comprehensive adult education. I
would almost like to say "compulsory" adult education, or better,
a cooperative *activity plan* or *active recreation*. This last is the
more important since present technology (let alone the advances
in the making) may cut down working hours and the new sciences
may increase life expectancy. It would be a major tragedy to be
unprepared for a creative, that is, active, use of the coming
leisure time.

Since pioneering days America has had its cooperative activities,
such as the town meetings in New England, work sharing at crop
time, barn-raising and other parties, utopian colonies, community
centers, freemasons, conventions of associations, labor unions,
women's clubs, YMCA, YWCA, religious sects—an infinite number of opportunities to meet and discuss diverse matters. These
are generally good pageantry and pastime but not always a humble
apprenticeship toward a creative, erudite life.

Group activity of the future must be more consciously aware
of the mechanics of its own operation as well as of its results.
Though the ancient civic centers, the Greek agora and Roman
forum, were rather good instruments for creating public opinion
and group consciousness of communal issues, it is doubtful that
the same type of civic instrument could be used for the same
purpose in our time. It is most probable that we have to go
through a period of trial and error—as in many other matters

Reprinted from *Vision in Motion* (Paul Theobald, 1947), copyright © 1947
Sibyl Moholy-Nagy. By permission of Mrs. Moholy-Nagy.

since the industrial revolution—before we can find the right framework for our own civic and "community centers." Some elements of a healthy approach existed in the now-suspended Federal Art Project, in some art centers and settlement houses of this country, partly in the Swiss La Sarraz Group of Madame du Mandrot, partly in the English health center of Drs. Williamson and Pearse (Peckham). Also the village colleges initiated by Henry Morris (Cambridgeshire), which provided workshops, laboratories, play, and health supervision for the urban and agricultural population of large areas, stimulated the participants not to "reception" but to creative expression.

The new activity "plan" must be more dimensional, an activity in relationships. It must bring about a complete integration of the technological and sociobiological values dormant in the industrial age. Instead of social climbing, charity, or misplaced personal sacrifice, it should lead to a happy participation. Instead of the cocoon type of isolation, it should generate a mutual exchange. It should break down general prejudices by eliminating unchecked misprints of the mind, reverberations of superstitions and gossip. It should bring an abundant life as well as intellectual perseverance.

The new activity plan must be understood as part of activized social living in the most varied and productive forms of culture and health. Instead of a passive flood over the eyes and ears by radio, television, cinema, and press, it must lead to an active participation in workshops and plays, symposiums and political discussions. This would create the stimuli for a rejuvenation of creative citizenship, spontaneity, and an understanding of the needs of the community. But all this must have a preparation. There must be a natural demand for the forms of realization. Such a demand can be created best when integrated education will be not an exception but the general rule.

Every civilization has to build up step by step its necessary working instruments. Young America achieved this mainly through the generosity of wealthy donors who erected scientific institutes, universities and colleges, museums, art institutes, and foundations—giving special contributions for various research projects. Most of these institutions are working on specialized tasks according to the haphazard interest of the patrons. However, what neither America nor any other continent has built up yet are thriving agencies which strive for coordination of activities, for a synthesis. Such agencies should be cultural working centers, institutes of workers who, by mastering their own fields, could embody all specialized knowledge into an integrated system through cooperative action.

Such experts are already working in different parts of the world. If earnest efforts were made to relate their findings and if a suitable environment could be found for their work, a deeper insight into urgent problems would result. Regional groups, of the type proposed, would serve as catalysts for this process of integration.

It is astonishing how differentiated knowledge can be in spite of a generally similar educational and social background. By directing interest to commonly accepted tasks and problems, this varied knowledge of the experts could easily be united and synthesized into a coherent purposeful unity focused on sociobiological aims. By collaboration between these regional centers on the different topics "to restore the basic unity of all human experiences," a hundred facts of living, work, emotional outlets, sublimations, recreation, and leisure could be worked out and translated into terms of common understanding.

As a first step for such a task, an international cultural working assembly could be established, composed of outstanding scientists, sociologists, artists, writers, musicians, technicians, and craftsmen. They would work either for a long or a limited period *together,* in daily contact, in their studios and laboratories. They would investigate the roots of our intellectual and emotional heritage. They could deal with such problems as the individual and the group; town and country planning; production and dwelling; prefabrication and standards; nutrition with its old and new theories; recreation and leisure; opto-phonetics; psychological and physiological color values; functions of museums; music; theater; cinema; television; the eternal problem of general and higher education; industry and agriculture; village colleges; sociography of towns, cities, countries, continents; the social phenomena of working processes; folklore; crime and rehabilitation; economics and government; etc.

The assembly could then continuously publish its findings in reviews and books, motion pictures and broadcasts.

It could plan exhibitions, plays, symposiums, and congresses; propose, demonstrate, and indicate settlement of issues of fundamental importance.

Together with its possible branches the assembly could represent a center of the highest aspirations. As the nucleus of a world-government it could prepare new, collective forms of cultural and social life for a coming generation.

In accepting the responsibility of initiative and stimulus, it could serve as the intellectual trustee of a new age in finding a *new unity of purpose;* not a life of metaphysical haze but one based upon the biological justice to develop all creative capacities for individual and social fulfillment. It could write a new charter of human life, culminating in the right to *and the capacity of* self expression (the best bond for social coherence) without censorship or economic pressure.

It could translate Utopia into action.

HOW DO WE REDUCE THE "INDEPENDENCE" OF TECHNIQUE?

by CHARLES R. DeCARLO

IN PRACTICAL TERMS the problem facing us as individuals and society is how to avoid the further institutionalizing of technique and science as separate and dominant instrumentalities. For it is as subordinate to the purposes of our most meaningful institutions that the functions of science and technique

Reprinted from *Motive* magazine (March–April, 1967, pp. 19–25). By permission of the publisher.

must be placed. The technical act must exist *within* the fabric of the larger and more humane institutions. To the extent, then, that an institutional form integrates technique into fabric it begins to suffer the dangers of deepening the dualism between spirit and matter, form and content, end and means. Yet we know the adaptations of science and technique are necessary components to the increasing growth and well-being of the society and the extension of the benefits of its value systems.

This, then, forces upon all of us the responsibility to consider always those human purposes which lie above the plenum of rational and technical operations in the institutional reality. The expansion of these rational and technical opportunities, including information processing, productive abundance, new discoveries in the life and behavioral sciences, offers the possibilities of life styles of incredible richness and awareness. The guidance and moderation of these opportunities or dangers can spring only from minds trained to embrace scientific attitudes and practice as lesser components in the total and divine form of the human being. As people are changed and educated, throughout life, they will be required to deal with a different world from that of several generations ago.

First, they will be moving into a world of work in which daily activity will depend much more upon the ability to think logically, to handle symbolic and abstract material, and to be capable of continued lifelong learning. The psychic and spiritual satisfaction of work will be different by a degree greater than that difference which we have experienced between ourselves and our grandfathers.

The second requirement that they will face is the ability to use leisure in a meaningful way. More people must have the ability and desire to probe questions of values and meaning, must be attuned to wider artistic, spiritual, and intellectual experiences. But this cannot be done in the context of purely intellectual growth; it is imperative that all the senses be developed to know and appreciate the world of nature around us.

Thirdly, there will be the requirement to live much of life in even closer contact with people—contacts which will take place within formal and informal organizations and communities of interest. As a result of this, man will face the problems of divided loyalties as his life becomes a complex of overlapping memberships in different organizations and groups of shared values. Problems of privacy, social grace, respect for others, will become important to him as they have to few others in history.

A final aspect will be the requirement to live under ever changing institutional values. Because of the continual expansion of life in a technological society, political and social institutions will have to change to keep pace. For example, we will see this through the continued demand for human rights throughout the world, through the increased expectations in the economic systems, through the development of new methods of productivity, new cultural attitudes, etc. Facing institutional, social, and political change without the guiding light of sound principles will lead to chaos.

In order to live in such a changing world, attention will have to be paid to the earliest preparation of the child in understanding those basic and enduring values which are the society's soul. The existence of a technological society places an intense premium upon the articulation of central and basic values against a background of a continuously changing future. The conservative traditions of religion and education must assume primacy, to guarantee humaneness in the emergent society and preserve the finest human values which man has distilled from his history. These values are simply stated but extremely difficult to attain.

The first value is the integrity of self. The qualities of self-awareness and self-assurance, of introspection and consciousness, are priceless ingredients of the meaningful personality. It should be possible to develop these qualities more fully in the future, a future in which systems and machines will give men time to examine much more of their life, its purpose, its extension. This will create a situation where the "unexamined life" becomes a monstrous act; for the greatest and most enduring educational imperative, and one which will remain, is that of the Delphic oracle "Know Thyself."

Secondly, we must find new ways to teach the dignity of the individual. Concepts of responsibility and respect for others, which are the essence of humanity, must be inculcated at every opportunity in the family and the formal educational environments.

Sensitivity to the needs of others, the ability to empathize with their gifts and joys, to ask of them while according them individual existence, must become a principal characteristic of the well-educated person.

Finally, and working in concert with the other two, is the ability to develop loyalty and appropriate commitment to larger organizational forms. To conform in ritual and practice, to contribute to the needs and success of the group, while preserving an interior freedom and integrity, mark the superior man. Too often the organization is seen as a device which destroys the individual and his dignity. This can be prevented only as the leaders of our great organizations make them social creations gifted with humane purpose and committed to the best values of the society. In the long sweep of time, it is value systems as reflected in social organizations and institutional patterns and shared by the individual, which will hold the society together and protect the ultimate freedom of the individual. Appropriate loyalty and commitment to such shared values is a prime requisite for institutional stability and undivided freedom in the future.

Thus we face a series of profound paradoxes; for in a technological society, the historical and human values which led to its being and which must be a vital and pervasive part of its process may apparently be in direct conflict with the quality of life as it is lived in that society.

A society which places a premium upon abstract and symbolic work must guarantee in the education of its children a strong relationship between "symbol" and "thing," between sense and sensibility. It must give equal attention to the development of artistic and non-verbal, as well as the logical and verbal, characteristics of the child. It must develop the full animal, spiritual, and intellectual qualities of a child, so that in his own continuing consciousness he may be possessed of the widest horizons of choice and feeling.

A society which places a premium upon loyalty and conformity to the larger organization must teach its children to hold dear their self-integrity and to accord dignity of self to others, sometimes at the expense of the immediate needs of the group. It must place highest emphasis upon individuality and freedom of decision in the face of the collective nature of the technical act.

A society which will be subject to continuous institutional and social change must teach its children a profound commitment to deep and enduring human values. The values, which men know deep in their hearts as guidelines for right action, must be articulated, revitalized, and made part of the educational process at all levels.

To the extent that a technological society takes on aspects of dehumanization, religious and educational leadership must counter by placing urgent and highest priority upon the human values in the educational process. Otherwise life *can* become inhumane, *can* become bound in technique, and *can* suffer confusion of purpose.

> Where is the life we have lost in living?
> Where is the wisdom we have lost in knowledge?
> Where is the knowledge we have lost in information?

It is incumbent upon religious leaders and educators to help prevent a future in which these questions need be asked.

SIGMA: A TACTICAL BLUEPRINT

---

by ALEXANDER TROCCHI

I<small>T IS OUR</small> contention that, for many years now, a change, which might usefully be regarded as evolutionary, has been taking place in the minds of men; they have been becoming aware of the implications of self-consciousness. And, here and there throughout the world, individuals are more or less pur-

Reprinted from *City Lights Journal No. 2,* edited by Lawrence Ferlinghetti. Copyright © 1964 by City Lights Books. By permission of the publisher.

posively concerned with evolving techniques to inspire and sustain self-consciousness in all men.

However imperfect, fragmentary, and inarticulate this new force may presently appear, it is now in the process of becoming conscious of itself in the sense that its individual exponents are beginning to recognize their involvement and consciously to concern themselves with the technical problems of mutual recognition and, ultimately, of concerted action.

History is of societies geared to and through their every institution affirmative of the past, which tends, whatever its complexion, to perpetuate itself. Thus there is a natural inertia in history. Conventions, and the institutions which lend them authority, crystallize. Change is resisted, particularly changes in ways of thinking. The change which concerns us here was first explicit in modern science; the same change has been announced for close on a century in modern art. A whole new way of thinking became possible with the twentieth century. Just as the substantial, objective world was destroyed by modern science, so all modern art has turned on the conventional object and destroyed it. Modern art is expressive of the evolutionary change we are speaking about; modern science furnishes us with the methods and techniques in terms of which we can postulate and resolve the practical problems of adapting ourselves to history in a new, conscious and creative way.

In looking for a word to designate a possible international association of men who are concerned individually and in concert to articulate an effective strategy and tactics for this cultural revolution (cf. *The Invisible Insurrection*), it was thought necessary to find one which provoked no obvious responses. We chose the word "sigma." Commonly used in mathematical practice to designate all, the sum, the whole, it seemed to fit very well with our notion that all men must eventually be included.

In general, we prefer to use the word "sigma" with a small letter, as an adjective rather than as a noun, for there already exists a considerable number of individuals and groups whose ends, consciously or not, are near as dammit identical with our own, groups which are already called X and Y and Z and whose members may be somewhat reluctant to subsume their public identities under any other name. If these groups could be persuaded of the significance of linking themselves "adjectively" to sigma, it would for the present be enough. Moreover, in the foreseeable future, we may very well judge it prudent to maintain multiple legal identities; doing so, we may avoid provoking the more obvious kinds of resistance.

Actually dispersed as we are, and will be until several self-conscious focal-points (sigma-centers) are established, effective communications are vital. All individuals and groups the world over must be contacted and henceforth invited to participate. People must be located and activated: we are confronted with the technical problem of elaborating ways of gearing the power of all of us individuals to an effective flywheel. Thus must be solved without requiring anyone to sink his identity in anything noxiously metaphysical.

In *The Invisible Insurrection* we touched on the kind of situation we wish to bring about. We conceived it to be a kind of spontaneous university. But the term "university" has some unfortunate connotations and is, besides, too limited to include the entire complex of vital and infectious human processes we have in mind to detonate first in England and subsequently throughout the world. The original spontaneous university (or sigma-center) will be a fountainhead only. We are concerned with cities and civilizations, not with "classrooms" in the conventional sense; nevertheless, we are at the beginning of it all and must commence with certain practical considerations. Our experimental situation, our international conference, must be located so that our "cosmonauts" can either congregate or be in contact.

It is not simply a question of founding yet another publishing house, nor another art gallery, nor another theater group, and of sending it on its high-minded way amongst the mammon-engines of its destruction. Such a firm (I am thinking in terms of the West for the moment), if it were successful in sustaining itself within the traditional cultural complex, would "do much good," no doubt. But it is not the publishing industry alone that is in our view out of joint (and has no survival potential); to think almost exclusively in terms of publishing is to think in terms of yesterday's abstractions. A softer bit and more resilient harness won't keep the old nag out of the knackery. Of course sigma will publish. When we have something to publish. And we shall do it

effectively, forgetting no technique evolved in yesterday's publishing. (Or we may find it convenient to have this or that published by a traditional publisher.) But it is art too in which we
are interested. With the leisure of tomorrow in mind, it is all the
grids of expression we are concerned to seize.

That is what we mean when we say "literature is dead"; not
that some people won't write (indeed, perhaps all people will), or
even write a novel (although we feel this category has about out-
lived its usefulness), but the writing of anything in terms of
capitalist economy, as an economic act, with reference to economic
limits, is not in our view interesting. It is business. It is a jungle
talent. We also wish to paint and we also wish to sing. We have
to think of a society in which leisure is a fact and in which a
man's very survival will depend upon his ability to cope with it.
The conventional spectator-creator dichotomy must be broken
down. The traditional "audience" must participate.

We might even say we don't know what we wish to do; we
wish, rather, continuously to consult with other intelligences on
an international and experimental basis. Amongst other things,
we believe in the vital relevance of pamphlets and pamphleteering,
but it is not that we shall bring out twelve (the round dozen!)
pamphlets on the fourteenth of September to "launch" our imprint
and proceed to send our private little ball spinning along the well-
worn grooves of the cultural pinball-machine: that would be to
invite the destruction of the intuition which drives us to articulate.
Nor can we limit ourselves, as far as printed matter is concerned,
to the traditional media. One interesting "publishing" project, for
example, would be to rent an advertisement panel in (say) four
of the London Underground stations for a trial period of one
year, and to print our weekly (or monthly) magazine poster-size.
Obviously, the weekly poster could be placed in other spots as
well. A broadsheet, personal size, could be sent to sponsors and
subscribers who might value a facsimile collection of the posters.
And why stop at London? (Undergrounds of the World Unite!)
The editorial job in such a project would be complex but not
impractical. Thirty or forty writers sympathetic towards sigma
could be solicited in advance. Other conventional projects, which
we shall discuss in more detail later, are: advertising space in
little magazines; in the personal columns of national newspapers;

all manner of labels, matchboxes, etc.; toilet paper (for the *New Yorker* reader who has everything); cigarette cards; the backs of playing cards; etc. Of course, we shall publish books as well; but the greater part of what we shall eventually decide to do will grow out of the conflux of creative ideas and goodwill that is sigma. To begin with, we must make a continuous, international, experimental conference possible; a permanent meeting of minds to articulate and promote the vast cultural change which UNESCO is prevented by its origins from effecting.

We must say to our sponsors: while we can envisage sigma's flourishing economically in the West, it is not primarily a business organization. We require a protected situation, a place to confer and corporately create. A great deal has already been done. But our strength lies not so much in what has so far been done purposively in our name in *the availability of other intelligences to our transcategorical inspiration*. All over the world today are little conflagrations of intelligence, little pockets of "situation-making." Some of the first theorists called themselves *"Situationistes."* Other individuals and groups who appear to us to have similar attitudes are presently being gathered into a comprehensive index which will serve as the basis for our communications. We have to evolve the mechanisms and techniques for a kind of supercategorical cultural organization. Some of its features we believe to be as follows.

(1) *Sigma as International Index*

The first essential for those whose purpose it is to link mind with mind in a supernatural (transcategorical) process is some kind of efficient expanding index, an international "who's who." It is a question of taking stock, of surveying the variety of talent and goodwill at our disposal. *Who* is with us? *Who knows* he is with us? Our general invitation might read something like this:

We should like to invite you to take part in an international conference about the future of things. The brief introductory statement enclosed (*The Invisible Insurrection*) should give you an idea of what we are about.

We have chosen the word sigma because as a symbol it is free of bothersome semantic accretions.

Actually dispersed as we are, and will be until several self-conscious focal points are established (in each of which an experimental situation is self-consciously in the process of articulating itself), effective communications are vital.

Now and in the future our center is everywhere, our circumference nowhere. No one is in control. No one is excluded. A man will know when he is participating without our offering him a badge.

We have decided that as far as it is economically possible you should receive all our future informations. Sigma's publications are in general given away free to those who participate in its activities.

The conference begins now and goes on indefinitely. We are particularly anxious to have your participation soon, as soon as possible.

sigma associates

We are writers, painters, sculptors, musicians, dancers, physicists, bio-chemists, philosophers, neurologists, engineers, and whatnots, of every race and nationality. The catalogue of such a reservoir of talent, intelligence, and power is of itself a spur to our imagination.

(2) *Sigma as Spontaneous University*

We can write off existing universities. These lately illustrious institutions are almost hopelessly geared and sprocketed to the cultural-economic axles of the status quo; they have become a function of the context they came into being to inspire.

Of the American universities, Paul Goodman writes: "Therefore we see the paradox that, with so many centers of possible intellectual criticism and intellectual initiative, there is so much inane conformity, and the universities are little models of the Organized System itself." Secession, the forming of new models; this is the traditional answer, and in our view the only one. So Oxford broke away from the Sorbonne and Cambridge from Oxford, and "the intellectual ferment was most vigorous, the teaching most brilliant, the monopoly of the highest education most complete, almost before a university existed at all." (Hastings Rashdall: *The Universities of Europe in the Middle Ages.*) The bureaucracies of the universities mesh with the bureaucracy of the state, mirror it in little; and the specific disease of bureaucracy is that it tends to spawn more of itself and function as a parasitic organism, inventing "needs" to justify its existence, ultimately suffocating the host it was intended to nurture. (Cf. the satire of William Burroughs.) The universities have become factories for the production of degreed technicians; the various governmental reports on them (particularly the Robbins Report), skating over the thick crust of centuries, call simply for more and more of the same.

The empty chapels of the Cambridge colleges are a significant symbol of the decline of the parent institution. Built originally to house the soul of the community of scholars, they are presently derelict. Quite recently, there was a newspaper report of a prize being offered to the student who wrote the best essay on what should be done with them. It was awarded to a student who suggested that they be converted to laboratories for science, dining halls and residential quarters for the students, libraries, etc. In short, what was once the vital spiritual center was to be turned over to material purposes; space is short, and imagination shorter. That something immaterial, something intangible, has been lost was overlooked. There would have been more hope for Cambridge, certainly more evidence of spirituality, if it had been decided to turn them into brothels.

Meanwhile, those who (rightly or wrongly) are deeply distrustful of the statistical method, clamoring for the abolition of college examinations, tend to overlook the disastrous influence the examination-dominated curriculum has upon the attitudes and habits of the student population at our universities. The competitive system encourages the clever tactician, the glib, the plausible. It is certainly painful and perhaps even dangerous for a student to become deeply interested in his subject, or he is constantly having to get ready to demonstrate his virtuosity; the students at our universities are so busy practicing appearances that one seldom meets one who is concerned with the realities. The entire system is a dangerous anachronism. Secession by vital minds everywhere is the only answer.

The more imaginative university teachers all over the world are well aware of these things. But they can do nothing until they can see a possible alternative. Sigma as spontaneous university is such an alternative. It can only grow out of the combined effort of individuals and groups of individuals working *unofficially* at supernational level. A large country house, not too far from London (and Edinburgh, and New York, and Paris etc.), is being sought for the pilot project.

While a great deal of lip-service is paid to the significance of a man's environment (especially during the early formative years), our societies push ahead willy-nilly boxing people into honey-comb apartment blocks to meet the immediate requirements of industry. For the moment, there is little we can do about this, but we can take care that the structural features of our sigma-centers are geared to and inspiring of the future as we imagine it can be rather than the past and present out of which men must evolve. Our experimental sigma-center must be in all its dimensions a model for the functions of the future rather than of the past. Our architects, arriving at the site with the first group of associates, will design the architecture of the spontaneous university for and around the participants.

The site should not be farther from London than Oxford or Cambridge, for we must be located within striking distance of the metropolis, since many of our undertakings will be in relation to cultural phenomena already established there, and so that those coming from abroad can travel back and forth from the capital without difficulty. Moreover, we have always envisaged our experimental situation as a kind of shadow reality of the future existing side by side with the present "establishment," and the process as one of gradual "in(ex)filtration." If we were to locate ourselves too far away from the centers of power, we should run the risk of being regarded by some of those we are concerned to attract as a group of utopian escapists, spiritual exiles, hellbent for Shangri-La on the bicycle of our frustration. Then, "The original building will stand deep within its own grounds, preferably on a riverbank. It should be large enough for a pilot-group (astronauts of inner space) to situate itself, orgasm genius, and their tools and dream-machines and amazing apparatus and appurtenances; with outhouses for workshops large as could accommodate light industry, the entire site to allow for spontaneous architecture and eventual town-planning," etc. (*The Invisible Insurrection.*)

Here our "experimental laboratory" will locate itself, our community-as-art, and begin exploring the possible functions of a society in which leisure is a dominant fact, and universal community, in which the conventional assumptions about reality and the constraints which they imply are no longer operative, in which art and life are no longer divided. The "university," which we suspect will have much in common with Joan Littlewood's "leisuredrome" (if she will forgive my coining a word), will be operated by a "college" of teacher-practitioners with no separate administration.

The cultural atrophy endemic in conventional universities must be countered with an entirely new impulse. No pedagogical re-arrangements, no further proliferation of staff or equipment or buildings, nor even the mere subtraction of administration of planning will help. What is essential is a new conscious sense of community-as-art-of-living; the experimental situation (labora-tory) with its "personnel" is itself to be regarded as an artifact, a continuous making, a creative process, a community enacting it-self in its individual members. Within our hypothetical context many traditional historical problems will be recognized at once as artificial and contingent; simultaneously we shall realize our ability to outflank them by a new approach; and certain more vital problems which today receive scant attention or none at all, together with others which in a conventional context cannot even be articulated, will be recognized as more appropriate to any possible future of mankind on this planet.

We must choose our original associates widely from among the most brilliant creative talents in the arts and sciences.

They will be men and women who understand that one of the most important achievements of the twentieth century is the wide-spread recognition of the essentially relative nature of all lan-guages, who realize that most of our basic educational techniques have been inherited from a past in which almost all men were ignorant of the limitations inherent in any language. They will be men and women who are alive to the fact that a child's first six years of schooling are still dedicated to providing him with the emotional furniture imposed on his father before him, and that from the beginning he is trained to respond in terms of a neuro-linguistic system utterly inadequate to the real problems with which he will have to contend in the modern world.

Our university must become a community of mind whose vital function is to discover and articulate the functions of tomorrow, an association of free men creating a fertile ambience for new knowledge and understanding (men who don't jump to the conclusion Kropotkin carried a bomb because he was an anarchist) who will create an independent moral climate in which the best of what is thought and imagined can flourish. The community which is the university must become a living model for society at large.

(3) *Sigma as International Cultural Engineering Co-operative*

(a) *The international pipeline*   When sigma-centers exist near the capitals of many countries, associate artists and scientists traveling abroad will be able to avail themselves of all the facilities of the local center. They may choose simply to reside there or they may wish to participate. If the visitor is a celebrity, it would probably be to his advantage to do any "interview" work (audio or video) in the sigma-center where "angle" and editing can be his own. Sigma will then handle negotiations with local radio and television. The imaginative cultivation of this international pipeline would be a real contribution to international understanding.

(b) *Cultural promotion*   This field is too vast to be treated fully here. It includes all the interesting cultural projects, conferences, international newspaper, publishing ventures, film and television projects, etc., which have been and will be suggested by associates during conferences. Many of these ideas, realized efficiently, would make a great deal of money. All this work would contribute to the sigma image.

(c) *General cultural agents*   Some of the associates, especially the younger ones who are not previously committed elsewhere, will be glad to be handled by sigma. Obviously, we shall be in a position to recognize new talent long before the more conventional agencies, and, as our primary aim will not be to make money, we shall be able to cultivate a young talent, guarding the young person's integrity.

(d) *General cultural consultants*   The enormous pool of talent at our disposal places us in an incomparable position vis-à-vis providing expert counsel on cultural matters. We can advise on everything cultural, from producing a play to building a picture collection. Apropos the latter, one of our proposed services is to offer an insurance policy to a buyer against the depreciation in value of any work of art recommended by sigma. It may frequently be advisable, economically or otherwise, for sigma to encourage some established company to undertake this or that cultural project: that is to say, sigma will not necessarily wait passively to be consulted. (Obviously, ideas ripe for commercial exploitation cannot be made public in this context.)

Conclusion

Perhaps the most striking example of the wrong-headed attitude towards art in official places is provided by the recent scuffle to keep the well-known Leonardo cartoon from leaving the United Kingdom. The official attitude has more in common with stamp-collecting than with aesthetics. The famous cartoon could have been sold abroad for around £1,000,000. For a small fraction of that sum, *perfect replicas* of it could have been made and distributed to every art gallery in the country. It is small wonder that the man in the street has such a confused attitude towards art. This confusion of value with money has infected everything. The conventional categories distinguishing the arts from each other, tending as they do to perpetuate the profitable institutions which have grown up around them, can for the moment only get in the way of creativity and our understanding of it.

The basic shift in attitude described in the foregoing pages must happen. IT IS HAPPENING. Our problem is to make men conscious of the fact, and to inspire them to participate in it. Man must seize control of his own future: only by doing so can he ever hope to inherit the earth.

PROPOSITIONS ABOUT TECH-
NOLOGICAL INNOVATIONS

by JAMES R. BRIGHT

THIS PAPER presents some research conclusions as a number of *Propositions* about technological innovation. The word "proposition" has been chosen since these conclusions are not "laws," for one can certainly cite exceptions. And to present them as "hypotheses" is to neglect the support of repeated observations found in studying xerography and some thirty other recent technological innovations. The work of other researchers also supports some of these propositions. Finally, "proposition" was chosen to convey an assertion of some force, with a modest level of confidence. The *Propositions* are directed at management, for it is the managers of business and government institutions that are the directors of society's technological and economic efforts. A second intended audience is the students of economic and social progress—the academicians and their industrial and governmental counterparts whose theories and ideas influence the policies and actions of management. The *Propositions* are in no sense offered as being final, complete, or universally valid. Some of them are only the starting point for further research. I intend that they be regarded as concepts, observations, and points of view that deserve consideration by the decision makers as they make choices to new technology.

1. *Technological Innovation—the Process of Translating Technical Knowledge into economic reality involves four major functions* (usually but not always in the following sequence): the *scientific* (search for knowledge), the *engineering* (reduction to

practice), the *entrepreneurial* (introduction to society), the *managerial* (optimization of usage). Each of these functions requires a different type of skill and knowledge may involve some changes of attitudes and values, and requires the manipulation of very different resources. Technological innovations are delayed or may fail because the person or group involved lacks the skill, the knowledge of the resources to carry out some portions of one or more of these functions.

W. R. MacLaurin pointed out that, in the case of radio, no one man ever carried out this full process (Armstrong, with FM radio, possibly might be an exception). Dr. Edwin Land of Polaroid fame is an unquestioned exception to this proposition. Doubtless there are a few more such individuals, but one must search long and hard to find them.

Conclusion: Management must realize that an innovation requires these four types of activities, roughly in the sequence mentioned. In proceeding with a radical technological innovation, management must continually assess the current leadership needs of the innovation process, and it must nurture the project by providing the necessary skills and leadership at the right times.

2. *The full Process of Technological Innovation usually takes upwards of 10 years; and a quarter of a century is not an uncommon time.* Although it is frequently stated that the time to innovate is much shorter today, these statements usually turn out to be based upon erroneous data or applicable to only a portion of the innovative process. To understand this proposition we must break down the process into its chronological stages. While the process of technological innovation can be divided in as few as three or as many as fifteen stages, I find the following eight-stage division most useful. It uses identifiable points, which facilitate measurement and comparison. These particular stages also reflect transitions of the innovation to the next of the four basic functions. Of course, I do not mean to imply that these stages always can be rigorously or sharply defined. I shall identify some exceptions to these sequences after reviewing them.

Stage 1—*Scientific suggestion, discovery and observation, or recognition of need*. Most innovations seem to begin with the latter, but there are notable exceptions such as atomic power, the laser, and penicillin.

Stage 2—*Development of theory or design concept*. While early theories or designs usually are imperfect, their definition leads to a focus of effort along certain lines. In many technical innovations, new scientific theory is not necessary or may be late in coming. Then a combination of known science and/or technology—a design concept—is the goal of this stage.

Stage 3—*Laboratory verification of theory or design concept*. This is the laboratory experiment which simply confirms the validity of the principle suggested in Stage 2.

Stage 4—*Laboratory demonstration of application*. Here the concept is first embodied in a bread-board model of the device, a sample material, or a laboratory model of the process, as it would be used (hopefully) by society. In other words, the concept is demonstrated in application form.

Stage 5—*Field trial or full scale trial*. The innovation next is developed to a level where it can be tried under operating conditions. Usually, it has passed the prototype stage but is short of being the marketable, commercial version. The stage is defined as the achievement of *technical success under normal operating conditions*.

Stage 6—*Commercial introduction*. This stage is marked by "first sale" (or operational use for the military) as distinct from experimental use. The line between Stages 5 and 6 is sometimes far from clear, and may be shifted simply by intent. We mean to imply, in Stage 6, that the innovation has been purchased in the belief that it is now applicable and reliable enough for everyday requirements.

Stage 7—*Widespread adoption*. A subjective judgement is required to mark this stage, and I have been unable to pin down a single common measure of accomplishment. Therefore we include several notions: (a) that the innovation is widely recognized as a practical device and not as experimental, (b) that the innovation has enough so as to achieve profits for the innovating firm, (c) that substantial numbers are in use.

Stage 8—*Proliferation.* The innovation is used in a number of devices and its principle is adopted for other purposes. The innovation spreads in two ways: (a) the original device is applied to a number of new uses (on more than an experimental scale), and (b) the technical or scientific principle is applied to other machines, processes, or materials. (E.g., (a) consider how radar spread from military uses to commercial planes, ships, air traffic control, police cars, and private boats; (b) consider how the microwave technology of radar was applied to commercial heating, to home ranges for cooking purposes, as well as to microwave communication systems.)

Obviously, these stages are not always sharply defined, false starts are made, and some stage may be rapidly bypassed. Most important, we must realize that though the main thrust of the innovation can be identified as having achieved a certain point, some components may be in very different and much earlier stages. And even when the basic innovation is clearly well along (as in the case of, say, the computer or television), the research and engineering development stages are filled with new technological elements (such as solid-state circuitry today), which leads to further drastic changes in the device or performance. Nevertheless, the fundamental notion of a "process of technological innovation," with identifiable stages, remains extremely useful.

Take the statement that "the time to innovate has been greatly reduced"—a statement that is frequently made and often supported by selected data offered by very competent technologists. However, when one applies these definitions carefully, a much more accurate picture emerges with significant managerial implications. It is true that the period from Stage 4, *Laboratory demonstration of use,* to Stage 6, *Commercial introduction,* can be and is shortened by the use of new management techniques such as parallel development, PERT, and related concepts. However, can we identify formal procedures that have been widely applied to speed the first three stages of innovation? By what means has industry speeded the last three? Only Governments have speeded progress from Stage 5 through Stage 7, for some innovations deemed socially desirable, such as agricultural, health, and environmental needs. Governments also have shortened the T/I process time by providing funding of R&D costs, by providing availability of the innovation, by education of users, and by legislation or taxation to speed adoption. But commercial equivalents generally do not exist. In practice, the concept of leasing and otherwise financing use by the customer may well speed Stages 6 and 7, but one doubts that leasing to speed diffusion is a conscious policy in more than a handful of cases.

Of course, Governments have speeded many innovations by funding the entire process. The classic case probably is atomic weapons, in which the U.S. Government picked up the innovation after Stage 2, *Development of theory,* and carried out multiple approaches to development through Stages 4, 5, and 6, and on a massive scale. Note, however, that in the case of nuclear power for civilian use, Stage 7 has been reached only recently. Nuclear power has been *over twenty years* in going from Stage 2 to Stage 7! The manager dealing with a radical innovation presented to him in the *Laboratory application* (Stage 4) must think of supporting it for roughly a decade to reach significant profits.

The manager can confirm this ten-year minimum for himself by simple estimates based on his own experience. Let us suppose that his technical people show him a laboratory model of the new technology, which successfully serves a promising and useful purpose. How long will it take to achieve a prototype for full scale or field trial? One to four years? *Assume two years.*

Then how much longer until a commercially salable product, with necessary adjuncts in the form of maintenance, user training aids, promotional support, etc., is ready for sale? One to four years? *Assume two years.*

Once first sale is made, how long will it be until the number of sales recovers costs and achieves a profitable position for the firm, or until the innovation is in widespread use? Three to ten years? *Assume six years.* Using these rough assumptions on the optimistic basis the total time is about ten years! Now allow for the fact that we may be lucky in shortening some of these phases, but are more likely to have underestimated at least one of them. Then a fifteen-year time span is a strong probability.

But notice that we ignored Stage 1, the birth of the concept,

Stage 2, the achievement of a theory or concept on which we would work, and Stage 3, the verification of theory or concept and time to reach Stage 4, laboratory demonstration. Surely this must usually involve five years or so. Therefore, our likely time span for the full process has extended to twenty years. (Although Carlson carried xerography through Stages 1–3 in three years, six more years went by until the innovation reached Stage 4. It took xerography around five to seven years (1950 to 1955–57) to move from first sale to wide adoption. It is thought-provoking to realize that Carlson began his work on xerography in 1934, so twenty years passed before this innovation achieved Stage 7. If we consider his original goal—the office copier—another five years was required and a quarter of a century went by.

Of course, management usually is confronted with a proposal already in Stage 3 or 4. Also we recognize that "success" may be adequately present long before the achievement of Stage 7, *Widespread adoption*. But, at the very best, this leaves management dealing with a process taking in the order of a decade! How does this fact sit with conventional management goals, resources, aspirations, and innovative procedures, and even management reward systems (based on last year's profits)? Not very well! More seriously, the present value theory which we teach our management students is totally inadequate for this spectrum of management decisions. If present value theory is applied to radical innovations it will discourage progress and will cause management to reject magnificent opportunities. It is only proper to agree that it probably will also forestall some painful errors for firms and individuals, and it will preclude those failures that inevitably apply to some percentage of attempts to deal with radical innovation.

Conclusion: Management decisions about radical technological innovations need to be made with an entirely different value system than is applied to most business problems. We are dealing with a ten- to twenty-five-year process, and it is wrong to use conventional business wisdom when relating oneself to this long process of *radical* technological innovation.

3. *Radical innovations often originate outside the traditional supplier-user sources.** In late 1968 we studied two current and little known innovations, and found the same phenomenon:

1. The *Rolligon* is a vehicle operating on very low pressure (2 p.s.i.) barrel-like bladders (tires). Its rough terrain capability is now finding success as a "swamp buggy" for oil exploration and construction work in jungles and swamps of the Gulf Coast and Southeast Asia. The idea originated in 1951, when a U.S. school teacher in Alaska observed the Eskimos handling whale boats on soft rollers made of inflated sealskins.

2. After a dozen years of work the world's first all-plastic airplane is about to be certified by the FAA (in Midland, Texas). This plane has a unique construction, based upon a stiff fiberglass shell filled with a cellular plastic core. The construction leads to outstanding strength-to-weight performance and manufacturing economies, plus numerous other advantages. The entire project was the brain child of a dentist, Dr. Windecker, who applied his knowledge of bone structure to achieve strength and light weight. He has been supported by the Dow Chemical Company and a group of oilmen and ranchers in the Midland area. These two examples are further evidence of this peculiar and fascinating proposition.

Conclusion: Firms and Governments should develop and exhibit more interest, respect and methodology in *searching* for techno-

* Innovation	"Logical originators" (Traditional suppliers and/or users)	Actual origin of the commercially prominent concept
Diesel locomotive	Steam-locomotive builders and railroads	Automotive firm
Kodachrome film	Photographic industry	Independent inventors (two musicians)
Xerography	Business-machine industry	Patent lawyer from electrical-components firm
Polaroid film	Photographic industry	Independent inventor
Phototypesetting	Printing-machine industry	Independent inventors
Computer	Business-machine industry	Universities and U.S. Army Ballistics Laboratory
Ground effects	Aircraft, automotive, or transportation industry	Private inventor supported by British Government
Transistor	Electrical component manufacturers	Bell Telephone Laboratories

logical opportunity and threat outside the traditional and logical sources, and among people who may have little in the way of conventional technical credibility.

All managers, particularly older, senior men who have built great enterprises around new technology, should be given periodic reminders that the technology that will replace theirs may well originate outside of their industry.

4. *The most important application of a new technology is not always that which was visualized first: and a corollary: Technological innovations frequently gain their first foothold for purposes that were originally not thought of or were deemed to be quite secondary.* This proposition is of utmost significance to management, and especially to market research inputs to management decisions. We are indebted to Rupert MacLaurin, whose classic study of radio led him to state that Marconi's shift from attempting to exploit applications of radio on land to ship communications "illustrates the principle that the most profitable outlet for an innovation is frequently not the one which is explored first."

Our study of contemporary innovations is replete with more confirmation of this phenomenon. We have redefined MacLaurin's observation because it has two quite different aspects—one dealing with that *first use,* which is so desperately needed to launch an innovation; and the second, with the *ultimate major use.* As examples of the first aspect: radio got its start at sea, rather than in replacing the land telegraph as Marconi had intended. Xerography failed initially in office copying but was rapidly adopted to make master plates for multilith duplicating machines. Its second major adoption was to make enlarged reproductions of engineering drawings that had been stored in microfilm.

And as examples of the second aspect: radio was conceived as a means of communication for private messages, but its great use was in sending public messages (broadcasting). The computer was originally thought of by many as a business machine that would mechanize much office paper work. However, it is clear that the computer is far more than that, and its great importance lies in the storage and manipulation of data and in problem solving and machine control capability. Indeed, we still do not know the ultimate importance of the computer, which is diffusing through society and performing hundreds of once unimagined services. And who will be bold enough to now predict the ultimate most important use of the laser, or of holography?

Conclusion: The sponsors of a radical technology should adopt a policy of searching for applications with an open mind toward new uses and a readiness to support trials in unexpected fields. The strategy should be one of exploration, rather than of single-minded commitment to one pre-determined usage. Therefore, market research studies should be taken with a very large grain of salt, for it is dubious that any one small group can imagine or discover the potential uses of a radical innovation that all of society will uncover. This is particularly true because other new technology and social developments create future needs that were unimagined when the early market studies were made. The market we can foresee today is likely to be drastically altered by changes during the decade in which the innovation grows to reality.

5. *Technological capabilities and parameters (such as power, speed, strength, etc.) advance in an exponential manner over time.* The fact that progress is of exponential nature is of utmost significance to decision-makers. Once certain troublesome features are surmounted, a technological capability increases at a rate that can only be described as explosive. This phenomenon can be seen in the speed of manned aerial vehicles, the computation time of computers, the miniaturization of solid-state circuitry, and many other devices. Judgments made about technical progress may be wildly off the mark, due to failure to appreciate this curve or to estimate its exponents.

Conclusion: In estimating future achievement, the nature of this exponential progress curve must be remembered. "Straight-line" progress can be anticipated initially, but when the crucial technical breakthroughs are made, progress will explode.

6. *Advances in technological capabilities often reach points of diminishing economic returns.* This is due to the cost of achieving the last incremental advance, or to inability to use the gain

for economic purposes. E.g., as transport speeds cut travel time from U.S. to Europe to, say, three hours, the relative advantage of a further cut to two hours is less. At some point the value of time is dissipated by other requirements of the system, such as waiting for baggage, or checking in. Or consider overnight air freight coast-to-coast. Overnight service has value to many firms, but five- to six-hour service arriving, say, at 4 a.m. has little or no additional economic value.

Conclusion: The immediate application of every additional technological gain may not have much economic value. However, the reason for this seems to be that other parts of the system (or society) are not yet in a position to benefit from the gain. In addition to the need for proper timing of the introduction, this proposition points to new opportunities in improving the ends of the system that are reducing the advantages of the advance.

7. *Accelerated and often unexpected progress comes about due to the impingement and convergence of one technology on another.* Thus, solid-state electronic circuitry provided the cost reduction, size reduction, and reliability gains essential for computer progress. Numerical control of machine tools was extremely limited until the generation of control tapes by computer became practical.

Conclusion: Many erroneous rejections of new technical possibilities or their markets occur because we tend to hold all other technology constant. We must always examine the possibility that other technological elements are also subject to exponential progress, and so may rapidly change the merits or feasibility of a particular technological innovation.

8. *The demonstration of a new technological concept is a most critical point to the progress of an innovation.* Demonstrations must be planned with great care because they can easily discourage support:

(a) Very few people can grasp the economic significance of a demonstration of a *scientific principle*. Few people can translate "principle" into "hardware."

(b) Failure in a detail is readily judged by observers to be a failure in basic concept.

(c) Successful demonstration of laboratory application or prototype easily causes one to underestimate the time needed to achieve commercialization and profits.

Conclusion: We need greater skill and thoughtfulness in appraising demonstrations.

9. *The mode of financing usage of the innovation of utmost significance to the rate of diffusion and to the financial returns to the innovating firm.* Few technological innovators have paid much attention to the design of the system by which users or consumers will pay for the use of their innovation. The importance of this area can be illustrated by the case of xerography. From 1960 to 1965 Xerox Corp. installed about 65,000 Model 914 Copiers in the USA. If these units had been sold for twice manufacturing cost, the gross revenue would have been about $330 million. If the units had been leased for $300 per month, as was considered at one time, the gross revenue would have been about $360 million, with the advantage that further annual lease fees would continue to accrue *and* the company would gain the cash-flow advantages of an enormous depreciation charge. However, using the charge-per-copy pricing system that was actually installed, the gross revenue was about $660 million with the same advantages of continuing revenue and cash flow from depreciation. Roughly, the additional revenue over these 5 years was at least $300 million *more* than the first two plans—a decision equivalent to doubling the value of the innovation!

Furthermore, there is no doubt that the very low cost of the charge-per-copy plan greatly encouraged adoption and speeded diffusion. Consider how slowly the computer would have spread had IBM only sold the machines.

Conclusion: The design of the method of charging for the use of the innovation deserves far more attention than it normally receives.

10. *A major weakness in our national support of the innovative process is the financing of innovation during progress after Stage 3*

(*Verification of theory*) *up to Stage 5* (*Full scale or field trial*). Universities, the U.S. Federal Government and Foundations have policies and funds to support technology in Stages 1 to 4 (and sometimes even further if they have sponsored the first portion of the process). There are also many financial and industrial institutions that will readily support an innovation that has reached Stage 5. But in between there is no formal effective support procedure by government or society in the USA.

Notice that scientific research is readily funded as an act of national faith and intellectual respectability, but the development of inventions and their launching into society as technical innovations is not often nationally supported. We do not fund this activity as an act of faith; and the private agency or individual who does so is not regarded as doing something particularly socially desirable and important. Instead, he is regarded as gambling on a long shot for personal gain, if not as a fool pouring money into a "crackpot" idea!

Furthermore, we leave this search for financial support of the innovation in the hands of the inventor. During this crucial time, in effect, society expects the inventor to drop his real forte (invention), and to become a promoter, entrepreneur, and financier. Why should the inventor, dedicated to a technological struggle and probably already under financial stress, be expected to be an effective fund raiser? Psychologically and intellectually he is not (usually) a good candidate for this job. Is it any wonder that social and economic progress is delayed?

The point is badly missed by American society. A panel convened by the United States Government, and with the help of distinguished industrialists and technicians, in January 1967, went on record stating that:

In view of present information on the potential availability of venture capital, the Federal Government should take no action with respect to the establishment of new federally supported programs for the furnishing of venture capital.

The panel showed a puzzling tender concern for inventors, for they made a number of excellent recommendations to help the inventors' financial position by allowing various tax exemptions and adjustments. They explicitly recognized the need to encourage invention and inventors. But *they missed the point that venture-capital agencies support inventors with only slightly more risk-taking propensity* than do conventional financial sources. They missed the point that *no venture-capital agency takes on an underwriting program unless it is highly confident that it will be a profitable venture.*

The panel jumped right past the fundamental distinction made above—that we presently do not have a good way of financing technological innovation from Stage 3 to Stage 5, as we do for basic research. The venture-capital schemes now in existence leave the inventor right where he was—searching and begging for supporters to help him move his invention from the laboratory to commercial introduction. These venture-capital agencies use the same old judgment criteria—"Can *we* make a profit out of this, and in a reasonably short time?" Thus the inventor does not receive the support that society gives to the researcher. If we are to have more innovation, we must give the inventor more support to invent, and not expect him also to be a financier and promoter.

Nothing above is intended to deny that inventors have a better chance today than did Carlson (xerography) of getting support from some source. The whole nation—government, industry, and financial leaders—are far more conscious of the opportunities in new technology. The point is that we in the USA do not yet have a good system of financing this critical portion of the innovative process. Indeed, as a national policy, we do not even recognize that there is an inconsistency in our support of the innovative process. One hopes that these "propositions" will help to persuade society that such a screening in the early stages of innovation is impossible, as well as undesirable, for it will cause a nation to forego some great opportunities.

THESE DAYS

by JOHN CAGE

Pᴀʀᴀʟʟᴇʟs may now be drawn between individual experience and social experience, for we have, through electronic technology, extended the central nervous system (Marshall Mc-Luhan). Mind, formerly housed in each person's head, is now also exteriorized, at home outside (nature, society) globally, and, more and more, outer-spatially, i.e., universally ("God" made "definite"—Buckminster Fuller).

Searching for alternatives to world violence, we can therefore take as directives proven means used now or formerly by individuals to "pacify" their minds. What were and/or are they?

Self-discipline. That is to say: self-alteration, particularly with regard to ego likes and dislikes, ego memory and resultant fixed habit ("Leave thy father and mother and follow Me." Disciple. Yoga: yoking, or, rather, making non-existent the ego. Cf. The ten oxherding pictures of Zen Buddhism. Once caught, the ox [the ego] is no longer visible. What happens? The oxherder, fat, smiling [cf. Konrad Lorenz, conclusion of *On Aggression,* re laughter, humor], returns to the village bearing gifts). The ego can act as a barrier to daily experience (the senses) by cultivating its judgment-making faculty; and as a barrier to nocturnal experience by paying no attention to the poetic warnings given by dreams. Disciplined (by means, traditionally, of myth, religion—e.g., meditation, sitting crosslegged—philosophical exercises—e.g., koan, Wittgenstein—arts, crafts—when these are not self-expressive, ego-flattering activities—the sciences—e.g., Thoreau: "I am sorrel; I am ice."—whatever to which one gives oneself away), the ego is no longer a barrier. One's attention is placed so that "ego" is open, fluent with its experience—dream or received through the senses—it doesn't sit in judgment, but joins in service to others—whether sentient or non-sentient (I'll go along, he said, with the here and the now).

Say one doesn't have the "strength" to discipline (change) himself. Then there are teachers (The world is never left without them. "I am with you always."). And there are chemicals, electrodes. We may be put away, changed in hospitals, or put ourselves away (drop-out, depend on drugs).

Enough for the instance of the individual. Time passes. What of all Mankind and the Earth he inhabits? Global (at least) Mind must be pacified. This will not be accomplished by means of politics: Buckminster Fuller points out, "Take away the energy-distributing networks and the industrial machinery from America, Russia, and all the world's industrialized countries, and within six months more than two billion swiftly and painfully deteriorating people will starve to death. Take away all the world's politicians, all the ideologies and their professional protagonists from these same countries, and send them off on a rocket trip around the sun and leave all the countries their present energy networks, industrial machinery, routine production and distribution personnel, and no more humans will starve nor be afflicted in health than at present." But it could be accomplished (Buckminster Fuller) by means of unemotional (cf. zazen, yoga) problem-solving (comprehensive design science), relating world resources to human needs, so that A.D. 2000, 100% of humanity will be "haves." Nations (i.e. ego) removed, regenerative—constantly accomplishing more with less—fluency of man and man, men and nature, made daily experience. World as a university from which no one graduates. Organization not for control of others, but for implementation of fullest life for others (e.g. air travel, telephone, water that's not polluted, air that's fit to breathe, clothing that suits whatever climate, absence of hunger)— Fuller: "As long as one human being is hungry, the entire human race is hungry."—the home (currently being Russia-U.S.A. designed as space-ship, wireless, and free of utility pipes) placed wherever one wishes to live or move, population stabilized (birth and death rates changingly balanced) and upgraded (eugenics), *use* instead of ownership, property globalized through electronics (there is only one Person, the One we are), etc.

We have, that is, nothing but alternatives to violence, things to which Global Mind may give attention. Time-consuming things rather than humanity destroying ones: Otherwise, Fuller warns, "Oblivion." Nothing's accomplished in the way of Global Discipline by being angry because world's angry (i.e. protest against war), or, rather, what's accomplished is to give further lease on life to divisive structures (nations, politics, finance) that would otherwise die a natural (i.e. technological) death. Recent instance: French riots; De Gaulle's position subsequently strengthened. Divisiveness is being weakened by technology: electrical power, by means of new dielectrics permitting 1,500-mile radius of transmission, now exceeds national boundaries.

We don't vote. Why? The election was national, concerned with power. Our attention's on the world. Concern is service, not power.

We cultivate getting things done by as many people as are interested in doing them without any one person's telling the others what to do.

We renounce laws which protect those who "have" from those who "have-not." If forced to obey them, we do so unseriously.

Substitute for laws: systems intelligently set-up so that they work for all, e.g., utilities.

There'll be violence (We're in the midst of what Fuller calls the critical period; at present 47% have and 53% don't; by '72 it'll be 50–50—end of critical period), but attention placed elsewhere will minimize it (Daniel in the Lion's Den).

GRAND STRATEGY

by R. BUCKMINSTER FULLER

IN ORGANIZING our grand strategy we must first discover where we are now, what our navigational position is in the universal scheme of evolution.

To begin our position-fixing we must first acknowledge that the cushion for our initial trial-and-error experiences is exhausted. The relative abundance of immediately consumable, obviously desirable, or utterly essential resources has been sufficient to allow us to carry on despite our ignorance, but only up to this critical moment—this cushion-for-error of humanity's survival and growth up to now was apparently provided just as a bird inside the egg is provided with liquid nutriment to develop it to a certain point. But then by design, the nutriment is exhausted at just the time when the chick is large enough to be able to locomote on its own legs. And so as the chick pecks at the shell seeking more nutriment it inadvertently breaks open the shell. Stepping forth from its initial sanctuary the young bird must now forage on its own legs and wings to discover the next phase of its regenerative sustenance.

My own picture of humanity today finds us just about to step out from amongst the pieces of our just-broken egg shell. Our innocent, trial-and-error-sustaining nutriment is exhausted. We are faced with an entirely new relationship to the universe. We are going to have to spread our wings of intellect and fly or perish—that is we must dare immediately to fly by the generalized principles governing the universe and not by the ground rules of yesterday's superstitious and erroneously conditioned reflexes.

As we attempt competent thinking, we immediately begin to reuse our innate drive for comprehensive understanding.

Reprinted from William Ewald, ed., *Environment and Change*. Copyright © 1968 by Indiana University Press. By permission of the publisher.

Your particular professional world is one in which the architects and planners, particularly the planners, though rated as
specialists, have a little wider focus than do the other professions.
Also as human beings you often battle the narrow views of specialists—in particular, your patrons the politicians—and the financial and other legal, but no longer comprehensively effective,
heirs to the great pirates' prerogatives. At least you planners are
allowed to look at *all* of Philadelphia, and not just to peek
through a hole at one house or through one door at one room in
that house.

We will begin by eschewing the role of specialists who deal
only in parts. Becoming deliberately expansive instead of con-
tractive, we ask, *"How* do we think in terms of *wholes?"* If it is
true that the bigger the thinking becomes, the more effective it
is, we must ask: "How big can we think?"

One of the modern tools of high intellectual advantage is the
development of what is called *general systems theory*. Employing
it, we begin to think of the largest and most comprehensive systems, and try to do so scientifically.

We start by listing all the important known variables that are
operative in the problem. But if we do not really know how big
"big" is, we may not start big enough and are thus likely to
leave unknown but critical variables outside the system which
will continue to plague us. Interaction of the unknown variables
inside and outside the arbitrarily chosen limits of the system are
probably going to generate misleading or altogether wrong answers. If we are to be effective, we are going to have to think in
both the biggest and most minute ways permitted by intellect
and by the information thus far won through experience.

Can we think of, and state adequately and incisively, what we
mean by *universe?* For *universe* is, at least inferentially, the biggest system. If we could start with universe we would automatically avoid leaving out any strategically critical variables.

We find no record as yet of man having successfully defined
the universe—scientifically and comprehensively to include the
nonsimultaneous and only partially overlapping, micro-macro,
always-and-everywhere-transforming, physical and metaphysical,
omnicomplementary but nonidentical events. Man has failed thus
far, as a specialist, to define the microcosmic limits of divisi-

bility of the nucleus of the atom, but epochally, *has* been able to define successfully the *physical universe*—but not the metaphysical universe—not universe itself as combining both the physical and metaphysical. The scientist was able to define physical universe by virtue of the experimentally verified discovery that energy can neither be created nor lost and therefore that energy is conserved and so *finite*. That means it is definable.

Einstein successfully defined the physical universe as $E = mc^2$. His definition was only a hypothetical venture until fission proved it to be true. The physical universe of associative and disassociative energy was found to be a closed, but nonsimultaneously occurring, system, with its separately occurring events being mathematically measurable, i.e., weighable and equatable.

But the *finite physical universe* did not include the metaphysical aspects of universe. All the unweighables, such as any and all our thoughts and all the abstract mathematics, are weightless. The metaphysical aspects of universe were therefore thought by the physical scientists to be "open" and therefore defied "closed systems" analysis.

I have found, however, as we shall soon witness, that *total universe*, including both its physical and metaphysical behaviors and aspects is *scientifically definable*.

Einstein and others have spoken exclusively about the *physical* department of universe in words which may be integrated and digested as: *the aggregate of nonsimultaneous and only partially overlapping, nonidentical but always complementary, omni-transforming, and weighable energy events*.

Eddington defines science as "The earnest attempt to set in order the facts of experience." Einstein and many other first-rank scientists noted that science is concerned exclusively with "facts of experience." Holding to the scientists' *experiences* as all-important, I define universe, including both physical and metaphysical, as: *the aggregate of all of humanity's consciously apprehended and communicated experiences with the nonsimultaneous, nonidentical and only partially overlapping, always complementary, weighable and unweighable, ever omni-transforming, event sequences*.

Each experience begins and ends, ergo, is finite. Because our apprehending is packaged, both physically and metaphysically, into time increments of alternate awakeness and asleepness, as well as into separate finite conceptions such as the discrete energy quanta and the atomic nucleus components of the fundamental physical discontinuity, all experiences are finite. Physical experiments have found no solids, no continuous surfaces or lines, only discontinuous constellations of individual events. An aggregate of finites is finite. Therefore, universe as experientially defined including both the physical and metaphysical is finite.

It is therefore possible to initiate our general systems formulation at the all-inclusive level of universe from which no strategic variables will be omitted.

There is an operational grand strategy of general systems analysis that proceeds from here. It is played somewhat like the game of "Twenty Questions," but GSA is more efficient—i.e., more economical—in reaching its answers. It is the same procedural strategy that is used by the computer to weed out all the wrong answers until only the right answer is left.

Having adequately defined the whole system, you proceed to subdivide progressively. This is accomplished through division into two parts, one of which, by definition, could not contain the answer, and discard of the sterile part. Each progressively retained live part is called a "bit" because of its being produced by the progressive bisection of the previously residual live part. The magnitude of such weeding problems is determined by the number of successive bits necessary to isolate the answer.

How many "bisecting bits" does it take to get rid of all the irrelevancies and leave in lucid isolation that specific information you are seeking?

We find that the first subdividing of the concept of universe— bit one—is into what we call a *system*. A system subdivides universe into all the universe outside the system (macrocosm) and all the rest of the universe which is inside the system (microcosm), with the exception of the minor fraction of universe which constitutes the system itself. The system divides universe not only into macrocosm and microcosm, but also coincidentally into typical *conceptual* and *nonconceptual* aspects of universe, i.e., an overlappingly associable consideration on the one hand, and on the other hand all the nonassociable, nonconsiderable, nonsimultaneously transforming events of nonsynchronizable, disparate wave frequency rates and ranges.

A *thought* is a *system* and is inherently *conceptual*—though often only dimly and confusedly conceived at the moment of first awareness of that as yet only vaguely describable thinking activity.

Because total universe is nonsimultaneous, it is not conceptual. Conceptuality is produced by isolation as is one single static picture held out from a moving-picture film-reel's scenario continuity.

Universe is an evolutionarily processed scenario without beginning or end, because the shown part is continually transformed chemically into fresh film and re-exposed to the ever self-reorganizing process of latest thought realizations which must continually introduce new significance into the freshly written description of the ever transforming events before splicing the film in again for its projection phase. One picture of the scenario about the caterpillar phase does not communicate its transformation into the butterfly phase, etc. And Heisenberg's principle of "indeterminism" which recognized the experimental discovery that the act of measuring always alters that which was being measured is turned into a continuous and never repeatable evolutionary scenario.

The question, "I wonder what is outside the outside-of-universe?" is a request for a single picture description of a scenario of transformations and is an inherently invalid question. It is the same as looking at a dictionary and saying "which word is the dictionary?" It is an incoherent question.

It is characteristic of "all" thinking, of all systems' conceptioning, that all the lines of thought interrelationships must return cyclically upon themselves in a plurality of directions, as do various great circles around spheres. Thus may we interrelatedly comprehend the *constellation*—or system—of experiences under consideration. Thus may we comprehend how the special-case economy demonstrated by the particular system considered also discloses the generalized law of energy conservation of physical universe.

Great circles provide the most economical (energy, effort) distances between any two points on a system's spherical surface; therefore nature, which always employs only the most economical realizations, must use those great circles which, unlike spiral lines, always return upon themselves in the most economical manner. All the systems paths must be topologically and circularly interrelated for conceptually definitive, locally transformable, polyhedronal understanding to be attained in our spontaneous thoughts.

Thinking, itself, consists of self-disciplined dismissal of both the macrocosmic and microcosmic irrelevancies, leaving only the lucidly relevant considerations. The macrocosmic irrelevancies are all the events too large and too infrequent to be synchronizably tuneable in any possible way with our *consideration* (a beautiful word meaning *putting stars together*).

The microcosmic irrelevancies are all the events which are obviously too small and too frequent to be differentially resolved in one way, to be synchronizably tuneable within the lucidly relevant wave-frequency limits of the system we are considering.

How many stages of dismissal of irrelevancies does it take, i.e., proceeding from universe (as I defined it), how many bits does it take to lucidly isolate all the interrelations of all the "star" identities in the constellation under consideration?

The answer is the formula $\dfrac{N^2 - N}{2}$ where N is the number of stars in the thought-discerned constellation of focal point entities comprising the problem.

"Comprehension" means identifying all the most uniquely economical interrelationships of the focal point entities involved. We may say

$$\text{Comprehension} = \frac{N^2 - N}{2}.$$

This is the way in which thought processes operate with mathematical logic. The mathematics involved consist of topology combined with vectorial geometry, which combination I call "synergetics," a word I will now define while clarifying its use.

The word *synergy* is obviously not a popular word. It is the only word in our language that means: *Behavior of whole systems unpredicted by the separately observed behaviors of any of the system's separate parts or any subassembly of the system's parts.* There is nothing in the *chemistry* of a toenail that predicts the existence of a human being.

I asked an audience of the National Honors Society in chemistry "How many of you are familiar with the word synergy?" and all hands went up. Synergy is the essence of chemistry. The tensile strength of chrome nickel steel, which is approximately 350,000 pounds per square inch, is one hundred thousand p.s.i. greater than the sum of the tensile strengths of each of all its alloyed-together, component, metallic elements. Here is a "chain" that is 50 percent stronger than the sum of the strengths of all its links. We think popularly only in the terms of *a chain is no stronger than its weakest link* which fails to consider the case of an endlessly interlinked chain of ever atomically renewed links of omni-equal strength and of an omni-directionally interlinked chain matrix of ever renewed atomic links in which one broken link would be, only momentarily, a local cavern within the whole mass having no weakening effect on the whole, for every link within the matrix is a high-frequency recurring, break-and-make restructuring of the system.

Since synergy is the only word in our language meaning *behavior* of wholes unpredicted by behavior of their parts, it is clear that society does not think there are behaviors of whole systems unpredicted by their separate parts. This means that society's formally accredited thoughts and ways of thinking and of accrediting others is grossly inadequate in comprehending the non-conceptual qualities of the scenario "universal evolution."

There is nothing about an electron alone that forecasts the proton, nor is there anything about Earth or the moon that forecasts the coexistence of the sun. The solar system is synergetic, unpredicted by its separate parts. But the interplay of sun as supply ship of Earth and the moon's gravitationally produced tidal pulsations on Earth all interact to produce the biosphere's chemical conditions which permit but do not cause the regeneration of life on spaceship Earth. This is all synergetic.

There is nothing about the gases given off respiratorially by Earth's green vegetation that predicts that those gases will be essential to the life-support of all mammals aboard spaceship Earth and nothing about the mammals that predicts that the gases which they give off respiratorially are essential to the support of the vegetation aboard our spaceship Earth. Universe is synergetic. Life is synergetic.

A SELECTION OF FURTHER READINGS

Research for this anthology provided me with a bibliography of books and essays relevant both to the topics of *Human Alternatives* and to visionary social thinking in general. The following list represents a supplement to those appended to *Beyond Left & Right* (Morrow, 1968) and *Social Speculations* (Morrow, 1971), and here too are given the sources of the epigraphs distributed throughout the preceding texts. As in the previous bibliographies, titles listed under one heading could just as feasibly be placed under another; and needless to say perhaps, no list of writings about human alternatives today could possibly be definitive or complete.

I. KNOWLEDGE

Bertalanffy, Ludwig von. *General Systems Theory*. N.Y.: Braziller, 1968.

Brockman, John. *37*. N.Y.: Holt, Rinehart & Winston, 1970.

Carpenter, Edmund, and Heyman, Ken. *They Became What They Beheld*. N.Y.: Outerbridge & Dienstfrey, 1970.

Churchman, C. West. *The Systems Approach*. N.Y.: Delacorte, 1968.

Frye, Northrop. *The Stubborn Structure*. Ithaca: Cornell Univ., 1970.

Gellner, Ernest. *Thought and Change*. Chicago: Univ. of Chicago, 1965.

Jantsch, Erich. *Technological Forecasting in Perspective*. Paris: Organization for Economic Cooperation and Development, 1967.

Krim, Seymour. *Shake It For the World, Smartass*. N.Y.: Dial, 1970.

Meethan, Roger. *Information Retrieval*. Garden City: Doubleday, 1970.

Nevitt, H. J. Barrington. "Problems of Communicating with People Through Media," *the*. Ottawa: Northern Electric, 1968.

Simon, Herbert A. *The Sciences of the Artificial*. Cambridge, Mass.: M.I.T., 1969.

Stulman, Julius. *Evolving Mankind's Future*. Philadelphia: Lippincott, 1967.

Toffler, Alvin. *Future Shock*. N.Y.: Random House, 1970.

Young, Michael, ed. *Forecasting and the Social Sciences*. London: Heinemann, 1968.

II. ORGANISMS

Brockman, John. *By the Late John Brockman*. N.Y.: Macmillan, 1969.

Comfort, Alex. *The Nature of Human Nature*. N.Y.: Harper & Row, 1967.

Delgado, José. *Physical Control of the Mind*. N.Y.: Harper & Row, 1969.

Dubos, René. *Man Adapting*. New Haven: Yale Univ., 1965.

———. *Man, Medicine, and Environment*. N.Y.: Praeger, 1968.

———. *So Human an Animal*. N.Y.: Scribner's, 1968.

Earisman, Delbert L. *Hippies in Our Midst*. Philadelphia: Fortress, 1968.

Eccles, J. C. *The Neurophysical Basis of Mind*. N.Y.: Oxford Univ., 1965.

Fairfield, Dick. "Training for Alternatives," *Alternatives*, 1 (Fall, 1969).

Firestone, Shulamith. *The Dialectic of Sex*. N.Y.: William Morrow, 1970.

Gregory, R. L. *Eye and Brain*. N.Y.: McGraw-Hill, 1966.

Halacy, D. S. *Cyborg: Evolution of the Superman*. N.Y.: Harper & Row, 1966.

Handler, Philip, ed. *Biology and the Future of Man*. N.Y.: Oxford Univ., 1970.

Hanna, Thomas. *Bodies in Revolt*. N.Y.: Holt, 1970.

Hardin, Garrett, ed. *Population, Evolution and Birth Control*. San Francisco: W. H. Freeman, 1964.

Huxley, Aldous. *Island*. N.Y.: Harper, 1962.

Koestler, Arthur. *The Ghost in the Machine*. N.Y.: Macmillan, 1967.

Kornbluth, Jesse, ed. *Notes from the New Underground*. N.Y.: Viking, 1968.

Laing, R. D. *The Self and Others*. N.Y.: Pantheon, 1969.

Leary, Timothy. *High Priest*. N.Y.: World, 1968.

Lilly, John C. *Human Biocomputer*. Big Sur, Calif.: Esalen Institute, 1967.

Lilly, John C. *The Mind of the Dolphin.* N.Y.: Avon, 1967.

Longmore, Donald. *Spare-Part Surgery: The Surgical Practice of the Future.* Garden City: Doubleday, 1968.

———. *Machines in Medicine.* Garden City: Doubleday, 1970.

Maslow, Abraham. *Religions, Values, and Peak-Experiences.* Columbus: Ohio State Univ., 1964.

———. *Toward a Psychology of Being.* Princeton: Van Nostrand, 1962.

———. "Lessons from Peak-Experiences," *Journal of Humanistic Psychology,* II/1 (1962).

Mead, Margaret. *Culture and Commitment.* N.Y.: Natural History, 1969.

Norton, Alan. *The New Dimensions of Medicine.* London: Hodder & Stoughton, 1969.

Pelletier, Wilfred. "Childhood in a Canadian Indian Village," *The,* 3 (1969).

Perls, Frederick S. *In and Out the Garbage Pail.* Lafayette, Calif.: Poor People, 1969.

Prehoda, Robert. *Extended Youth.* N.Y.: Putnam's, 1968.

Rimmer, Robert. *The Harrad Experiment.* N.Y.: New American Library, 1966.

———. *Proposition 31.* N.Y.: New American Library, 1968.

Rogers, Carl, et al. *Person to Person.* Lafayette, Calif.: Real People, 1967.

Rosenfeld, Albert. *The Second Genesis.* Englewood Cliffs: Prentice-Hall, 1969.

Rubenfield, Jerry. "There Is Only One Kind of Love," *Vision,* I/1 (1969).

Schmeck, Harold. *The Semi-Artificial Man.* N.Y.: Walker, 1965.

Schock, Nathan W. *Perspectives in Experimental Gerontology.* Springfield, Ill.: Charles C Thomas, 1966.

Schoenfeld, Eugene, M.D. *Dear Doctor Hippocrates.* N.Y.: Grove, 1968.

Schutz, William C. *Joy: Expanding Human Awareness.* N.Y.: Grove, 1968.

Smith, David E., ed. *The New Social Drug.* Englewood Cliffs: Prentice-Hall, 1970.

Tart, Charles, ed. *Altered States of Consciousness.* N.Y.: Wiley, 1969.

Von Hoffman, Nicholas. *We Are the People Our Parents Warned Us Against.* Chicago: Quadrangle, 1968.

Warshofsky, Fred. *The Control of Life.* N.Y.: Viking, 1969.

Winick, Charles E. *The New People.* N.Y.: Pegasus, 1968.
Wooldridge, Dean E. *Mechanical Man.* N.Y.: McGraw-Hill, 1968.
Young, J. Z. *A Model of the Brain.* N.Y.: Oxford Univ., 1964.
———. and Margerison, Tom, eds. *From Molecules to Man.* N.Y.: Crown, 1969.

III. ECONOMICS

Anderson, Allan H., et al. *An Electronic Cash and Credit System.* N.Y.: American Management Association, 1966.
Boulding, Kenneth, E. *Beyond Economics.* Ann Arbor: Univ. of Michigan, 1969.
Bowen, Howard R., and Magnum, Garth L., eds. *Automation and Economic Progress.* Englewood Cliffs: Prentice-Hall, 1966.
Fein, Louis. "The P. I. Bill of Rights," in *Technology and Education in the 21st Century.* Washington, D.C.: Communication Service Corp., 1967.
Meier, Richard L. *Science and Economic Development.* Rev. ed. Cambridge: M.I.T., 1966.
Schmookler, J. *Invention and Economic Growth.* Cambridge: Harvard Univ., 1966.
Simpson, David. "The Dimensions of World Poverty," *Scientific American,* CCXIX/5 (Nov., 1968).
Stone, Richard, ed. *A Computable Model of Economic Growth.* Cambridge: M.I.T., 1964.
Theobald, Robert, ed. *Committed Spending.* Garden City: Doubleday, 1968.

IV. POLITICS

Bertram, Christoph. "Models of Western Europe in the 1970's—The Alternative Choices," *Futures,* I/2 (Dec., 1968).
Bloomfield, Lincoln. *Western Europe in the mid-70's: Scenarios.* Cambridge: M.I.T., 1968.
———, ed. *Outer Space.* Englewood Cliffs: Prentice-Hall, 1962.
Brzezinski, Zbigniew. *Between Two Ages.* N.Y.: Viking, 1970.
Buchan, Alastair, ed. *Europe's Futures—Europe's Choices?* London: Chatto & Windus, 1969.
Calder, Nigel, ed. *Unless Peace Comes.* N.Y.: Viking, 1968.
Dror, Yehezkel. *Public Policymaking Reexamined.* San Francisco: Chandler, 1968.

Godron, Kermit, ed. *Agenda for the Nation*. Washington, D.C.: Brookings Institution, 1968.

Goldsen, J. M., ed. *Outer Space in World Politics*. London: Pall Mall, 1966.

Goodall, Marcus C. *Science and the Politician*. Cambridge, Mass.: Schenkman, 1965.

Goodman, Mitchell. *Movement Toward a New America*. Philadelphia, Pa.: Pilgrim Press, 1970.

Gross, Bertram M. *The State of the Nation*. London: Tavistock, 1966.

Kahn, Herman. *The Emerging Japanese Superstate*. Englewood Cliffs, N.J.: Prentice-Hall, 1970.

Long, Priscilla, ed. *The New Left: A Collection of Essays*. Boston: Porter Sargent, 1969.

Mau, James A. *Social Changes and Images of the Future*. Cambridge, Mass.: Schenkman, 1968.

Morenoff, Jerome. *World Peace through Space Law*. Charlottesville, Va.: The Michie Co., 1967.

Morgenthau, Hans J. *A New Foreign Policy for the United States*. N.Y.: Praeger, 1969.

Morse, Chandler, et al. *Modernization by Design*. Ithaca: Cornell Univ., 1969.

Nelson, Richard R., et al. *Technology, Economic Growth and Public Policy*. Washington, D.C.: Brookings, 1967.

Nieburg, H. L. *In the Name of Science*. Chicago: Quadrangle, 1966.

Panero, Robert B. "A Dam Across the Amazon," *Science Journal*, V/9 (Sept., 1969).

Reischauer, Edwin. *Beyond Vietnam: The United States and Asia*. N.Y.: Knopf, 1967.

Riencourt, Amaury de. *The American Empire*. N.Y.: Dell, 1970.

Servan-Schreiber, Jean-Jacques. *The American Challenge*. N.Y.: Atheneum, 1968.

Shils, Edward. *Political Development in the New States*. N.Y.: Humanities, 1962.

Theobald, Robert, ed. *Social Policies for America in the Seventies*. Garden City: Doubleday, 1968.

V. EDUCATION

Abt, Clark C. *Serious Games*. N.Y.: Viking, 1970.

Adelman, Howard, and Lee, Dennis, eds. *The University Game*. Toronto: House of Anansi, 1968.

Birnbaum, William M. *Overlive.* N.Y.: Delacorte, 1969.

Brewster, Kingman, et al. *Educating for the Twenty-First Century.* Urbana: Univ. of Illinois, 1969.

Eurich, Alvin C. *Reforming American Education.* N.Y.: Harper & Row, 1969.

————, ed. *Campus 1980.* N.Y.: Delacorte, 1969.

Gattegno, Caleb. *Toward a Visual Culture.* N.Y.: Outerbridge & Dienstfrey, 1969.

Gross, Ronald, ed. *The Teacher and the Taught.* N.Y.: Delacorte, 1969.

————, and Gross, Beatrice, eds. *Radical School Reform.* N.Y.: Simon & Schuster, 1970.

Hirsch, Werner A., et al. *Inventing Education for the Future.* San Francisco: Chandler, 1967.

Johansen, Waldemar, et al. *Technology and Education in the 21st Century.* Washington, D.C.: Communication Service Corp., 1967.

Kean, Richard, ed. *Dialogue on Education.* N.Y.: Bobbs-Merrill, 1967.

Krech, David. "The Chemistry of Learning," *Saturday Review* (Jan. 20, 1968).

Leonard, George. *Education and Ecstasy.* N.Y.: Delacorte, 1969.

Oettinger, Anthony G., with Marks, Selma. *Run, Computer, Run.* Cambridge: Harvard Univ., 1969.

Overhage, Carl F. J., and Hartman, R. Joyce, eds. *Intrex.* Cambridge: M.I.T., 1967.

Patterson, Franklin, and Longworth, Charles R. *The Making of a College.* Cambridge: M.I.T., 1967.

Stein, Maurice, and Miller, Larry. *Blueprint for Counter Education.* Garden City: Doubleday, 1970.

Wolff, Robert Paul. *The Ideal of the University.* Boston: Beacon, 1969.

VI. PLANNING

Anderson, Stanford, ed. *Planning for Diversity and Choice.* Cambridge: M.I.T., 1969.

Ayres, Robert U. *Technological Forecasting and Long-Range Planning.* N.Y.: McGraw-Hill, 1969.

Brand, Stewart, ed. *Whole Earth Catalog: Access to Tools.* Menlo Park: Portola Institute, 1969.

Bright, James R. "Some Management Lessons from Technological Innovation Research," *Long-Range Planning*, II/1 (Sept., 1969).

Davenport, William H., and Rosenthal, Daniel, eds. *Engineering: Its Role and Function in Human Society.* N.Y.: Pergamon, 1967.

Doxiadis, Constantinos A., et al. "Technology and Social Goals," *Ekistics* (Sept., 1967).

Feinberg, Gerald. *The Prometheus Project.* Garden City: Doubleday, 1969.

Fuller, R. Buckminster. *Operating Manual for Spaceship Earth.* Carbondale: Southern Illinois, 1969.

———. *Utopia or Oblivion?* N.Y.: Bantam, 1969.

———, with Jerome Agel and Quentin Fiore. *I Seem To Be a Verb,* N.Y.: Bantam, 1970.

Licklider, J. C. R. "Interactive Dynamic Modeling," in George Shapiro & Milton Rogers, eds., *Prospects for Simulation and Simulators of Dynamic Systems.* N.Y.: Spartan, 1967.

Meier, Richard L. *Developmental Planning.* N.Y.: McGraw-Hill, 1965.

Michael, Donald N. *The Unprepared Society: Planning for a Precarious Future.* N.Y.: Basic, 1968.

Theobald, Robert. *An Alternative Future for America.* Two vols. Chicago: Swallow, 1969–70.

Winthrop, Henry. "Social Philosophy for an Age of Technology," *Ventures in Social Interpretation.* N.Y.: Appleton, 1968.

CONTRIBUTORS

DAVID T. BAZELON, born in Shreveport, Louisiana, in 1923, has taught literature, practiced corporate law, and contributed essays on various subjects to many magazines. A sometime Fellow of the Institute for Policy Studies in Washington, he is currently teaching law at Rutgers University. His books include *The Paper Economy* (1963) and *Power in America* (1967).

JAMES R. BRIGHT, formerly the editor of *Modern Material Handling,* is currently a Professor at Harvard Graduate School of Business Administration and a Distinguished Visiting Professor and Associate Dean at the University of Texas. He wrote *Automation and Management* (1958).

JOHN CAGE, internationally known as a composer and esthetic philosopher, has in recent years been devoting more of his attention to social philosophy. His writings are reprinted in *Silence* (1961) and *A Year from Monday* (1967), as well as in *John Cage* (1970), a documentary monograph edited by Richard Kostelanetz.

EDMUND CARPENTER, born in Rochester, New York, in 1922 took his Ph.D. in anthropology from the University of Pennsylvania. He has made prize-winning films, conducted field research in the Arctic, Siberia, Borneo and Outer Mongolia, and taught at the University of Toronto, Fordham and the University of California at Santa Cruz. His books include *Aivilik* (1958), *Eskimo* (1959), *Anerca* (1960) and an anthology co-edited with Marshall McLuhan, *Explorations in Communication* (1960).

GRENVILLE CLARK took his law degree at Harvard in 1906 and subsequently practiced law and worked in government. One of the earliest American "peace" scholars, he wrote *A Plan for the Peace* and co-authored, with Louis B. Sohn, the much-reprinted *World Peace Through World Law* (1958).

DANDRIDGE M. COLE, born in 1921 in Sandusky, Ohio, was at his death in 1965 a space programs analyst with the General Electric

Missile and Space Division. After earning his A.B. in Chemistry from Princeton and his M.A. in Physics from the University of Pennsylvania, he taught science at the Academy of New Church and Phillips-Exeter. His books include *Exploring the Secrets of Space* (1963, with I. M. Leavitt) and *Beyond Tomorrow* (1965).

CHARLES R. DeCARLO, currently president of Sarah Lawrence College, was previously director of automation research at IBM. He holds a B.S. in engineering and a Ph.D. in mathematics from the University of Pittsburgh, and he has written widely on technology and society.

JOHN DIEBOLD, president and founder of The Diebold Group, Inc., an international management consulting company, took an economics degree from Swarthmore College, an engineering degree from the U.S. Merchant Marine Academy and an M.B.A. from the Harvard Business School. His books include *The Automation Factory* (1952), *Beyond Automation* (1964), and *Man and the Computer* (1969).

DON FABUN, currently Director of Publications for Kaiser Aluminum, took his bachelor's degree in Journalism from the University of California at Berkeley. Since 1952, he has been the editor of *Kaiser Aluminum News,* indubitably the most forward-looking publication of its kind. He lives presently in Berkeley, California.

GERALD FEINBERG took his B.A., M.A., and Ph.D. degrees at Columbia University, where he is now Professor of Physics. He has written on scientific subjects for many publications and *The Prometheus Project* (1969) is his first book for general readers.

J. H. FREMLIN is Professor of Physics at the University of Birmingham, England, where he is particularly concerned with applied nuclear science in biology and medicine. He has contributed to *The New Scientist*.

R. BUCKMINSTER FULLER, born in 1895 in Milford, Massachusetts, attended Harvard and the U.S. Naval Academy, taking no degrees. Since then, he has designed a radically original automobile in the 1930's, invented both a system of mapping and the geodesic principles of building construction, envisioned whole cities, and lectured around the world. Currently Professor of Comprehensive Anticipatory Design Science at Southern Illinois University, he has written a long poem, *Unfinished Epic of Industrialization* (1963), and five major books: *No More Second-hand God* (1962), *Education Automation* (1962), *Ideas and Integrities* (1963), *Nine Chains to the Moon* (1938; reprinted, 1963), and *Operating Manual to the Spaceship Earth* (1969).

CALEB GATTEGNO, born in Alexandria, Egypt, in 1911, has taught at universities in Cairo, Liverpool and London, as well as translated two books of Jean Piaget into English. Since 1966, he has been living in the United States, directing a New York organization called Schools for the Future, Inc. His books include *Toward a Visual Culture* (1969), and *What We Owe Children* (1970).

ALLEN GINSBERG, perhaps the most famous American poet, has also written and spoken on social problems and frequently participated in radical activities. His books of poetry include *Howl and Other Poems* (1956), *Empty Mirror: Early Poems* (1961), *Kaddish and Other Poems* (1961), *Reality Sandwiches* (1963), and *Planet News* (1968).

PAUL GOODMAN, one of the great American intellectual vagabonds, has lectured at countless universities and published over a score of books, covering nearly as many subjects. Among the more speculative are *Growing Up Absurd* (1960), a novel entitled *The Empire City* (1959), *Utopian Essays and Practical Proposals* (1961), *The Community of Scholars* (1962), *Like a Conquered Province* (1967), and *Communitas* (1948; revised, 1960). The last was co-authored with his brother, the architect Percival Goodman.

HERMAN KAHN, director of the Hudson Institute of Harmon, New York, was born in Bayonne, New Jersey, in 1922, and was educated at U.C.L.A. and California Institute of Technology. Among his writings are innumerable essays and reports, mostly privately published, and four controversial books: *On Thermonuclear War* (1960), *Thinking About the Unthinkable* (1962), *On Escalation* (1965) and, with Anthony J. Wiener, *The Year 2000* (1967). He was also the primary contributor to *Can We Win in Vietnam?* (1968).

ALLAN KAPROW, best known as the originator of that mixed-media art called "Happenings," is currently associate dean at the California Institute of the Arts. Recipient of an M.A. in Art History and orginally a painter, he was previously a Professor of Art at the State University of New York at Stony Brook. His writings include many essays and *Assemblage, Environments & Happenings* (1966).

TIMOTHY LEARY taught and researched psychology at Harvard before founding the League for Spiritual Discovery and other "psychedelic" organizations. A popular lecturer, he has also written several books, including *High Priest* (1968) and *The Politics of Ecstasy* (1968), and co-edited *The Psychedelic Reader* (1965).

STANLEY LESSE is editor-in-chief of the *American Journal of Psychotherapy* and WILLIAM WOLF is secretary of the Association for the Advancement of Psychotherapy in New York. They contributed to the International Future Research Inaugural Conference, whose papers were reprinted in *Mankind 2000* (1969), edited by Robert Jungk and Johan Galtung.

SEYMOUR MELMAN, Professor of Industrial and Management Engineering at Columbia University, has written *Dynamic Factors in Industrial Productivity* (1956), *Decision-Making and Productivity* (1958), *The Peace Race* (1961) and other books, as well as edited *Inspection for Disarmament* (1958) and *No Place to Hide* (1962).

L. MOHOLY-NAGY, born in Hungary in 1895, was a painter, sculptor, film-maker, photographer, critic, teacher, stage designer, typographer, and much else. At the time of his premature death, in 1946, he was head of the Institute of Design in Chicago. His influential expository books include *Painting, Photography, Film* (1925), *The New Vision* (1929), and *Vision in Motion* (1947).

ANTHONY G. OETTINGER, born in Nuremberg, Germany, in 1929, is currently Professor of Linguistics and Gordon McKay Professor of Applied Mathematics, Harvard University, as well as a Research Associate of the Program on Technology and Society. In 1966, he became president of the Association for Computing Machinery.

JOHN R. PLATT received his B.S. in Physics from Northwestern (1936) and his Ph.D. from the University of Michigan in 1941, at the age of twenty-two. Currently Professor of Physics and Research Biophysicist, and Associate Director of the Mental Health Research Institute at the University of Michigan, he has written, among other books, *Free Electron Theory of Conjugated Molecules* (1964) and *The Step to Man* (1966).

JOHN W. SENDERS is a principal scientist and manager of engineering psychology at Bolt, Beranek and Newman, Inc. in Cambridge, Mass., as well as a senior research associate and lecturer in psychology at Brandeis University.

RENATO SEVERINO, trained as an architect, is a partner in COMTEC in Rome, Italy. He contributed to the American Institute of Planners' Fiftieth Year Consultation, reprinted in *Environment and Change* (1968) edited by William Ewald.

HERBERT A. SIMON, born in Milwaukee, Wisconsin, in 1916, is Professor of Administration and Psychology and Associate Dean of the Graduate School of Industrial Administration at Carnegie-Mellon University. His books include *Models of Man* (1956), *The Shape of Automation* (1965), and *Sciences of the Artificial* (1969).

ROBERT THEOBALD, born in India in 1929, has been living in the United States since 1957. A free-lance lecturer and consultant, he has written *The Rich and The Poor* (1960), *The Challenge of Abundance* (1961) and *Free Men and Free Markets* (1963), and edited several important anthologies.

ALEXANDER TROCCHI, born in Scotland, edited *Merlin* in Paris in the fifties and currently lives with his American wife in London. His writings include the novels *Cain's Book* (1960) and *The Outsiders* (1961).

VLADIMIR ZWORYKIN, born in Mourom, Russia, in 1889, was Vice-President of the Radio Corporation of America Laboratories from 1947 to 1954. An initiating scientist in the development of television, he has also written numerous essays on technical and social subjects.

A Note about the Author

RICHARD KOSTELANETZ has written *The Theatre of Mixed Means* (1968), *Master Minds* (1969), *Visual Language* (1970), and *Metamorphosis in the Arts* (1971), and co-authored *The New American Arts* (1965), as well as edited documentary monographs on *Moholy-Nagy* (1970) and *John Cage* (1970) and several anthologies—among them *Beyond Left & Right* (1968), *Imaged Words & Worded Images* (1970), *Possibilities of Poetry* (1970), and *Social Speculations* (1971). His articles and critical essays have appeared in magazines here and abroad, and he has also published fiction and visual poetry.

Born in 1940 in New York City, where he now lives, Kostelanetz studied at Brown, Columbia, and London universities. Recently a Guggenheim Fellow, he is currently co-editing *Assembling,* an annual of otherwise unpublishable literature, and completing, among other projects in process, both an extended fiction and a history of recent American thought.